WOMEN AND POVERTY

WOMEN
AND
POVERTY

Edited by Barbara C. Gelpi,
Nancy C.M. Hartsock, Clare C. Novak,
and Myra H. Strober

The University of Chicago Press
CHICAGO AND LONDON

Most of the essays in this volume originally appeared in the Winter 1984 issue of SIGNS: JOURNAL OF WOMEN IN CULTURE AND SOCIETY (10:2). There are two exceptions: Diana Pearce's article first appeared in SIGNS 10:3, and Muriel Nazzari's article was first published in SIGNS 9:2.

The University of Chicago Press, Chicago 60637
The University of Chicago Press, Ltd., London
© 1983, 1984, 1985, 1986 by The University of Chicago
All rights reserved. Published 1986
Printed in the United States of America
95 94 93 92 91 90   5 4 3 2

Library of Congress Cataloging-in-Publication Data

Women and poverty.

   "Most of the essays in this volume originally
appeared in the winter 1984 issue of Signs, volume 10,
number 2"—T.p. verso.
   Includes bibliographies and index.
   1. Women—Economic conditions. 2. Women, Poor.
3. Women—Employment. 4. Women heads of households.
I. Gelpi, Barbara Charlesworth.
HQ1381.W63   1986   305.4   86-6907
ISBN 0-226-28726-2 (alk. paper)
ISBN 0-226-28727-0 (pbk. : alk. paper)

Cover design by Dennis McClendon.

Contents

Introduction

Over the past decade, numerous governmental and academic studies have described women's poverty and analyzed the ways in which race and class, along with gender, make women particularly subject to economic victimization. Although extremely useful, such descriptions and analyses do not generate an impetus toward social change unless coupled with strategies for empowering women of all classes and races to combat the actuality or the threat of poverty. These two themes—victimization and empowerment—run through this collection of *Signs* essays, most of which appeared in a special issue on women's poverty.

Nowhere are these concerns more dramatically expressed than in the first-person testimony from the 1983 California hearings on women's poverty. The accounts by California women were selected in part to add the dimension of personal experience to the analyses made elsewhere in this volume and also to indicate areas of concern that the articles we publish here cannot adequately cover. We put forward this testimony, along with an introduction by Elaine Zimmerman chronicling the development of the Women's Economic Agenda Project, to indicate the kinds of actions women have initiated and to encourage groups in other parts of the country to set up similar projects.

Although our coverage cannot be complete, women's economic and political situations are amply and depressingly documented by the articles in this book. An assessment of the information they contain requires taking into account not only the effects of inflation since these articles appeared but also the way in which poverty is defined. As of April 1986, the poverty line for a family of four stands at $11,000 a year.[1] However, the method of computation used to arrive at that figure raises questions about its accuracy. The Social Security Administration calculates the poverty line by computing the costs of feeding a family of four and then

1. *Federal Register* 51 (February 11, 1986): 5106.

multiplying this figure by three. However, utilities, rent, taxes, and other necessary expenses may take up more than two-thirds of the family budget. Thus, some experts conclude that a poverty line pegged at less than $12,000 a year may underestimate the number of people living in poverty.[2] Even if we do rely on official measures to identify those in poverty, however, statistics show that in 1984 women represented 63.5 percent of all adults who were poor.[3]

In the opening essay, Mary Corcoran, Greg Duncan, and Martha Hill tell us that poverty is both more widespread and less fixed than popularly imagined and call attention to important racial differences in the incidence of poverty: 70 percent of black children, compared to 30 percent of white children, were poor at some time over the past ten years. Joan Smith notes how the growing wage differential between manufacturing and service industries, the increase in part-time jobs relative to full-time ones, and the increase in service jobs relative to manufacturing jobs affect women's income. Because both white women and women and men of color are disproportionately employed in the service industries and as part-time workers, these shifts mark an expansion of the low-wage sector of the economy. Deborah Zinn and Rosemary Sarri help us understand why many women have found it necessary to take such poorly paid jobs when they point out that no state allows a family receiving AFDC (Aid to Families with Dependent Children) to receive other assistance in cash or in kind that will bring its total income up to the poverty line. Work incentives, which were part of AFDC before Ronald Reagan took office, meant, in fact, that employers could pay poor workers lower salaries; thus these incentives functioned as a government subsidy of the low-wage sector. The changes made under the Reagan administration—such as tightening the requirements for welfare eligibility and eliminating the practice of disregarding certain earned income when eligibility is determined—have functioned, then, both as a cut in wages for women workers and as a way of making the work force even more captive because the need for jobs is more desperate. Indeed, women's wages are so low that, as Corcoran, Duncan, and Hill point out, women's full-time employment itself provides no automatic solution to female poverty. Yet, Roslyn Feldberg's analysis shows that, if working women got men's wages, the number of poor families would drop by half. And—a point not well covered in this issue—many older women's social security benefits would be far greater than they are.

The situation of women who receive AFDC and other government benefits has clearly worsened since Reagan took office. Aid to Families

2. See Stephen J. Rose, *The American Profile Poster* (New York: Pantheon Books, 1986).
3. Victor R. Fuchs, "The Feminization of Poverty?" (Stanford University, Department of Economics, May 1986).

with Dependent Children caseloads have dropped up to 14 percent in some states.[4] Twenty percent of all children now live in households with incomes below the poverty line, as compared to 14 and 16 percent during the 1970s.[5] Zinn and Sarri document the suffering these changes have caused. Half of the families questioned in their study not only had run out of money at some point in the year before the interview but also had run out of food at least once during that time. Associated with such extreme hardship is the high incidence both of health problems and of troubles with older children among these families. It is important to note as well that women's economic situation has political consequences. For one, poor women seldom have the time or resources to participate more than minimally in politics. Moreover, as Barbara Nelson shows, the nature of the liberal political system itself disempowers women.

Women, of course, are poor not just in advanced industrial countries but in other parts of the world as well. Mari Clark discusses some of the ways women's poverty in Kenya has been promoted by colonial practices. There, too, households headed by women more frequently than those headed by men are impoverished, and they lack access to resources necessary to improve their lot. Jana Everett and Mira Savara report a similar situation in India. There, women's current status is indicated by a decline in the female population in proportion to the male, women's decreased labor force participation rate, and an increasing literacy gap between men and women. But, by examining bank loans to poor women, Everett and Savara show that the addition of very small amounts of money for maintaining and expanding small businesses can empower women and free them from dependency on local moneylenders. Of great interest and usefulness also is Muriel Nazzari's analysis of the ways in which the implementation of socialist theory in the Cuban Revolution has benefited Cuba's working women and of the ways in which it has preserved their inequality and perpetuated their personal dependence on men.

In the past, dependence on individual men for subsistence has impoverished women as individuals. But impoverishment remains—even grows—as social arrangements change. Zillah Eisenstein argues that we are witnessing a reorganization of patriarchy in which the state is attempting to counter challenges represented by the increase of women working for wages and by changes in family forms. Because, as Feldberg points out, women now have less access to a "family wage" and therefore greater dependence on what they can earn themselves, they have far less money

4. U.S. House of Representatives, Committee on Ways and Means, *Children in Poverty* (Washington, D.C.: Government Printing Office, 1985).

5. John L. Palmer and Isabel V. Sawhill, *The Reagan Record: An Assessment of America's Changing Domestic Priorities* (Cambridge, Mass.: Ballinger Publishing Co., 1984), p. 192.

available to them. Thus, Corcoran, Duncan, and Hill point to the fact that poverty does not come from lack of education and training or from a transgenerational culture of poverty. Divorce, rather, is the strongest predictor that children (with their mothers) will fall into poverty.

Indeed, all households without access to a man's earnings are much likelier to be poor. For example, one in three of all households with a female householder was designated as poor in 1984, as compared to one in eleven with a male householder. In that year, almost one-half of all people living in poverty were in a household with a female householder, a marked rise from one-third in 1965, a year in which the total number of poor was approximately the same. In 1984, 6.8 million children were in families principally supported by women, and 3.1 million of these children were living in poverty.[6] The impoverishment of female-headed families was due both to women's low wages and to the strain of raising children on a low income, often without child-support payments from the father. Impoverishment and dependence now reflect women's practical exclusion from the family wage and at the same time their inclusion in the labor force on terms that falsely assume them to share in a family (i.e., a man's) wage.

The current attention to women's poverty, then, exposes the unjust and gendered nature of the false separation between public and private spheres. Women's lives are held as defined by their attachment to the private sphere, and, in general, their low wages are not seen as an important public concern. Nelson points out that legislative changes in women's working conditions (i.e., their situation in the public world) have traditionally been justified by the fact that women are mothers—that is, they belong to the private world. And it is as mothers that they can claim AFDC and many other government benefits. Furthermore, as Smith points out, women's low wages reflect a societal judgment that they are marginal figures in the wage labor market. Diana Pearce's essay "Toil and Trouble: Women Workers and Unemployment Compensation" makes a related point: unemployment compensation programs designed to aid male heads of households are biased against women by their very structure.

The current discussion of women's poverty recognizes that patriarchy is a system subject to change over time—one in which, despite their victimization, women have indeed some power to effect change. One form this struggle takes is the transformation of state actions and policies. Eisenstein and Nelson point out that the liberal democratic state has

---

6. U.S. Department of Commerce, Bureau of the Census, *Money Income and Poverty Status of Families and Persons in the U.S., 1984*, in *Current Population Reports*, series P-60, no. 149 (Washington, D.C.: Government Printing Office, 1985), table 15, pp. 22–23; table 18, p. 29.

traditionally failed to include women and includes them now only with a certain amount of difficulty. Yet aspects of the liberal political system, in its evolution into the welfare state, have been subversive of patriarchy. As a result, feminists can use the principles of liberal democracy to challenge recent efforts to return society to a former, more explicitly patriarchal mode.

Ultimately, women's poverty and the contemporary debate it has provoked open the way to deeper questions about capitalism, liberal democracy, and patriarchy. Women's situation is the nexus of a series of contradictions. The capitalist market claims to set the value of labor by supply and demand; yet it reproduces a gender and race hierarchy in its system of wages.

The expanding service sector and other low-wage industries depend on the wage labor of women, especially women (and some men) of color. Here, too, there has been a decline since 1980 in the ability of a full-time worker to support a family: in the 1970s, such a worker earning the minimum wage would have fallen just short of the income necessary to support a family of four at or above the poverty line. Since 1981, because the minimum wage has remained fixed while costs have risen, the gap between income and necessary expenditures has widened substantially. One of the societal supports for low-wage industries is the widespread conviction that workers in them are not "really" part of the wage labor force. The ideology of liberal democracy insists that every citizen is equal; yet its proponents have established a two-tiered system of state benefits that reproduces the gendered public-private hierarchy and allows women benefits only because of their status as family members.

Attention to women's poverty, then, is not simply a depressing recitation of the facts and figures. It raises new and fundamental issues about our social and political system and should lead us to explore alternatives. Sheila Kamerman presents one set of strategies in her argument that the United States should emulate other industrial countries in removing the stigma of AFDC while providing universal child benefits, adequate health care, and housing subsidies. Feldberg suggests another possibility in her discussion of comparable worth, a policy instituted now in several states for public-sector workers. Yet a third alternative is grass-roots efforts such as the Women's Economic Agenda Project, whose purpose is the eradication of poverty through women's political empowerment.

* * *

The collection, review, and editing of this volume took years of collegial effort. We are grateful to the many co-workers who helped us during that long process: former *Signs* managing editor, Susan L. Johnson, intern Frances Dinkelspiel, and associate editors Jane Fishburne

Collier, Estelle Freedman, Carol Nagy Jacklin, Barrie Thorne, Gaye Tuchman, Margery Wolf, and Sylvia Yanagisako. We also thank the anonymous reviewers who evaluated these articles and the others submitted for the "Women and Poverty" issue of *Signs*.

The Economic Fortunes of Women and Children: Lessons from the Panel Study of Income Dynamics

Mary Corcoran, Greg J. Duncan, and Martha S. Hill

Most of our knowledge about the economic fortunes of women and children comes from case studies, special-purpose surveys such as National Longitudinal Surveys, or cross-sectional data. Each source has certain limitations. Case studies often provide richly detailed pictures of a few individuals who may not, however, be representative of larger groups. Analyses of special-purpose longitudinal surveys may yield generalizations about only limited segments of the population. Cross-sectional data provide snapshot pictures of an entire population but tell us little about the dynamic processes that affect their lives.

Because most social science theories of human behavior are dynamic rather than static, they must be tested through repeated observations of the same people. An extra year of data on one set of individuals is considerably more valuable than new data on a different cross section. This is particularly important when the process under analysis takes an extended period of time. For instance, investigations of the causes, extent, and consequences of long-run welfare dependency must be conducted over an extended period and even across generations if competing theories are to be tested adequately. This requirement also holds for studies of changes in family composition (e.g., marriage, childbirth, marital breakups), which should be based on comparisons of a family's situation before and after change.

Equally important, any study of the economic well-being of women

The research reported in this article was supported by the Department of Labor, the Sloan Foundation, the National Science Foundation, the Ford Foundation, the Department of Health and Human Services, and the National Academy of Science. None of these institutions is responsible for any opinions or errors within.

7

and children should look at entire families—particularly at any male adults present, for they are often key economic influences. Because families change over time through marriage, childbirth, children's departure from home, and marital disruptions, monitoring economic well-being requires following all family members as these changes occur.

Each year since 1968, the Panel Study of Income Dynamics (PSID) has followed the economic fortunes of a nationally representative sample of American families.[1] Since the PSID tracks all individuals who have left the homes of the original 1968 sample, it is an unbiased, self-replacing, and representative sample of families each year. The procedure of following all original family members also makes the PSID a unique data set for monitoring the causes and effects of family composition change. Further, since the study originally oversampled poor and minority households, it provides a large enough black subsample to permit separate analyses by race.

The main content of the PSID interviews is an annual measurement of a set of trend items that indicate changes in income sources, family composition, employment, earnings, and hours spent working, commuting, doing housework, and caring for children. While these variables have been elaborated and changed somewhat over time, most are comparable from year to year. Also, PSID interviewers collected extensive background information about the head, and some about the spouse, of each original family, a procedure repeated for the head and spouse of each new family surveyed. Information about children's schooling, about housing and transportation, and about income and occupation are available each year. Finally, in 1976, the PSID added a special interview with wives that included questions about their past work history and fertility.

Thus, the Panel Study of Income Dynamics is unique among longitudinal data sets in combining a national sample, years of annual interviews with many similar questions about work and income, and information about all members of the initial sample of families. These factors give the PSID a versatility unparalleled by other studies and also make it an exceptionally good vehicle for exploring the economic situations of women and children, as the findings reported below indicate.

Sex-based Differences in Wages

The Lord spoke to Moses and said, "When a man makes a special vow to the Lord which requires your valuation of living persons, a male between twenty and sixty years old shall be valued at fifty silver

---

1. The design and content of the PSID are described in an 8-vol. set of documentation available from the Institute for Social Research, University of Michigan, Ann Arbor, Michigan 48106.

shekels. If it is a female, she shall be valued at thirty shekels."
[Lev. 27:1–4]

The biblical practice of setting the value of a woman's work at about three-fifths that of a man's seems to persist in modern times. Census Bureau figures show that on average, for every dollar men earned per hour, women earned $.63 in 1949, $.65 in 1959, and $.63 in 1969.[2] Some attribute this wage gap to discrimination. An alternative explanation—popular with employers, emphasized by economists, and prevalent in recent government policy statements—is that men's higher earnings reflect their higher level of job-related skills. Because women allegedly choose to sacrifice career advancement for home responsibilities, they are thought to lack equal skills.

Demands of child care and other home responsibilities may influence women's acquisition of job skills in several ways. First, most women do not work continuously after leaving school but, instead, fulfill family and child care responsibilities by interspersing periods of employment with periods of nonmarket work. If women expect to have a less regular pattern of labor-force participation, then they will have a shorter wage-earning career than will men. Reducing the period during which a woman will benefit from her investment in job-related skills may produce a clear economic incentive for her to acquire fewer of those skills.[3] Second, women may find that their skills become rusty (and hence less valuable) if they temporarily leave the labor force to have and raise children. Third, many women workers must balance the demands of work and family and may be forced to accept lower-paying jobs in order to be closer to home, to have suitable work schedules, or to allow for high absenteeism when their children are ill.

In sum, the human capital explanation posits that most, if not all, of the earnings gap between the sexes is a consequence of the home responsibilities assumed by women. Saying that the wage differentials are justifiable, however, in no way implies that the choices made by women are unwise. Women's actions are seen merely as responses to the incentives

2. U.S. Department of Labor, *Manpower and Training Report of the President* (Washington, D.C.: Department of Labor, 1973). These ratios have been adjusted for differences in educational attainment. Victor R. Fuchs finds that adjustments for schooling and age produce hourly wage ratios of .61 in 1959 and .64 in 1969 ("Recent Trends and Long-Run Prospects for Female Earnings," *American Economic Review* 64 [1974]: 236–42). Fuchs is also responsible for uncovering the biblical verse that opens this section.

3. This result follows from the view that job skills are acquired at some cost to the worker and can therefore be considered an investment. Costs can be direct (tuition for formal course work) or indirect (the opportunity cost of forgoing a high salary in a job with little future in favor of an initially lower salary in a job that does promise future advancement).

created by their current responsibilities and future plans. Men faced with similar incentives would be expected to make similar choices.[4]

The PSID data are well suited to testing this explanation.[5] In 1976 a special questionnaire asked male and female household heads and spouses explicitly about work history, interruptions in work, absenteeism, and self-imposed restrictions on work hours and job location. Thus, the PSID provides measures of an extensive number of qualifications for a nationally representative sample of men and women across a broad age range.

We investigated the human capital explanation by calculating the difference in average skill levels of men and women as measured by five criteria: education, work experience, work continuity, self-imposed work restrictions, and patterns of absenteeism (see table 1). Then we calculated the economic value of each particular factor, that is, the extent to which it increased earnings. The degree to which a particular attribute contributed to the wage gap was measured by multiplying the economic value of that attribute by the actual difference in the average amounts of that attribute possessed by men and women.[6] If the sex-based wage differential is "justifiable" and our list of factors is complete and well measured, then sex differentials in these factors should "explain" most of the gap.

Many of the differences between women and white men were consistent with cultural stereotypes. A majority of the women surveyed had not worked continuously after school completion; much of their work experience was part-time; a substantial minority of those who did work placed limits on when, how much, or where they worked; and a substantial

4. Women's low incentive to acquire skills may be reinforced by the expectation that discrimination will reduce the likely value of those skills in the workplace. This argument is not an integral part of the skills explanation, although some proponents may support it.

5. The research summarized below is reported in Mary Corcoran, "The Structure of Female Wages," *American Economic Review* 68, no. 2 (May 1978): 165–70, and "Work Experience, Labor Force Withdrawals, and Women's Earnings: Empirical Results Using the 1976 Panel Study of Income Dynamics," in *Women in the Labor Market*, ed. Cynthia Lloyd, Emily Andrews, and Curtis Gilroy (New York: Columbia University Press, 1979); Mary Corcoran and Greg J. Duncan, "Work History, Labor Force Attachment, and Earnings Differences between the Races and Sexes," *Journal of Human Resources* 14, no. 1 (Winter 1979): 3–20; Mary Corcoran, Greg J. Duncan, and Michael Ponza, "Work Experience, Job Segregation and Wages," in *Sex Segregation in the Work Place: Trends, Explanations, Remedies*, ed. Barbara F. Reskin and the National Research Council Committee on Women's Employment and Related Social Issues (Washington, D.C.: National Academy Press, 1984), and "A Longitudinal Approach to White Women's Wages," *Journal of Human Resources* 18, no. 4 (Fall 1983): 497–520.

6. For example, suppose that men's average education level exceeded that of women by one year. The influence of that difference on the wage gap would depend on the value of a year's worth of education. If average wages of men and women differed by $2.00 per hour and an additional year of education were "worth" $2.00 per hour, then all of the wage gap could be explained by the education difference. If additional years of education were worth $.25 per hour, then one-eighth of the gap would be accounted for by the education difference.

minority stayed home from work to care for sick children. Also, black women averaged a year less schooling than did white men. Yet these differences in work patterns and experience will explain wage differences only if those factors in themselves have a substantial effect on earnings. If, for example, workers who placed restrictions on work hours or job location were not paid less than other workers, then women's tendency, on average, to self-impose more restrictions would not explain why they earned less than white men.

The last two columns of table 1 show the results of combining information on differences in education, work experience, work continuity, job restrictions, and absenteeism within the race-sex subgroups with the estimated effects of these factors on earnings. We reached these estimates through a statistical analysis that adjusts for differences in all other variables listed in table 1. The figures in the right-hand columns represent the fraction of the wage gaps explained by each of the skill measures. The totals shown indicate the overall explanatory power of all skills combined.

As expected, differences in work experience explained a significant portion of the wage gap between white men and women, largely because women had acquired less tenure and were more likely to have worked part-time. Altogether, differences in work experience accounted for 29 percent of the wage gap between white men and white women and 17 percent between white men and black women.

Surprisingly, the large differences that existed in male and female patterns of job tenure did little to explain the wage gap between white and black women and white men. Although discontinuous employment did reduce women's work experience, they apparently were not handicapped by having "rusty" skills when they returned to the work force. After adjusting for the effects of lost experience, we found that labor-force interruptions never significantly lowered wages for either women or white men. Delays in starting work after school completion did lower white women's wages slightly.

It is also surprising that the large sex differences in male and female decisions to self-impose job restrictions and to stay home to care for family members explained almost none of the wage gap. Women and white men who were frequently absent from work or who had restricted work hours or job locations did not earn consistently less than did equally qualified workers who imposed no limitations and had attended work regularly.[7]

7. Since it takes time for employers to reflect their evaluation of individual performance in salary and promotion decisions, it may not be surprising that we found no relation between current pay and records of absenteeism. However, additional analysis has also shown that wages are not related to past absenteeism (see Richard D. Coe, "Absenteeism from Work," in *Five Thousand American Families—Patterns of Economic Progress*, vol. 6, ed. Greg J. Duncan and James M. Morgan [Ann Arbor, Mich.: Institute for Social Research, 1978]).

Table 1

Effect of Differences in Human Capital Measures on Wage Gaps between White Men and Women

	Mean Values of Human Capital Measures			Percent of Wage Gap Accounted for by Human Capital Measures*	
	For White Men	For White Women	For Black Women	Between White Men and White Women	Between White Men and Black Women
Education (years)	12.9	12.7	11.8	2	10
Work experience:					
Years of experience prior to present job	11.3	8.1	9.3	4	2
Years in present job	8.7	5.7	6.5	16	10
Proportion of total working years employed full-time............	.91	.79	.83	9	5
Work continuity:					
Years out of the labor force after completing school	.7	3.2	3.1	2	1

12

Length in years of most recent work interruption	1.0	2.5	.5	1	0
Percent who interrupted work two or more times	2.8	11.8	3.7	1	0
Self-imposed job restrictions:					
Percentage who placed limitations on work hours or location	15	34	22	3	0
Percentage working part-time voluntarily	1	15	9	−2	0
Annual rates of absenteeism (hours):					
Due to own illness	37	43	58	0	0
Due to illness of family members	4	12	25	−1	−2
Total				35	26

NOTE.—Our sample consisted of male heads of households, female heads of households, and wives aged sixteen to sixty-four in 1976 who were employed at least 500 hours in 1975. The table reads (e.g., across the first row): "Schooling of white men averaged 12.9 years, compared with averages of 12.7 and 11.8 years for white and black women, respectively. The schooling differences between white men and white women accounted for 2 percent of the earnings gaps between them. This difference explained 10 percent of the gap between white men and black women."

*This figure is calculated by the following formula: $G_Z = (\bar{Z}_{WM} - \bar{Z}_{WW}) \hat{B}_{WM} (\ln \bar{W}_{WM} - \ln \bar{W}_{WW})$, where G_Z = proportion of wage gap between white men and women accounted for by variable Z, $\bar{Z}_{WM}$ = white male mean on Z, $\bar{Z}_{WW}$ = white female mean on Z, $\bar{W}_{WM}$ = white male mean on hourly wage, $\bar{W}_{WW}$ = white female mean on hourly wage, $\hat{B}_{WM}$ = coefficient obtained from regressing ln (hourly wages) on a set of independent predictors containing Z. For details, see Mary Corcoran and Greg J. Duncan, "Work History, Labor Force Attachment, and Earnings Differences between the Races and Sexes," *Journal of Human Resources* 14, no. 1 (Winter 1979): 3–20.

13

Even women who voluntarily chose to work part-time earned no less per hour than other women.

Perhaps our most important finding is that, taken together, all these large differences between women and men explain only about one-third of the wage gap between white men and white women and only about one-quarter of the wage gap between white men and black women. Even after accounting for sex differences among a wide range of factors that influence skill measures, we still see that white men enjoy a large advantage in earnings over women. This casts considerable doubt on the argument that women "deserve" to earn less than men because women sacrifice career advancement in order to meet family responsibilities.

Family Composition and Economic Well-Being

A woman's earnings may, however, represent only one component of her overall economic status. Many women live in families in which a male wage earner contributes the largest component of family income; family income dynamics, then, is the key to understanding their economic position.[8] Some might argue that if the economic benefits provided by marriage were added to married women's earnings, their overall economic position might be quite similar to that of men.

The PSID provides longitudinal data on family incomes, which enables those studying economic inequality not only to determine the structure of a family's income and to compare it at multiple points in time but also to analyze the economic mobility of the family as a whole and of its individual members. By following a panel of families over time, the PSID

8. This section summarizes research from Mary Jo Bane, *Here to Stay: American Families in the Twentieth Century* (New York: Basic Books, 1976); Jacob Benus and James N. Morgan, "Time Period, Unit of Analysis, and Income Concept in the Analysis of Income Distribution," in *The Personal Distribution of Income and Wealth*, ed. James D. Smith (New York: Columbia University Press, 1975); Richard D. Coe, Greg J. Duncan, and Martha S. Hill, "Dynamic Aspects of Poverty and Welfare Use in the United States" (paper delivered at the Conference on Problems of Poverty, Clark University, August 1982); Greg J. Duncan, "The Implications of Changing Family Composition for the Dynamic Analysis of Family Well-Being" (paper delivered at the Conference on Analysis of Panel Data on Income, London, June 1982); Martha S. Hill, "Trends in the Economic Situation of U.S. Families and Children" (paper delivered at the Conference on Families and the Economy, National Academy of Science, Washington, D.C., 1982); Jonathan P. Lane and James N. Morgan, "Patterns of Change in Economic Status and Family Structure," in *Five Thousand American Families—Patterns of Economic Progress*, vol. 3, ed. Greg J. Duncan and James N. Morgan (Ann Arbor, Mich.: Institute for Social Research, 1975); George Masnick and Mary Jo Bane, *The Nation's Families: 1969–1990*, Joint Center Outlook Reports (Cambridge, Mass.: Joint Center for Urban Studies of MIT and Harvard University, 1980); James N. Morgan, "Change in Global Measures," in *Five Thousand American Families—Patterns of Economic Progress*, vol. 1, ed. James N. Morgan et al. (Ann Arbor, Mich.: Institute for Social Research, 1974).

also raises a whole new set of questions about our conception and analysis of the "family." In a cross-sectional study, determining family composition is not problematic since at any point, all individuals can be classified uniquely as members of a particular family. However as the PSID demonstrates, a family can at any time splinter through divorce, separation, or the departure of children. Two distinct families can merge through marriage, cohabitation, the return of a child after a temporary absence, or more complicated rearrangements. In fact, one major finding of this study is that families do undergo considerable change over time. By the thirteenth year of the PSID, only 11.9 percent of the existing families had not changed in composition, and 57.1 percent were headed by someone other than the original sample head.

These fluctuations in family structure have important implications. Although measures of the level of family economic status (e.g., family income, family per capita income) may be the outcomes of interest, the family itself is not usually the appropriate unit of analysis. If, however, we choose to look at individuals, then each can be associated with a family at a given point in time and with the economic well-being of that family. This strategy has the added advantage of allowing us to test whether changes in family composition predict changes in economic well-being for women and children.

Greg J. Duncan examined the level, trend, and stability of family income for men, women, and children from 1974 to 1979.[9] Both the level and stability of per capita family income (measured as income relative to needs)[10] were greater for white men than for either women or children. The economic benefits of marriage did not, on average, compensate women for their low relative earnings. Black children had the least per capita income and the least financial stability.

Family composition changes were important in determining changes in economic well-being. Duncan estimated growth rates in family income and in family income relative to needs over the period 1971–78 for male heads of household, female heads of household, and children.[11] He then used dummy variable regression to estimate the effect of family composition changes on family income growth after adjusting for education, age, and race. For men, such changes had a negligible effect on per capita income growth; in contrast, a shift in family composition had a powerful effect on the economic status of women and children. Indeed, the ex-

9. See Duncan (n. 8 above).

10. Needs are defined using the Orshansky Poverty Index, explained in Molly Orshansky, "Counting the Poor," in *Poverty in America*, ed. L. Ferman, J. Hornblack, and A. Haberc (Ann Arbor: University of Michigan Press, 1968).

11. See Duncan (n. 8 above).

planatory power of family change variables was many times higher than the explanatory power of changes in the labor-force participation of men and women. The effects of four major changes in family makeup are explained below in order of importance.

Divorce and remarriage.—Divorce often leads to a sharp drop in family income and per capita income for an ex-wife and, if present, her children. She loses her former husband's wages for the support of her newly formed family, which in almost all instances includes the divorced couple's children as well. Alimony and child support payments from an ex-husband are rare and, even if paid, usually do not represent more than a fraction of the lost income. Although most divorced women enter or remain in the labor force, their low level of earnings and part-time work arrangements result in a dramatically lower income level for the family. Private transfer payments from other relatives or friends are rare. Roughly one-fifth of ex-wives receive public transfer payments in the year following a divorce, but they do not replace much of the lost income.

The ex-wife's new family is smaller following her husband's departure, but the loss of his income is much greater than the drop in needs, producing almost as sharp a decline in per capita family income as in family income alone. The economic status of the ex-husband, in contrast, typically improves substantially for the same reasons. His newly formed family (which usually comprises just himself for a brief period, then another spouse) has fewer needs, since it is greatly reduced in size.

Marriage or remarriage sharply improves the economic status of female-headed households because a male wage earner's contribution to the total family income is typically much greater than the growth in family needs following his arrival. Remarriage is much more common for divorced men than for divorced women and considerably more frequent for white women than for black women.

Departure of children.—Children departing their parental homes experience a sharp drop in family income level but little net change, on average, in their per capita family income level. The newly formed family loses the parents' income but proportionately lowers its needs standards as well. The economic well-being of family members left behind typically increases modestly since, on average, the departing children have added more to the family's needs than to its income.

Birth.—Births often lead to modest reductions in a family's economic well-being. Needs increase with the addition of a new family member, and income often falls if a mother drops out of the labor force to care for the child.

Widowhood.—The death of a spouse is most common for an elderly woman, whose income and needs both decrease so that her economic position changes very little.

Poverty

The "culture of poverty" thesis, dominant both in social science research on poverty and in public policy debate, was developed from anthropological case studies of poor, urban families in a number of countries. It contends that the qualities developed and reinforced in the environment in which the poor live prevent them from taking advantage of economic opportunities. Poverty is seen as a self-perpetuating state; the present generation of poor locked into it bequeath it to their children. Proponents of this argument vary in their estimates of the proportion of poor people to which this pattern applies.

Bradley Schiller has classified this argument as a "flawed character" explanation of poverty. The problem is seen not as a lack of opportunities for the poor but as their failure to seize opportunities because they lack diligence and initiative. According to this argument, poverty is more a function of the way people think than of their physical environment; the implication is that to cure poverty one has to change the attitudes of the poor. As Oscar Lewis put it: "Once [the culture of poverty] comes into existence, it tends to perpetuate itself from generation because of its effects on children. By the time slum children are age six or seven, they have usually absorbed the basic values and attitudes of their subculture and are not psychologically geared to take full advantage of changing conditions or increased opportunities which may occur in their lifetime."[12]

A new flawed-character argument has now become prominent in public debate on poverty. In a recent *New Yorker* series and in a new book, Ken Auletta writes about the "underclass"—a group permanently mired in poverty.[13] He primarily describes relatively young, able-bodied adults and leaves the impression that many of the long-term poor fall into four subgroups: "hostile street criminals," "hustlers," welfare mothers, and the "traumatized." Much of Auletta's work is based on case studies of participants in a supported work program for the hard-core poor.

Lewis and Auletta present compelling and eloquent descriptions of a set of poor people; such case studies easily command public attention—particularly when few data exist about the dynamics of poverty. But the individuals they describe may be very unrepresentative of the larger groups with which the public tends to identify them. A major advantage of the PSID is its more complete picture of the nature, extent, and

---

12. Bradley R. Schiller, *The Economics of Poverty and Discrimination*, 2d ed. (Englewood Cliffs, N.J.: Prentice-Hall, Inc., 1976); Oscar Lewis, *La Vida* (New York: Random House, 1966), p. 50.

13. Ken Auletta, *The Underclass* (New York: Random House, 1982).

duration of poverty as experienced by real but representative families over time.[14]

We find that poverty is more widespread but much less persistent than is popularly imagined. Poverty spells often begin with a job loss or a marital breakup and end when an individual takes a new job or remarries. Even the small group of persistently poor individuals do not reflect the demographic makeup or economic experiences of either Auletta's "underclass" or Lewis's slum families.

For example, consider the incidence of poverty over the ten-year period 1969–78. In 1978, 6.8 percent of the PSID sample were poor.[15] If poverty were permanent, then those individuals—and thus 6.8 percent of the entire population—should have been poor for every one of those ten years. Similarly, if poverty were entirely transitory, then poverty in one year would be no predictor of later poverty, and 52 percent of the population would have been poor at least once.[16] In fact, one-quarter of the population were poor at some time during the years from 1969 to 1978, suggesting that poverty is a widespread risk. But of that group, the majority were only poor one or two years, and only about one-tenth (2.6 percent of the entire population) were poor at least eight years.[17]

The persistently poor were thus only a small subset of those who ever experienced poverty, and they did not fit easily into the underclass stereotype. One-third were elderly or lived in households headed by an elderly person. More than one-quarter were children, fewer than one-third lived in large urban areas, and more than one-quarter lived in families in which the head had worked a substantial amount in at least five out of the ten years. By following the economic fortunes of both children

14. This section summarizes research by Richard D. Coe, "A Preliminary Empirical Examination of the Dynamics of Welfare Use," in *Five Thousand American Families—Patterns of Economic Progress*, vol. 9, ed. Daniel H. Hill, Martha S. Hill, and James N. Morgan (Ann Arbor, Mich.: Institute for Social Research, 1981), "Dependency and Poverty in the Short and Long Run," in *Five Thousand American Families—Patterns of Economic Progress*, vol. 6, ed. Greg J. Duncan and James N. Morgan (Ann Arbor, Mich.: Institute for Social Research, 1978), and "The Poverty Line: Its Functions and Limitations," *Public Welfare* (Winter 1978), pp. 32–36; Coe, Duncan, and Hill (n. 8 above); Hill (n. 8 above); Martha S. Hill, "Some Dynamics of Poverty," in Hill, Hill, and Morgan, eds.; Frank Levy, "The Intergenerational Transfer of Poverty," Working Paper 1241–02 (Washington, D.C.: Urban Institute, January 1980, mimeographed), and "How Big Is the American Underclass?" rev. version (Urban Institute, Washington, D.C., 1976, mimeographed).

15. This figure is based on the PSID. The Census Bureau reported a higher incidence of poverty for 1978—11.4 percent of the population. For a number of reasons, however, these figures are not comparable.

16. The 52 percent figure is equal to $\Sigma_{i=1}^{N} (.068)(.932)^{i-1}$.

17. This one-tenth figure is the ratio of experiencing long-term poverty (2.6 percent) to ever experiencing poverty (25 percent).

and parents with PSID data, Frank Levy found that, after forming their own households, at least four-fifths of the children from poor families moved out of poverty; many had incomes substantially above the poverty line. This offers little support for the idea that, among most of the poor, poverty is transmitted from one generation to the next. PSID data on the achievement motivation, sense of personal efficacy, and future orientation of all household heads in the early years of the survey also indicate that these attitudes had small and generally insignificant effects on later changes in individuals' economic status; at least as measured in the PSID, these factors did not account for failure to achieve, as some flawed-character theories might predict.

If the culture-of-poverty and underclass arguments do not apply to many of the long-term poor, then what does explain persistent poverty, and how might one combat it? One way to answer this is to look at the demographic characteristics of the persistently poor.

First, one-third of the persistently poor are elderly, a group in which women are overrepresented. Second, the remaining 65 percent live in households headed by a woman, and 70 percent of these are headed by a black woman. Most of these heads of household have the double economic burden of children at home who increase needs and decrease a single parent's ability to work.

This overrepresentation of female-headed households among the persistently poor underscores our earlier conclusion that changes in family composition greatly affect women's and children's economic well-being. Given Norton and Glick's prediction that 40 percent of all first marriages will end in divorce, we could expect considerable damage to the standard of living of women and children in these homes.[18] In fact, Richard Coe, Greg Duncan, and Martha Hill report that for children, divorce is the strongest single predictor of poverty.[19] Remarriage does considerably improve women's and children's standard of living; but of course not all divorced women do remarry. The period during which they head households without access to a man's income—whether brief or extended—is financially difficult. Frank Levy's analyses suggest that even if poor women who head households were able to work, many of them would be unlikely to find a job paying enough to remove them from poverty. Thus again, we need to understand more about women's low wage rates if we are to help them and their children move out of poverty.

Using PSID data to examine the economic experiences of children over a ten-year period, Martha Hill found that they were slightly more likely to experience poverty than the general population.[20] But her most

18. Arthur J. Norton and Paul C. Glick, "Marital Instability: Past, Present and Future," *Journal of Social Issues* 32 (1976): 5–20.

19. Coe, Duncan, and Hill (n. 8 above).

20. Hill, "Trends in the Economic Situation of U.S. Families and Children" (n. 8 above).

dramatic finding was that black children were considerably more likely to live in poverty than white children. Over a ten-year period, 70 percent of black children were poor at some time, and 30 percent were poor in at least six of the ten years; comparable estimates for white children were 30 percent and 2 percent, respectively. Clearly we are far from eliminating the gap between black and white children's economic experiences during childhood, an aim of the social programs of the 1960s and 1970s.

Welfare Dependency

Central to the recent conservative attack on welfare programs—particularly AFDC and food stamps—is the argument that these programs foster the growth of a "welfare class," people trapped in a system that perpetuates their poverty and dependency. Martin Anderson, former domestic policy advisor to Reagan, summarizes this view: "In effect we have created a new caste of Americans—perhaps as much as one-tenth of this nation—a caste of people free from basic wants but almost totally dependent on the State, with little hope or prospects of breaking free. Perhaps we should call them the Dependent Americans."[21]

Understanding welfare dependency is clearly important for an understanding of women's and children's well-being, since they form the majority of AFDC recipients. Conservatives argue that typical welfare recipients live in families headed by a woman, who persistently depends on welfare and raises children who will do the same. They also suggest that welfare discourages working and remarriage and encourages divorce, separation, and illegitimate births.

The PSID data on long-run patterns of welfare use simply do not support many of these stereotypes, also found in case-study accounts such as Auletta's.[22] Like poverty, welfare use is widespread; between 1969 and 1978 one-fourth of the population lived in families that received welfare income at some point.[23] But welfare dependency was not extensive. If dependency is defined as reliance on welfare income for more than half of total family income in any year, then only one-third of those receiving

21. Martin Anderson, *Welfare* (Stanford, Calif.: Hoover Institution Press, 1978), p. 56.
22. This section reviews research by Coe, "A Preliminary Empirical Examination . . . ," "Dependency and Poverty . . . ," and "The Poverty Line" (all in n. 14 above); Coe, Duncan, and Hill (n. 8 above); Martha Hill and Michael Ponza, "The Intergenerational Transfer of Welfare: Does Dependency Beget Dependency?" (paper delivered at the Southern Economic Association meeting, Washington, D.C., November 1983); Levy, "The Intergenerational Transfer of Poverty," and "How Big Is the American Underclass?" (both in n. 14 above); Martin Rein and Lee Rainwater, "Patterns of Welfare Use," *Social Science Review* (December 1978), pp. 511–34; Isabel V. Sawhill et al., *Income Transfers and Family Structure* (Washington, D.C.: Urban Institute, 1975).
23. This group of welfare recipients overlaps with, but is not identical to, the group of poor individuals identified between 1969 and 1978.

welfare throughout this period were dependent on it. Using this definition, only 2 percent of the population were dependent on welfare for
eight or more of the ten years between 1969 and 1978. (About 1 percent
were dependent in all ten years.) Thus, most welfare recipients are not on
the rolls for a long time, and most are not completely dependent on
welfare income. Instead, welfare recipients are more likely to mix work
and welfare or to alternate between them.

The PSID data also give little or no support to the contention that
patterns of welfare dependency are intergenerational. Most women who
had left the homes of parents who received welfare income were not likely
to be receiving welfare themselves. Nor did they appear more likely to
receive public aid than otherwise similar women whose parents did not
receive welfare income. In general, parents' overall economic status
proved a more powerful determinant of their children's welfare use than
did their history of welfare assistance.

Another important charge leveled against the current welfare system
is that it has the unintended side effects of encouraging divorce and
separation, discouraging remarriage, or encouraging illegitimate births.
The PSID evidence indicates few, if any, effects of this kind.[24]

We conclude that the welfare system successfully reaches a large
number of the poor without promoting dependency. But admittedly
there is a small group persistently dependent on welfare. As with the
persistently poor, these welfare recipients are disproportionately female,
black, and with children in the home. Any solutions for this group must
deal with the burdens of child care and the low wage positions of blacks
and women. Without major societal changes, direct income transfers may
be the most efficient solution.

Conclusion

The PSID data have enabled a more complete description and analysis of the long-term economic processes affecting the economic fortunes
of women and children and have been useful in dispelling some prominent myths about poverty, welfare, women's wages, and race differences.
In summary, this research indicates the following:

1. The argument that women earn less than men because they
acquire fewer work skills does not hold up under empirical scrutiny.
Although there are large differences between men's and women's work

---

24. Evidence from the negative income tax experiments suggests that these income
maintenance plans may lead to higher rates of marital dissolution than the current system of
AFDC, SSI, and other welfare programs. Evidence from the PSID provides little support for
the hypothesis that couples living in states with the most generous AFDC benefits are more
likely to split up than couples living in less generous states.

skills, our data show that two-thirds of the wage gap between white men and white women and three-quarters of the gap between white men and black women cannot be accounted for by sex differences in skills, work participation, or labor-force attachment.

2. Families change considerably over time, which profoundly affects the economic fortunes of women and children. Often a divorced mother faces the double economic bind of assuming complete responsibility for her children's care while attempting to make up for her ex-husband's lost income with small child support payments and poorly paid wage labor.

3. Arguments about the culture of poverty and the underclass are not consistent with evidence from the PSID about the extent, duration, and nature of poverty. Poverty and welfare use are more pervasive, but much less persistent, than is commonly thought. There is little evidence of extensive welfare dependence or of the transmission of poverty and welfare status from parents to children. There is also little evidence that good attitudes enable people to overcome poverty or that welfare encourages family instability.

4. Women and children have a much lower and more unstable per capita family income over time—and a higher risk of falling into poverty—than do white men. Black children are the group most at risk. Their six-year average per capita income is less than half that of white men. Clearly race differences have not narrowed to the point that black and white children enjoy similar economic security during childhood.

These findings have important implications for public policy debate. Arguments for welfare cuts on the grounds that the poor are "undeserving" and lack initiative are contradicted by our evidence that many recipients of public aid mix work with welfare; the long-term poor most in need of aid, in fact, tend to be elderly people and women with children. Even if we were willing to compel female heads of household to work full-time, our study suggests that they could not make enough to escape poverty. Welfare reform proposals based on assumptions that the availability of AFDC funds encourages welfare dependency within and across generations or that it causes marital instability are simply untenable in light of our research.

Evidence from the PSID also challenges the notion that women's low earnings are due to the voluntary sexual division of labor in the home, a claim often used to justify abandoning equal opportunity and affirmative action programs for women. Such a strategy, we believe, would most likely further exacerbate the economic inequalities based on sex and age reported here. One route to improving women's and children's economic well-being would be to reduce "undeserved" sex differences in earnings. Another might be some kind of social insurance program for divorced women that provided more generous benefits than those currently available from alimony or AFDC.

Finally, our findings confirm that it is not yet time to pull back on compensatory and affirmative action programs for blacks. Policies that discontinue the government's role in alleviating or redressing race-based childhood inequalities could be very costly politically for a society that places great symbolic value on "equal opportunity."

Institute for Social Research
University of Michigan

Turning Back the Clock on Public Welfare

Deborah K. Zinn and Rosemary C. Sarri

The number of persons below the official poverty line in the United States has increased dramatically since 1980, rising from 30 to 34 million, or 15 percent of the population. Women and children have entered the ranks of the poor at a rate that greatly exceeds that observed for men or the aged. This trend has been accelerated by the recent decrease in public aid programs aimed at poor women and children.[1]

Historically the federal government has only reluctantly extended income supports to its needy citizens—even when those in need are children, unable to support themselves. Women have often had the primary responsibilities for socializing and financially supporting their children, responsibilities that they have been expected to fulfill without

This research report was funded in part by grants from the Ford and Shiffman foundations and the Ruth Mott Fund. We are indebted to other staff members of the working welfare women project: William Barton, Nicky Beisel, Jacques Boulet, Amy Butler, Deborah Eddy, Sue Lambert, Aisha Ray, Carol Russell, and Joan Weber. We also thank Agnes Mansour, Mark Murray, and Joseph La Rosa of the Michigan Department of Social Services, and last, but not least, the women who gave us freely of their time and knowledge and without whom this study would not have been possible.

1. U.S. Department of Commerce, Bureau of the Census, *Money Income and Poverty Status of Families and Persons in the U.S., 1982*, in *Current Population Reports*, series P-60, no. 140 (Washington, D.C.: Government Printing Office, 1983), table 15, p. 22; Sheldon Danziger, "Budget Cuts as Welfare Reform," *American Economic Association Papers and Proceedings* 73 (May 1983): 65–70.

the assurance of long-term public income support. Even today, in no state can a family with AFDC income support receive cash grants or in-kind transfers that will bring its total income up to the poverty level.[2]

Presidents Nixon and Carter established reform of the Aid to Families with Dependent Children (AFDC) program as a major social policy goal. However it was Ronald Reagan who engineered the most significant changes in welfare policies in recent history. Within his first year in office, he introduced "reforms" that Congress passed into law as the Omnibus Budget Reconciliation Act of 1981 (OBRA) and that were subsequently implemented in states and localities nationwide.[3] In contrast to the controversial Nixon and Carter proposals, which would have extended benefits as well as federal responsibility, the Reagan changes significantly reduced expenditures in social welfare programs serving the poor.

Especially hard hit by OBRA policies were poor working women. The costs of the AFDC program were cut primarily by raising the tax rate on the earned income of welfare recipients and by establishing lower and more restrictive gross income limits. Congruent with the trend toward increased employment of women outside the home, 27 percent of the adult AFDC population was in the labor force at the time of the OBRA cut (14 percent working and 13 percent actively seeking work).[4] All AFDC women also raise families; therefore, a significant proportion was performing two demanding roles.

Despite compelling data to the contrary, Ronald Reagan and his administration have accepted the conservative thesis that those supported by public aid will not attempt to become self-supporting and will become divorced from the world of work.[5] Moreover, they postulate that women receiving assistance will evidence increased psychological deficiencies and deviant behavior and will transmit patterns of dependency to their children. The view that working women with children are better off coping with sharply decreased incomes than with the potential risk of psychological harm from welfare assistance has led to policy changes whereby poor

2. U.S. Commission on Civil Rights, *A Growing Crisis: Disadvantaged Women and Their Children* (Washington, D.C.: Government Printing Office, May 1983), pp. 5–7.

3. A comprehensive description and analysis of OBRA is presented in John L. Palmer and Isabel V. Sawhill, *The Reagan Experiment* (Washington, D.C.: Urban Institute, 1982). One of the most complex statutes implemented in recent history, OBRA incorporates changes in more than 200 categorical and block grant programs. Consequences for AFDC recipients have differed widely within and among the states, which have implemented OBRA with substantial variation.

4. U.S. Department of Health and Human Services, *1979 AFDC Recipient Characteristics Study*, pts. 1, 2 (Washington, D.C.: Government Printing Office, 1982), pp. 45–47.

5. For two of the more thoroughgoing critiques of welfare support to working women and their children, see Martin Anderson, *Welfare: The Political Economy of Welfare Reform in the U.S.* (Stanford, Calif.: Hoover Institute Press, 1978); George Gilder, *Wealth and Poverty* (New York: Basic Books, 1981).

working women (the "marginally" poor) are not allowed to participate in AFDC or related income supports.

Clearly, conservative advocates of such policies do not recognize the extensive work efforts of these women or the ways in which their efforts are diminished by women's virtual restriction to low-paying, sex-segregated occupations with few or no employee benefits.[6] No consideration is given to environmental factors affecting AFDC recipients' well-being, such as economic recession, double-digit unemployment, or sex discrimination in employment. Also ignored is the fact that 40 percent of all AFDC recipients who leave the program have incomes below the poverty level in the years following receipt of AFDC support.[7]

This article challenges conservative assumptions about welfare and examines the effects of recent federal changes in OBRA on working recipients who were terminated from AFDC.

AFDC Policy from 1935 to OBRA of 1981

The federal AFDC program has been providing payments to families since its passage in 1935 as part of the Social Security Act. At that time, the Depression brought to federal and state governments an increased recognition of both the victimizing economic circumstances beyond individual control and the government's responsibility for the well-being of families. The program has remained fundamentally unchanged throughout its almost fifty-year history: a means-tested program for providing income to women who are the sole heads of families.[8] However, with the 1960s came major liberalizing trends. Congress gave states the option of extend-

6. U.S. Commission on Civil Rights, *Unemployment and Underemployment among Blacks, Hispanics, and Women* (Washington, D.C.: Government Printing Office, November 1982). The median yearly income in 1981 for families maintained by women was $10,960, in contrast to the comparable figure of $19,887 for families headed by a single male and $25,065 for married two-parent families (U.S. Commission on Civil Rights, *A Growing Crisis: Disadvantaged Women and Their Children*, p. 33; *Perspectives on Working Women: A Databook*, bulletin 2080 [Washington, D.C.: Bureau of Labor Statistics, August 1983], table 1, p. 3). For more on occupational segregation and resultant income differentials, see Valerie Oppenheimer, *Female Labor Force in the United States* (Berkeley, Calif.: Institute of International Studies, 1970); Martha Blaxall, ed., *The Implications of Occupational Segregation* (Chicago: University of Chicago Press, 1976).

7. Mary Jo Bane and David Ellwood, *The Dynamics of Dependence: The Routes to Self-Sufficiency* (Cambridge, Mass.: Urban Sysytems Research, 1983).

8. For more on the history of AFDC, see Josephine C. Brown, *Public Relief, 1929–1939* (New York: Holt & Co., 1940); Winifred Bell, *Aid to Dependent Children* (New York: Columbia University Press, 1965); Frances Fox Piven and Richard A. Cloward, *Regulating the Poor* (New York: Random House, 1971); Gilbert Y. Steiner, *The State of Welfare* (Washington, D.C.: Brookings Institution, 1971); Martha N. Ozawa, *Income Maintenance and Work Incentives* (New York: Praeger Publications, 1982).

ing benefits to families headed by unemployed males and initiated the Medicaid and food stamp programs. Benefit levels increased only incrementally, but the number of persons qualifying for and participating in AFDC rose, causing concern about the burgeoning welfare rolls.[9]

The Work Incentive Program (WIN) was started in the late 1960s to help women acquire work skills and to act as a job placement agency for employers who wanted to hire the low-wage workers who made up the welfare rolls. In 1971, for the first time, federal AFDC policy required women whose children were over the age of six to work outside the home.[10]

Concomitant with federal work requirements, Congress established as work incentives new policies for the treatment of earnings. Under these revised provisions, women who got jobs after having received AFDC benefits could retain part of their earnings without a dollar-for-dollar reduction in benefits; their tax rate was no longer 100 percent. This policy was referred to as the "thirty and one-third" income disregard: AFDC administrators subtracted the first thirty dollars of earned income and one-third of the remainder from a woman's gross wage before calculating her grant reduction. Women could also deduct work expenses. However, as a woman's wages increased, her grant amount was gradually lowered until she reached a cutoff for AFDC eligibility.

Women with children under six could choose to take employment or to remain at home until their children entered school. This option provided some security for job seekers, who knew they could temporarily rely on welfare if necessary. For women who were the sole supporters of families, the AFDC program was an important financial backup—it would not necessarily support their families adequately, but it would keep them from destitution.

"Work incentives" for AFDC recipients were also subsidies to employers who could be assured that their employees would not have to survive solely on the wages and benefits offered. Aid to Families with Dependent Children provided health insurance and child care to all recipients through the Medicaid program and Title IV-A, respectively. The work requirements ensured a more stable work force by eliminating women's option to remain full-time homemakers.

With Reagan's election came changes in almost all federal social programs, including AFDC. Congress passed the OBRA changes of 1981 as part of an overall plan to cut governmental costs, shift responsibility for social programs to the state and local levels, and target the remaining programs toward the "truly needy." In essence, OBRA turned back the clock on welfare policy, profoundly affecting eligibility of working

9. Piven and Cloward, pp. 183–99.
10. Ozawa, p. 30.

women and their families. The earned income disregards and work incentives of the 1960s were largely eliminated. Since many ancillary programs such as food stamps, Medicaid, and child care are related to categorical eligibility for AFDC, working women cut from the AFDC program were often cut from these other benefits as well.[11]

In addition OBRA reduced or eliminated other programs providing important benefits for low-income families and children: prenatal, maternal, and child health care; school lunch allowances; and day care. The Children's Defense Fund estimates that approximately one and one-half million children were in families whose AFDC benefits were reduced; federal program cutbacks directly affected 5–6 million children overall.[12] Although OBRA was based on the premise that states should accept primary responsibility for welfare, few have been able to compensate for the loss of federally supported programs, which were cut swiftly during the recession.[13]

In its study of the effects of AFDC policy changes, the Center for the Study of Social Policy summarized the following OBRA changes that had the greatest effects on AFDC recipients with earnings:

1. Establishment of a cap on eligibility [for families whose gross income exceeds] 150% of the state need standard, . . . the amount of money each state establishes as necessary for a family of a given size to meet basic living costs. Prior to the OBRA policy changes, a family with modest earnings and high work-related expenses (transportation, childcare, etc.) might have qualified for AFDC based on low "countable" income (gross earnings minus work expenses).

2. Elimination of the $30 and one-third disregard after four months . . . thereby sharply reducing and in some cases eliminating AFDC benefits to working parents after [this period]. Also . . . the earned income disregard is applied to net income rather than gross income. This change reduces the value of the disregard, since it is now applied to a smaller amount of earnings.

3. Standardization of work expenses at $75 per month [for full-time workers and $50 per month for part-time workers] and capping of child care expenses at $160 per month [for each child]. Previously, working recipients could deduct reasonable work-related expenses such as taxes, transportation, and uniforms when their benefits were calculated. This new rule eliminates this flexibility.

4. Advance counting of any Earned Income Tax Credit (EITC),

---

11. Our research showed that women terminated from AFDC often were not informed of their possible continued eligibility for these ancillary programs or of benefits for which they were known to be legally eligible.

12. Children's Defense Fund, *A Children's Defense Fund Budget: An Analysis of the 1984 Budget* (Washington, D.C.: Children's Defense Fund, 1983).

13. Palmer and Sawhill (n. 3 above), p. 328.

[refundable to earners] with annual incomes below $10,000 and at least one dependent child. . . . Whereas under previous law the tax credit was only considered as income if an AFDC recipient actually applied for and received it, the new policy requires that the EITC be counted as income in determining AFDC benefits whether or not it is actually received. In some cases the recipient may not receive the tax credit, yet the AFDC grant is now automatically reduced.[14]

The following sections of this article set forth the results of a recent study conducted at the Institute for Social Research of the University of Michigan that examined the impact of OBRA policies on working women and sought to determine how these women attempted to maintain individual and family well-being when confronted with the termination of their AFDC benefits and Medicaid insurance. In some cases housing, energy, child care, and/or school lunch allowances were also eliminated.

Our guiding hypothesis was that both objective factors—such as economic need—and subjective factors—such as perceived stress—would influence the well-being of a poor family faced with AFDC termination. Therefore, in order to understand the additive effects of OBRA cuts, we chose to investigate the total picture of family life. Thus although OBRA did not create many or all of the poverty-related problems discussed below, it did exacerbate them by reducing family benefits from a program already beleagured by low benefits and philosophical controversies.

Methodology

In 1982 we selected six Michigan counties to serve as the geographical population for our study. Three of the counties had low rates of unemployment (around 9 percent); three had high rates (around 20 percent). Wide variations in employment rates throughout Michigan counties in 1982 (6–34 percent) made this factor a critical sampling variable. We chose counties as the unit for analysis because public social service programs are administered by county agencies that retain some decision-making authority about services and service delivery.

With the cooperation and assistance of the Michigan Department of Social Services, we identified 3,200 women in the six counties who were possibly terminated from AFDC between September 1, 1981, and April 1, 1982, because of OBRA policies. After selecting samples randomly by county, we screened all women and then obtained complete interviews from 316 recipients cut from AFDC due to OBRA. Most interviews were

14. The Center for the Study of Social Policy, *Effects of Federal AFDC Policy Changes: A Study of a Federal-State "Partnership"* (Washington, D.C.: Center for the Study of Social Policy, March 1983), pp. 7–9.

completed in the respondents' homes. The refusal rate was 8.4 percent and we were unable to locate some women who had moved. These latter recipients were replaced with other randomly selected cases. The sample used in this article includes 279 respondents who were single heads of households terminated because of OBRA policies pertaining to working women.[15]

We first examined each woman's initial important decision to continue or discontinue work, then her strategies to overcome problems in balancing work, income, and family needs. The latter step was essential to our study, for as Deborah Belle, Diana Dill, and their colleagues observed in a study of AFDC Boston families and stress, the environment of low-income women frequently opposes their efforts to overcome problematic situations.[16] Strategies that are effective in more hospitable social contexts may fail for this sample of working AFDC recipients.

Findings

Respondents' Personal and Social Characteristics

The median age of the respondents was 33 years; 37 percent were women of color. Three-fourths had high-school degrees; 30 percent had some postsecondary education; 12 percent were enrolled in school when we interviewed them.

Sixteen percent identified themselves as married or presently living with a "significant other." The average household had 2.1 children in residence, but, on the average, families had listed only 1.8 children in their formal AFDC unit at the time of their termination. Most of the children not included in the formal count were stepchildren, nieces, or nephews. The majority of other adults living in the household added to its income, although their contribution was often small and sporadic.

Given our difficulties in locating and contacting respondents, we were not surprised by their reported high levels of mobility. Twenty-three percent had moved one or more times in 1982. Twenty-seven percent of the households had one or more persons move in with them,

15. Ten percent of the overall sample was terminated because of the application of the "stepfather" rule and is excluded from our remaining analysis. Many families in this group had far higher household incomes at termination than those headed by females, but several returned to AFDC when their husbands deserted as a result of increased financial problems. Many of these families then received far higher AFDC benefits than they had prior to termination. Undoubtedly, the social costs of family disruption were great for these women and children.

16. Deborah Belle, ed., *Lives in Stress* (Beverly Hills, Calif.: Sage Publications, 1982); Diana Dill et al., "The Impact of the Environment on the Coping Efforts of Low Income Mothers," *Family Relations* 29 (October 1980): 503–9.

and 21 percent had someone move out. Many respondents moved in with parents, siblings, and friends in order to stretch meager resources.

Women in this sample, on the average, first went on AFDC at the age of twenty-four. Of those not married at the time of the interview, 72 percent reported having applied for AFDC following the breakup of a previous marriage or partnership—which made each a single head of household. Mary Jo Bane and David Ellwood reported that poverty "spells" begun under these circumstances last longer than poverty spells attributable to other causes, especially if young children are involved.[17]

Respondents' Welfare Use and Experience

By December 1981, two months after OBRA policy changes were implemented in Michigan, 78 percent of our sample had been terminated—primarily because they earned income over 150 percent of the state's standard of need. Michigan was experiencing a severe recession—state funds were short and deficits were growing. Thus, not surprisingly, AFDC cases were dropped as quickly as possible and without consideration of familial needs.

Although most women knew that their benefits had been eliminated by cutbacks in social welfare spending, few respondents understood the details of their terminations. Only 8 percent appealed the decision of the Department of Social Services. Only two-fifths said they were informed that they might be eligible for food stamps even though ineligible for AFDC.

Forty-seven percent reapplied for welfare after being terminated, and an additional 40 percent said that they wanted or needed to reapply —an overall total of 84 percent. Those who did reapply were most apt to cite health insurance as the reason for need (40 percent). Overall, 36 percent did not have health insurance coverage for their children. More than half of the respondents visited the local social services office at least once to inquire about or reapply for benefits.

Among the 53 percent who did not reapply, 70 percent said that they did not do so because they thought they were ineligible, a realistic assumption. Because working women could not return to AFDC easily in Michigan, the return rate severely underestimates the poverty and suffering of families who remained off AFDC—David Stockman's so-called success cases. Furthermore, many former recipients reported that they would not return to AFDC no matter how great their distress because of the degrading eligibility procedures and the lack of surety about their continuing eligibility.

The return rate to AFDC for women in our sample was 24 percent over an eighteen-month interval (see table 1). Among those who received

17. Bane and Ellwood (n. 7 above), pp. 17–19.

some type of welfare support for at least one month between termination and interview, 43 percent received food stamps and 32 percent received Medicaid. However, within this group some continued to obtain food stamps and Medicaid (for a limited period up to four months) after initial termination of their AFDC cash benefits. Even though two out of five children in this sample had no health insurance, and need for medical coverage was stated as the most important reason for reapplication, most women were not reinstated. Beyond the 24 percent who obtained Medicaid when their AFDC benefits were reinstated, only an additional 10 percent were able to reapply and receive Medicaid alone (without AFDC) through the Medicaid for the medically indigent program, an optional program in which Michigan participates.

Respondents' Economic Well-Being

One irony in OBRA as well as in other welfare-related legislation is that working women who receive only a small portion of their income from AFDC are categorically labeled as welfare recipients, rather than as employees or the "deserving poor." To place welfare receipt in perspective, the average monthly AFDC grant at the time of the OBRA cuts was $173, the average food stamp grant $40, and the recipient's average earned income $609. During the year following a working woman's termination, her average monthly income dropped to $771 from the $822 monthly total of food stamps, AFDC grants, and wages quoted above. The average annual income received in 1982 by the women cut from welfare ($9,250) was almost three times less than the median income for white, two-parent families that year ($26,019) and below the poverty level for a nonfarm family of four ($9,862).[18]

Table 1

Respondents Who Received Welfare Assistance after AFDC Termination
(*N* = 279) (%)

Benefits Received	For at Least One Month*	Without Interruption	Following Reinstatement in Program
AFDC	24	...	24
Medicaid only	32	22	10
Food stamps	43	12	33
One or more programs	56	28	40

*If an individual was both continued and reinstated, she is counted only once in this column.

18. Tom Joe et al., *Working Female-headed Families in Poverty* (Washington, D.C.: Center for the Study of Social Policy, 1984), p. 10; U.S. House of Representatives, Committee on

The respondents, whose average gross wage was $5.40 per hour, were primarily in low-paying service or retail trade related occupations. They received 74 percent of their total income through their employment earnings, which were of overriding importance in determining economic well-being. When earned income is low, even a small amount of additional income can represent a high and important proportion of total income. On the average, when these women lost AFDC benefits, they lost 21 percent of their income, with one month's (or less) notice. Often they also lost all medical coverage through Medicaid and child care payments, of extreme importance in ensuring the health and well-being of children.

How did women respond when faced with sharply decreased resources? The immediacy of their reactions testifies to the importance of lost income as well as to the women's concern about their well-being. As table 2 indicates, most quickly sought to improve their employment situation; 32 percent searched for a new job, and 18 percent sought help from their children's father.

Their efforts brought limited success. Only 4 percent of these women were able to change jobs within three months after the OBRA cuts, while 6 percent became unemployed. Sixty-nine percent reported no job change,

Table 2

Responses to AFDC Termination
(*N* = 279)

	%
Women's immediate responses:	
Became ill, upset, or depressed	57
Applied for a better job or sought full-time work	38
Searched for a new job	32
Asked children's father for financial support	18
Sought training	12
Appealed termination	8
Wage earners' responses after three months:	
Experienced no change in job	69
Increased working hours	14
Became unemployed, laid off	6
Changed job	4
Had working hours reduced by employer	3
Took an additional job	2
Voluntarily reduced working hours	1
Other	1

Note.—Totals exceed 100 percent because respondents may have more than one response.

Ways and Means, *Background Material on Poverty* (Washington, D.C.: Government Printing Office, October 1983), p. 4.

but 14 percent had been able to increase their working hours. When asked why they decided to continue working rather than to return to AFDC, more than one-third said that they had no choice; however, 29 percent said that they did not want to return to AFDC, and 18 percent said specifically that they felt people should work (see table 3). These responses reflect an implicit understanding of the larger forces restraining these women's choices—lack of opportunities for women with families, high unemployment rates, restrictive welfare policies, and individual commitment to self-support. Only 22 percent said that they continued working because they enjoyed their jobs, an understandable figure given the types of jobs that most held and their remuneration.

These results reinforce our earlier observation that work plays a primary role in the lives of these women, who are often described simply as "welfare recipients." Thus, despite a decrease in income, benefits, and security, most women in our sample contined working, thereby providing for their families as well as they could.

In 1982 these women also attempted to stretch their remaining dollars. Seventy percent obtained used clothes; many attempted to save food dollars by getting emergency food supplies, buying remaindered food at reduced prices, or shopping at food co-ops. A small percentage who could not meet their bills wrote checks without sufficient funds or moved to avoid paying rent.

How did OBRA affect the relationship between these women and the labor market? Employers both lost and gained from these federal changes. When women workers lost AFDC payments, child care allowances, and Medicaid coverage, their employers in effect no longer had federal subsidies for their poor wage and benefit policies. However, this loss was limited because employers were not strongly pressured by government, organized labor, or the affected women either to increase wages or to provide benefits.

Table 3

Wage Earners' Reasons for Continued Employment Three Months
after AFDC Termination
($N = 263$)

	%
Had no other choice	42
Did not like receiving AFDC assistance	29
Liked job	22
Felt that people should work	18
Felt earnings were adequate	15
Wanted employee benefits	5

NOTE.—Totals exceed 100 percent because respondents may have more than one reason.

Employers gained (particularly when unemployment rates are taken into account) by having a larger captive work force. The women terminated by OBRA policies needed their jobs more than ever after losing the backup security of welfare eligibility. Women who were previously mistakenly labeled as dependent on welfare now became truly dependent on employers who had a demonstrated lack of interest in their economic well-being.

Family Stress

A number of noneconomic and quasi-economic problems added to the daily living situations these women confronted. In order to see clearly the impact of a significant reduction in economic resources on a family, we must look at other stresses that also contribute to its total life picture. This aspect of our study sets it apart in a very important way from other studies described below that have investigated the effects of OBRA. The simple assessment of whether or not a family returns to AFDC is alone not sufficient to indicate the effect of this federal legislation. Although we would not contend that OBRA caused the problems mentioned in this section, the presence of other problems certainly mediates the impact of OBRA.

Crises resulting from lack of money were almost routine for these families. Nearly nine out of ten ran out of money at least once in the year prior to the interview. When asked if they had run out of food, half indicated they had at least once; a quarter stated that they had run out of food more than seven times. Many families regularly relied on free food distribution centers when their own food and financial resources were exhausted. Several interviewers visited households in which there was no food and where respondents were extremely anxious about meeting their children's needs.

Because respondents were employed, child care was a major problem. Half of the respondents had children under twelve years of age and needed child care in order to work. On termination from AFDC, they discovered severe cutbacks in programs such as Title XX funded day care; they then became more reliant on informal caregivers, such as relatives and older siblings (48 percent), or on private sitters (37 percent). The remaining 15 percent relied on public services, such as Headstart or recreational programs. Informal arrangements tended to be less stable than those with private sitters and often were an imposition on relatives or siblings, who might have desired to spend their time in other ways.

Women also encountered a variety of serious problems with their older children. More than one-third were called to school in 1982 for special conferences, and 21 percent reported that their children had been suspended at least once. A small number of children had been expelled, referred to the juvenile court, committed to institutions, and/or victimized by crime. The numbers, although small, exceeded those one would expect to observe in an average family. Thus mothers had special worries about, as well as responsibilities for, their older children.

Health and health care were matters of critical concern, and if a woman had a seriously ill child or was ill herself, she took every action possible not to lose Medicaid—even if that meant giving up employment income that was higher than the welfare benefits she could obtain. Although comparable studies on the health characteristics of the population of this study are unavailable, it is important to consider that serious chronic illnesses—cancer, diabetes, epilepsy, hypertension, sickle cell anemia, and arthritis/rheumatism—afflicted one in seven respondents. Mental distress and illness were prevalent. Fifty-eight percent reported one or more of the following: frequent or severe headaches, sleeping disorders, frequent stomach upsets, tension and nervousness, and depression or anxiety. Over 5 percent were hospitalized one or more days during 1982.

Lack of health insurance was a major problem. One in five had Medicaid coverage, and an additional 29 percent reported some paid coverage through their employment. Another 21 percent purchased medical insurance through their employers but paid an average of $374 per year for it. Twenty-eight percent had no coverage; an additional 8 percent had coverage for themselves but not for their children. Thus nearly two in five did not have health insurance for their whole family. Nearly half (49 percent) said that they simply could not afford health care when they were ill. Even those with Medicaid reported difficulty locating a physician who would accept Medicaid payment. Given these circumstances, it was not surprising that 27 percent reported that their children had not seen a physician for a physical examination during 1982, and 34 percent said that they had not seen a dentist for a checkup.

When faced with this complex blend of economic, child care, and health problems, the social support networks of these women took on increased importance. Women with parents, grandparents, siblings, or children nearby relied on them heavily for housing, money, food, child care, transportation, and sympathetic counsel, as table 4 shows. Friends also provided frequent support, usually through advice and cheer rather than material assistance. Social workers, ministers, and health personnel were less frequently contacted by women in our sample in time of crisis.

Discussion and Implications

Our picture of working women terminated from AFDC benefits by OBRA challenges the myth that all women receiving welfare assistance have poor educations and a large number of dependents. The women in our sample had neither of these handicaps in the labor market, yet few were adequately able to meet the basic needs of their families—food, shelter, clothing, and preventive and necessary health and dental care— in the year following termination of AFDC payments. Less than half were able to earn enough to keep their families above the poverty level, and approximately two-fifths were without health insurance for themselves and/or their children. Cutbacks in federally supported child care during the working day also jeopardized their assurance of basic safety for their children.

The deprivation of most of these women and their children was compounded by reductions in other social programs and by the economic recession. Throughout the country unemployment was a constant threat and a frequent reality; this problem was particularly acute in Michigan, where the rate of unemployment has been a double-digit figure for more than fifty-four consecutive months in the period from January 1980 to August 1984.[19]

Given that working women of all races suffer wage discrimination even in the best of economic times, the respondents in our study faced a difficult decision about continuing work when faced with a loss of AFDC supplements to their earnings. Prior to OBRA's passage, researchers and policymakers debated whether workers would attempt to return to AFDC rolls once they were terminated. Those who contended that women would obtain adequate income and benefits through full-time employ- ment failed to note that many AFDC recipients eligible for termination

Table 4

Respondents' Social Support Networks in Crises
(*N* = 279) (%)

Support Persons Contacted	Following AFDC Termination	Following Most Serious Problem in 1982
Parents, siblings, or other relatives	76	70
Friends	63	52
Children	49	48
Boyfriend or partner	36	42
Physician, nurse, or clinic	10	21
Social worker or counselor	14	13
Police officer	...	9
Minister	8	8
Lawyer	...	7

19. Michigan Employment and Security Commission, Bureau of Research and Labor Statistics, *Civilian Labor Force, October 1983* (Lansing: Michigan Employment Security Com- mission, February 1984); Michigan Employment Security Commission statistician, tele- phone conversation with authors (July 31, 1984).

were already employed full-time but could not earn sufficient income through the jobs and compensation typically available to low-income working women. In contrast, Tom Joe and Frank Farrow asserted that the tax rates on earnings in relation to AFDC benefits were such that women in the majority of states would determine that it was to their advantage to quit work and seek full AFDC benefits.

Neither assertion was accurate as far as can be determined to date. Early surveys such as those from Norman Wyers and Robert Holloway, Richard Nathan and Fred Doolittle, Ira Muscovice and William Craig, and the Research Triangle Institute indicate that the working poor were faring "satisfactorily" because only 10–15 percent returned to the AFDC rolls, approximately the "normal" return rate each year. A later survey by Sandra Danziger and her associates reports that 33 percent of those terminated returned at least once during an interval of over slightly one year, in comparison with the return rate we observed of 24 percent over an eighteen-month interval.[20]

The question we must ask is, Does a low return rate indicate a high number of so-called success cases? Our study indicates that those who were not reinstated in welfare programs experienced the suffering and deprivation of continued poverty. Those who had relatives with resources to share fared better than those with only friends and neighbors to rely on; those who remarried were able to improve their economic status. Yet such coping strategies can be of only limited effectiveness in protecting women from the threat of poverty. Until the earnings of women supporting families are adjusted according to the principle of comparable worth so that they come closer to the amounts earned by white males, working women will face serious problems in independently achieving economic stability and well-being.

The AFDC reductions under OBRA exacerbated a social problem formerly on the decline.[21] Although pre-1981 programs had not eliminated poverty, they were incrementally moving toward increased income for poor persons. From 1965 to 1980, the number of poor people below the official poverty level fell by 25 percent from 15.6 percent of the

20. Norman Wyers and Robert Holloway, *Women and Children on Welfare in 1982: After the Cuts* (Portland: Portland State University School of Social Work, December 1982); Robert Nathan and Fred Doolittle, *The Consequences of Cuts: The Effects of the Reagan Domestic Programs on State and Local Governments* (Princeton, N.J.: Princeton University Press, 1983); Ira Moscovice and William Craig, "Meeting the Needs of the Working Poor: The Impact of the Omnibus Budget Reconciliation Act" (University of Minneapolis Center for Health Service Research, May 1983, mimeographed); C. Usher, *Evaluation of the 1981 AFDC Amendments: Final Report* (Research Triangle Park, N.C.: Research Triangle Institute, 1983); Sandra Danziger et al., *Poverty and Welfare Recipiency after OBRA: Some Preliminary Evidence from Wisconsin* (Madison: University of Wisconsin Institute of Research on Poverty, 1983).

21. U.S. House of Representatives, pp. 45–47.

population to 11.7 percent. From 1980 to 1983, the proportion rose to 15 percent—almost eliminating the gains of the previous fifteen years.[22]

Today children in the United States have the highest rate of poverty of any subgroup in the population: 23 percent of all children are poor. A massive effort is needed if the next generation is not to be jeopardized by the suffering now being experienced by children and their mothers who live in poverty. As Sheila Kamerman and Alfred Kahn persistently remind us, our industrialized peer countries view income support for all women with children as an important responsibility.[23] There must be a similar recognition in this, one of the wealthiest countries in the world, that women with children have certain periods in their lives—particularly when the children are young—when they are vulnerable and need support.

School of Social Work and Institute for Social Research
University of Michigan

22. U.S. House of Representatives, Committee on Ways and Means, *Poverty Rate Increase Hearings, October 18, 1983 and November 3, 1983* (Washington, D.C.: Government Printing Office, 1984), p. 42.

23. Sheila B. Kamerman and Alfred J. Kahn, "Income Transfers and Mother Only Families in Eight Countries," *Social Service Review* 57 (September 1983): 448–64; Sheila B. Kamerman, "Women, Children, and Poverty: Public Policies and Female-headed Families in Industrialized Countries" (in this book).

Women, Children, and Poverty: Public Policies and Female-headed Families in Industrialized Countries

Sheila B. Kamerman

Single-parent, female-headed families are at risk of poverty and are causing concern in all advanced industrialized countries. A committee set up by the British government in the early 1970s to study the problems of these families issued a well-publicized report in July 1974.[1] Although the recommendations made in the report have not yet been carried out, discussion continues about the need for more concerted attention to this problem. The Commission of the European Communities launched a major effort in the late 1970s aimed at assessing the extent of poverty and the composition and characteristics of the poor in member countries. Its report, issued in 1981, states that the incidence of poverty in much of the Community is "above or far above average" in households with a female head, one-parent families with more than one child (overwhelmingly female-headed), and households with a head, whether aged or not, who is not in the labor force.[2]

I wrote this article while a fellow at the Center for Advanced Study in the Behavioral Sciences. I would like to acknowledge, with gratitude, the support of the Foundations Fund for Research in Psychiatry.

1. Morris Finer et al., *Report on the Committee on One-Parent Families*, Cmd. 5629, 5629-1 (London: Her Majesty's Stationery Office, 1974).

2. A poverty-level income is defined as less than half the median income in the individual countries. See Commission of the European Communities, *Final Report from the Commissioners to the Council on the First Programme of Pilot Scheme and Studies to Combat Poverty* (Brussels: Commission of the European Communities, 1981). Continued attention in the European Economic Community to the problems of one-parent families in poverty has led to a special detailed report published at the end of 1983 and a meeting of experts in 1984. See Commission of the European Communities, *One-Parent Families and Poverty in the EEC* (Copenhagen: Commission of the European Communities, December 1982).

Several countries outside the Community, including as geographically disparate a group as Australia, Canada, and Sweden, have also noted a growth in the proportion and numbers of female-headed families with children and in the disproportionate risks of poverty these families experience. In Sweden, a Royal Commission was established in the late 1970s to focus specifically on the needs and problems of this family type. The federal Australian government set up a research program to examine mother-only families. A special group was assigned a similar task by the provincial government of Ontario, Canada.

Historically, those making policies related to female-headed families were concerned about the problems of widows with children. However, the growth in social insurance coverage (survivors insurance under social security) for these families and the increase in benefit levels, coupled with a significant decline in the number of widows with young children in most countries, has left such families a protected though minor group. In contrast, the growth in numbers of separated, divorced, and never-married mothers has made the families for which they have responsibility a far more significant type in most advanced industrialized countries. At the same time, these families' vulnerability to poverty has remained the same or has even increased.

The trend in all industrialized countries toward more mother-only families and a relatively high incidence of poverty among these families create important questions. What is the role of public policy in raising the income of these families in various countries? More specifically, which policy strategies are used, which are most effective, and what data exist to document relative degrees of effectiveness? Are there lessons that the United States can learn from the policies of other countries?

Welfare in the United States

Single-parent, female headed families constituted almost half of all poor families in the United States in 1982. Even though they are only about one-fifth of all families with children, they represented more than half (53 percent) of all poor families with children.[3] Furthermore, not only are female-headed families with children disproportionately at risk of poverty in the United States, but also the percentage that are poor has increased significantly in the last few years. Children living in this type of family are particularly at risk, and the numbers of children in such families have doubled since the end of the 1960s.

---

3. U.S. Department of Commerce, Bureau of the Census, *Money Income and Poverty Status of Families and Persons in the U.S., 1982*, Current Population Reports Series P-60, no. 140 (Washington, D.C.: Government Printing Office, 1983), table 18.

In the United States, the major program designed to help mother-only families is Aid to Families with Dependent Children (AFDC), the means-tested public assistance program established in 1935 as part of the Social Security Act and modified somewhat during the intervening years. Aid to Families with Dependent Children and its supplement, food stamps (the latter being the only completely federal program for economic relief to all low-income individuals and families), are the programs commonly called "welfare"; together, they constitute the core of U.S. policy for single mothers and their children. Dissatisfaction with AFDC abounds because of its costs, its administrative complexity, the inadequacy of benefits for families with no other source of income, the inequities resulting from its availability primarily to single-mother families and not to equally poor two-parent families, and the inequities created by the variation in benefit levels from state to state. The result is a general consensus among both conservatives and liberals—even if not for the same reasons—that welfare is a "mess."

Repeated efforts at reforming welfare over the past decade and a half have all been dismal failures. The proposals have been doomed because they were viewed as too expensive, or the benefit levels they offered were too low, or they failed to provide an adequate work incentive, thereby making it potentially more attractive for those qualifying for benefits to apply for AFDC rather than to obtain work.

In contrast to earlier reform efforts aimed at establishing a national program with uniform criteria for eligibility, uniform benefit levels, and a clear work incentive, changes initiated by the Reagan administration took a very different tack. The major goals have been: (1) to eliminate the federal role in AFDC entirely and assign full responsibility to the states, and (2) to eliminate the use of AFDC as a supplement to low wages. Thus far Congress has rejected the first but acquiesced in the second. Among the specific policy changes proposed by Reagan and adopted by Congress have been: basing the welfare grant on the applicant's income of the prior, rather than the current, month; lowering the age used as definition of a child from twenty-one to eighteen; offering AFDC benefits to women pregnant with their first child only at the third trimester of pregnancy; prohibiting AFDC payments to strikers and their families; including a step-parent's income in the determination of eligibility for AFDC; and limiting benefit levels in the states by restricting them to 150 percent of the state's definition of "need." The most important conceptual change, however, was the elimination of the use of AFDC as an income supplement. This was accomplished by changing the policy whereby women leaving AFDC to work could disregard the first thirty dollars plus one-third of their gross earnings, in addition to taxes, work expenses, and child care expenses, before their income was counted against their welfare grant. Now, the amount discounted as work expense is limited to a maximum of seventy-five dollars per month and the period in which it is possible to disregard income is limited to the first four months of employment. Application to do so again may only be made a year later. Moreover, funds to cover child care expenses are now limited to a maximum of $160 per month per child (far less than the average child care costs nationally).[4]

Thus far it appears that despite changes in the income disregard system that in effect reduce the incentive to seek a job and leave AFDC, few women have chosen welfare over work. A U.S. General Accounting Office report of a study carried out in late 1983 to determine the impact of these policy changes had this conclusion: those women dropped from welfare rolls stayed off welfare but ended up with earnings that left them poorer than before and often without any health insurance.[5] At the same time, benefit levels of those receiving AFDC have not begun to keep up with inflation, and in no state do benefits by themselves, even including food stamps, provide sufficient income to maintain a family above the poverty threshold ($9,862 for a nonfarm family of four in 1982). Recently the poverty rate for mother-only families has increased, and the dissatisfaction with welfare continues—and grows.

The Focus of a Cross-national Study

We need to know more about the situation of these families—and of other families likely to be at risk of poverty, such as two-parent families in which the father is the sole earner and is unemployed or underemployed, or in which the family includes several children. Information is particularly scarce on the effects of the public policy responses to their needs. In an effort to acquire some, Alfred Kahn and I, with the support of the U.S. Social Security Administration, carried out a cross-national study of public income transfer policies in eight advanced industrialized countries. We considered income transfers in a number of forms—social insurance benefits such as unemployment insurance; public or social assistance benefits such as the means-tested AFDC program and food stamps in the United States; family allowances such as the special non-income-tested cash benefits given to families with children; and income taxes, social security contributions, and tax benefits. The countries studied were Aus-

4. For a description of the changes and an analysis of their impact, see U.S. Congress, Congressional Budget Office, *Major Legislative Changes in Human Resource Programs since January 1981*, Staff Memorandum, August 1983, and John L. Palmer and Isabel V. Sawhill, *The Reagan Experiment* (Washington, D.C.: Urban Institute, 1982), chap. 12.

5. "Many Who Lose Aid Work More but Stay Poor," *New York Times* (April 1, 1984). For a full report, see U.S. General Accounting Office, *An Evaluation of the 1981 AFDC Changes: Initial Analyses* (Washington, D.C.: GAO, 1984).

tralia, Canada, France, Federal Republic of Germany (subsequently referred to as Germany), Israel, Sweden, the United Kingdom, and the United States. All eight countries are relatively similar—industrialized and wealthy—but differ, among other things, in the extent and explicitness of their commitment to "family policy."[6] Because the United States is so large, and because the states rather than the federal government determine eligibility criteria and benefit levels for AFDC (this country's major relevant transfer program), we selected two jurisdictions for study: New York, one of the most generous states, and Pennsylvania, a state ranking above about two-thirds of the states in maximum AFDC benefit levels.[7]

The study considered how various types of families with young children (those with one or two parents; those with one, two, or four children—and with no children, to provide contrast), with different labor force status among parents (employed, unemployed, not in the labor force), and with six different wage levels (ranging from no wage to three times average wage) fared economically. Its focus was their situation at the end of a year of receiving earnings and government income transfers after payment of taxes. A second focus was on the types of transfers used in different countries as well as on the alternative approaches employed in providing transfers. We drew up a selection of fifteen family types, making them standard in marital status, labor force status, number and age of children, work history, and wage as proportion of each country's average wage (see table 1). Only cash transfers (money or its equivalent) were considered, and among these, only "entitlements"—benefits awarded as a matter of legal right, such as social security or unemployment insurance or AFDC—were included. We did not take into account in-kind benefits such as national health insurance, Medicaid, and subsidized child care services; nonentitlement programs such as "Section 8" (subsidized) housing in the United States; or fringe benefits at the workplace. Although these benefits are admittedly important in gauging any standard of living, the difficulties in contrasting income standards across

6. The term "family policy" is used to describe governmental laws, regulations, and so forth that affect the family as an institution or individuals in their roles as family members. Family policies may involve explicit and specific laws or constitute aspects of a variety of governmental actions. Our concern in selecting countries was to include a "sample" from among those with an explicit "family policy" such as Sweden, France, and Germany, as well as those rejecting the concept, such as the U.S. and Britain. For some discussion of family policy, see Sheila B. Kamerman and Alfred J. Kahn, eds., *Family Policy: Government and Family in Fourteen Countries* (New York: Columbia University Press, 1978), or Sheila B. Kamerman and Alfred J. Kahn, *Child Care, Family Benefits, and Working Parents* (New York: Columbia University Press, 1981).

7. Subsequently, we added two states with the third and fourth lowest AFDC benefits, Tennessee and Alabama. Needless to say, the U.S. looks even worse when we consider the condition of families in these two states.

countries encouraged us to limit our focus to cash transfers, which provide the most feasible basis for comparison.

We identified ten major income transfer programs in the countries studied (see table 2). Not every program exists in every country. For purposes of comparison we assumed that all who qualified for a benefit both claimed and received it, although we realize that this is not necessarily the case.

For purposes of comparative analysis, the study used as a baseline for each country the net average production worker's wage (APWW) in that country. This yardstick has been shown to be useful in research conducted by the Organization for Economic Cooperation and Development (OECD), an economic alliance of the twenty-four leading Western industrialized countries and Japan. We compared the end-of-year income (earnings and transfers less income taxes and social security contributions) of each family type in each country and then contrasted the income of similar family types in each of the eight countries. Although the standard is conceptually the same in all countries, it clearly does not have the same monetary value everywhere, since wages and costs vary as does the per capita gross national product (GNP). Furthermore, the countries also vary in the extent to which health care, transportation, food, and

Table 1

Family Types Studied

1a.*	Single mother; not in labor force; two children, aged two and seven
1b.†	Same attributes as 1a; the court has ordered support payments but the father does not pay
2a.*	Single mother separated from spouse; employed at half APWW;‡ two children
2b.*	Same attributes as 2a; father's support payments equal twice the amount paid for child allowance for one child, one year
3a.	Two parents; one employed earner at APWW; two children
3b.*	Same attributes as 3a; earner works irregularly at half APWW
4a.*	Two parents; one unemployed earner; two children
4b.*	Same attributes as 4a; unemployed earner in a work-training program
4c.*	Same attributes as 4a; unemployed earner out of work thirteen months
5a.	Two parents, one employed earner at APWW and another at half APWW; two children
5b.	Same attributes as 5a; one employed earner at APWW and another at twice APWW
5c.	Same attributes as 5a; one earner unemployed and the other at half APWW
6.*	Two parents; one employed earner at APWW; four children
7a.	A married couple; one earner at APWW; no children
7b.	Two parents; one employed earner at APWW and another at three-quarters APWW; mother home on maternity leave after birth of first child
7c.	A married couple; the husband unemployed, the wife earning APWW§

*"Vulnerable" families, that is, those most threatened by poverty.
†We dropped this family type in the final analysis because its income was the same as that of family 1a.
‡Average Production Worker's Wage.
§This family is a standard for basis of comparison.

Table 2

"Core" Income Transfer Programs, by Country

Country	Family (Child) Allowance	Housing Allowance	Social Assistance	Child Support (Government)	Unemployment Insurance	Other Unemployment Benefits	Family Allowance Supplement	Food Stamps	Refundable Tax Credits	Maternity Benefits
Sweden	X	X	X	X	X	X*	...	...	...	X
Federal Republic of Germany	X	X	X	X	X	X†	...	...	...	X
United States (New York)	...	...	X	...	X	...	...	X	X	X
United States (Pennsylvania) ..	...	...	X	...	X	...	...	X	X	...
France	X	X	X	X‡	X	...	X	...	...	X
Canada	X	...	X	...	X	...	...	...	X	X
Australia§	X	...	X	...	...	X†	...	...	...	...
United Kingdom ..	X	X	X	...	X	...	...	...	...	X
Israel	X	...	X	X	X	...	...	...	...	X

NOTE.—In this and all other tables, I list countries in descending order of per capita GNP for 1979. I have used the generic terms for programs and have ignored significant distinctions. For example, the British child benefit is not the same as the German child allowance; the Swedish advance maintenance grant is quite different from the Israeli alimony payment—as the text subsequently shows.

*Labor market assistance.
†Unemployment assistance.
‡Beginning in 1985.
§I classify certain Australian benefits as employment assistance and social assistance, although the use of such labels for these income-tested benefits is debatable.

housing are partially or fully subsidized. However, our approach does illustrate how families fare in relation to a standardized income measure.

Research teams from each participating country collected data for the year 1979; Kahn and I served as directors. Eight of the fifteen hypothetical families selected for attention were particularly vulnerable to poverty, and thus of special concern to policymakers in all industrialized countries. All eight were either mother-only families in which the mother was not working or earning a low wage; two-parent families in which the sole earner, the husband, was either unemployed or underemployed; or large families. The other seven types represented "control" families whose income was expected to be adequate either by virtue of wage level, absence of children, or number of wage earners in the family. Three of the eight "vulnerable" families were mother-only families.[8]

Public Policies and Mother-only Families

The numerical importance of female-headed families with children ranges among the countries from Sweden, where about a quarter of all families with children are of this type, to Israel, where only 4 percent are, most of these headed by widows. Nevertheless, this family type is an important target for social policy in at least seven of the eight countries (see table 3). The hypothetical mother of such a family in this study is separated from her husband and raising two children, two and seven years old. In all countries, policies affecting her would have the same result whether she were divorced, deserted, never married, or separated. Only if she were widowed would the response be different—and more generous. She has no income from any source except her own earnings, where present, and government-provided benefits.

This family type is entitled to transfers under three sets of circumstances: when the mother is not in the labor force and the family has no income; when the mother is working, but for modest wages; and when the absent father pays some child support, but family income is still low. How does this family fare in each country and what contributes to the different economic outcomes?

Families with a Mother at Home

First consider a hypothetical family in which the mother is not in the labor force. She worked for two years, full-time, at three-quarters of an

---

8. For a more detailed description of the study design and method, as well as a more extensive discussion of study findings, see Alfred J. Kahn and Sheila B. Kamerman, *Income Transfers for Families with Children* (Philadelphia: Temple University Press, 1983).

Table 3

Families with Children: Family Structure, Labor-Force Participation Rate of Parents, and Family Size for All Countries Studied, 1979

Country	Two-Parent Families (% of All Families)	Single-Parent Families (% of All Families)	Female-headed Families (% of All Families)	% of Single Mothers in Labor Force	% of Single Mothers at Home	% of Married Mothers in Labor Force	% of Married Mothers at Home
Sweden	73	27	24.4	86	14*	64	36
Federal Republic of Germany	89	11	9	63	37†	41	59
United States	80.5	19.5	17.5	68	32	54	45‡
France§	87	13	13	69	31	41	59
Canada	87.7	12.3	10.6	63	37	58	42
Australia	87‖	12.7‖	10.8	43	57	45	55
United Kingdom	87.5‖	12‖	10.4	49	51	60	40
Israel	95.7	4.3	4	69#	31	37	63

Sources.—Data supplied by country research teams; U.S. data from Bureau of the Census and Department of Labor.

*Many of these are in school or training programs.

†This includes a significant group of widows (27.8 percent), whose labor-force participation rate is only 43 percent in contrast to over 70 percent for all other single mothers (including family 1a).

‡In a little less than 1 percent of the two-parent families, neither parent is in the labor force.

§1981 data.

‖Because of rounding, these figures do not total 100 percent.

#Includes non-Jews.

average wage until the birth of her second child; she has not worked since. Families such as this one headed by at-home mothers constitute a minority of mother-only families in every country studied with the exceptions of Australia, where they are 57 percent of such families, and the United Kingdom, where they are only slightly more than half (51 percent). However they are a significant minority—about one-third—in all the other countries except Sweden, where they are only 14 percent.

A family such as this has very limited income in most countries (see table 4, family 1*a*). Only in Sweden does its income even approximate an average production worker's wage; and only in France and Germany, the two other countries with the largest family policy commitments, is this family's income level equal to more than half an average wage. In the others, the low standards are relatively similar; transfer payments provide this family with income that represents about half an average wage. Pennsylvania, the lowest-ranking jurisdiction, provides even less than half in the way of benefits, and most U.S. states would not be this generous.

What policy instruments yield these results? The countries in the British income maintenance tradition—the United States, Canada, the United Kingdom, Israel, and perhaps Australia[9]—still rely very heavily on public (social) assistance (means-tested cash benefits) for providing the basics to families headed by at-home mothers and, perhaps as a consequence, provide smaller transfer payments than the three countries with explicit family policy commitments. All countries except the United States offer universal family allowances (or child allowances, child benefits) that are not income-tested. France adds an income-tested supplementary family allowance, with an income ceiling set at a sufficiently high level so that over three-quarters of all families with three or more children or one child under age three qualify for the benefit. The food stamp allotment in the United States plays approximately the same role as family allowances in Israel, Germany, and the United Kingdom in the total income picture.

Sweden, the most generous country in relation to this and most other types of families in need, packages four different benefits to provide the family with income that is almost twice that made available in countries using primarily social assistance. In Sweden social assistance makes up about one-third of this family's income, while a significant child-support program ("advance maintenance") constitutes another 30 percent. Also significant is Sweden's major income-tested housing allowance; this supplement to the universal family allowance reached half of all families with children in 1979.

---

9. Classifying Australia as a country in the British tradition is debatable in view of its unique history. See Kahn and Kamerman, pp. 115–26.

Table 4

End-of-Year Income for a Mother and Two Children
as a Percent of Average Production Worker's Wage (APWW), Net

Country	Family 1a (Mother at Home)	Ranking	Family 1b (Mother at Home, Receiving Child Support)	Family 2a (Mother Earning Wages)	Ranking	Family 2b (Mother Earning Wages, Receiving Child Support)	Ranking
Sweden	93.8	1	93.8	123.1	1	123.1	1
Federal Republic of Germany	67.3	3	67.3	70.9	7.5	76.3	8
United States (New York)	54.9	4	54.9	100.8	2	100.8	3
United States (Pennsylvania)	44.0	9	44.0	69.2	9	75.3	8
France	78.6	2	79.1	87.8	3	103.4	2
Canada	52.5	5	52.5	75.9	6	75.5	8
Australia	50.0	7.5	50.0	78.8	5	82.1	5
United Kingdom	51.7	6	51.7	83.0	4	91.6	4
Israel	50.0	7.5	50.0	71.5	7.5	80.1	6

NOTE.—There is a court support order for family 1b, but the father does not contribute. Since this had no impact on family income, family 1b was dropped from subsequent analysis. Mother in family 2a earns half APWW. Ranks defined as ties unless the ratios (annual income as percentage of net APWW) differ by 1 percent.

France, the country ranking second in generosity to these and most other families, relies even less on social assistance than does Sweden. It employs a cluster of family allowances—including a major income-tested housing allowance program, the universal allowance, and the income-tested supplementary allowance—that make a significant contribution to family income. Its sole-parent allowance, which in some ways resembles AFDC, provides over half the income for a family headed by a mother at home. However, this benefit is only available for a maximum of one year if the youngest child is age two or older, or—if the child is younger—until she or he is three years old. Because the benefit is means-tested and discretionary, it is stigmatized. Relatively few women use it.

In Germany, a mother such as the one we describe is still eligible for unemployment insurance because of her wage work within the last three years. This benefit, together with family and housing allowances more modest than those provided by France or Sweden, makes social assistance unnecessary. However, if we disregard unemployment benefits and compute only the social assistance benefits that would be applicable in this case, the resulting family income, although somewhat lower, would still rank third highest among those offered by the other countries.[10]

In Australia, all relevant benefits are income-tested, except for family allowances. Although more generous than Pennsylvania, Australia ranks with Israel near the bottom of the list, through its support package of both family allowances (a modest grant) and what is called a Class A Widow's Pension (resembling other systems of public assistance). Of special interest is a refundable dependent child's tax credit available in the province of Ontario, Canada; this constitutes two annual lump payments from the national government and from the province, which together exceed the Canadian family allowance.

We also analyzed how a court support order in each country would affect the income of this family if the father were not providing payments. Although each country treats this issue differently, their policies have the same effect on family income: no change (see table 4, family 1*b*). The reasons for this uniformity are as follows: in Sweden both parents would have the same entitlements; the existence of a court order of child support for one family and not for the other would not lead to any difference in family income. In Israel the amount we specified for the court order was less than this mother would receive from social assistance; therefore, she receives assistance, ending up with the same benefit received by the family with no court order. In Germany, as mentioned earlier, a mother

10. Moreover, when unemployment insurance benefits end, this mother would qualify for unemployment assistance—an income-tested benefit that maintains Germany's third-place ranking for this family.

in this situation would be receiving unemployment insurance, a far more generous benefit than the modest amount ordered by the court. None of the other countries had such a special child support program as yet in the year of the study.

Families with a Wage-earning Mother

At least two-thirds of the single mothers are in the labor force in six of our eight countries, and far more in Sweden. What would happen to family income in the household described above if the mother were to find work at a salary equal to half an average wage (see table 4, family 2a)?

For most, the improvement in family income would be substantial. In New York, the mother's wages would increase her family's income by almost 90 percent, and in Sweden, by almost one-third. However, the improvement is small in Germany, because her gain in salary would be offset by a loss of unemployment insurance (uniquely available for the German family). It is modest also in France, where the loss of the single-parent allowance and the addition of a relatively low wage results in an approximately 12 percent net income increase. (The single-parent benefit, however, is of very limited duration.) The child allowance and the housing allowance entitlements continue in both these countries.

What policy instruments yield these results? Child allowance, housing allowance, and the advance maintenance allowance (child support) continue unchanged in Sweden, although the family loses social assistance. As a result, a Swedish family headed by a wage-earning mother ends up with income more than 50 percent higher than a similar family in any other country. An identical U.S. family continues to receive AFDC and food stamps, both reduced, and the working mother remains eligible for the earned income tax credit. In Canada, such a family retains eligibility for family allowance, assistance, and tax credits, and experiences only a modest assistance decrease. Nor are there basic entitlement changes in France (family allowance, family allowance supplement, housing allowance); however, the mother's salary does not replace the lone-parent allowance and leads to a partial reduction in the housing allowance. Australian eligibility continues for family allowance and the Class A Widow's Pension (really a governmental income-tested child support program). Yet the salary entitles the wage-earning mother to a sole-parent tax rebate and thus improves the family's ultimate income despite a decrease in the widow's pension. Child benefits continue in Britain, but supplementary benefits (the basic public assistance program) are discontinued; however, rent or rate rebates—the British version of a housing allowance—partially balances this loss for those who apply and receive it (a qualification that pertains in the case of each of these supplements). Eligibility for child allowance, but not for social assistance, continues in Israel.

Families with an Absent Father Providing Child Support

In this third variety of a female-headed family with children, we consider the effect of a father's monthly contribution to the family's earned income of a sum equal to twice the monthly child allowance for a first child (or a second child, where a first child is not eligible, or the AFDC budget amount for a child in the United States).

Most families are not much better off, if at all, although there are exceptions (see table 4, family 2*b*). The father's contribution merely decreases the advance maintenance allowance in Sweden but changes nothing else; goes directly to the agency to meet half the costs of AFDC in New York; eliminates AFDC and food stamps in Pennsylvania; decreases the housing allowance in Germany; wipes out social assistance and worsens the tax situation a bit in Canada; and helps budgets somewhat in Britain and Israel. France is the major exception: the contribution does not affect eligibility for the family allowance, family allowance supplement, and housing allowance; family income actually increases.

Programs That Matter to Single-Parent Families

Several programs are clearly important to these single-parent families: family or child allowances, housing allowances, advance maintenance or child-support allowances, social or public assistance, and, in the United States, food stamps and the earned income tax credit (a refundable tax credit, also available in Canada, for low-income, working parents). Family allowances, provided everywhere but in the United States, are the cornerstone of child and family policies wherever they exist. Housing allowances, although familiar to us in this country, are available only to a small proportion of those who qualify (thus they are not part of U.S. entitlement programs). Advance maintenance payments are receiving increased attention in several countries; this is an especially important benefit for mother-only families in Sweden. The economic standing of most families receiving these benefits is far superior to that of similar families in the United States, who are dependent largely on public assistance. A brief description of these three programs follows.

Family allowances, or child allowances or child benefits, are cash benefits or payments extended by the government to families with children. They are usually provided as flat-rate benefits with a specific amount paid for each child in a family. In some countries the amounts vary by the age, ordinal position, and/or number of children. In contrast to most other public income transfer payments, family allowances are usually not indexed, but are usually tax-free and non-income-tested. In addition they are generally awarded until a child completes compulsory schooling or no longer must attend school; however, in some cases the benefit can be extended if the child is a full-time student.

These allowances exist as a statutory (government) benefit in sixty-seven countries, including every industrialized country save the United States. Except in Australia, where their size is modest, they constitute between 13 and 27 percent of family income for the non-wage-earning mother, and between 10 and 24 percent for the wage-earning mother with a modest salary. Designed to assist parents in a small way with the economic costs of rearing young children, family allowances obviously play a far more significant role in the income of single-parent, female-headed families—which tends to be low in all countries—than in the income of two-parent families. Moreover, some countries provide a supplementary grant for the first child in a single-parent family, or for low-income families.

First used in France in the 1930s as a wage supplement and a device for avoiding across-the-board wage increases for all workers, and employed subsequently (if unsuccessfully) as a pronatalist device, family allowances have emerged over the last two decades as an important income supplement for wage earners with children. Despite the failure almost everywhere to index these benefits, and despite their consequent erosion by inflation, countries have regularly increased benefit levels. In Israel, where the benefit is fully indexed, it has also been integrated into the income tax system, so that beneficiaries receive either a direct cash transfer (if they have no tax liability) or a tax credit. The family allowance is the foundation of France's income transfer system for families with children. Using a combination of universal and income-tested benefits, the French assure their single-parent families without wage earners a standard of living surpassed only in Sweden. Yet, even in France, the benefit fulfills a transitional function, enabling a mother to be supported while in training and helping her to enter or reenter the labor force. The underlying assumption is that this mother will be working either when her child is three or within one year after first receipt of the single-parent allowance. (Free, publicly subsidized preschools are available to all children above the age of two whose parents wish them to attend.) Once the lone parent allowance ends, or when the mother is working and no longer qualifies on an income basis, the universal family allowances remain, as they do even if the single mother remarries. The objective is to provide an income supplement for low or modest wage earners and to create a work incentive while protecting the economic well-being of children.

Housing allowances are only one component of an array of policies that all the countries studied provide in order to increase the availability of housing and to assist in home purchase and even in mortgage guarantees. Our concern here is not with such policies but rather with the monetary or tax benefits to which an individual family that rents or owns its dwelling is entitled under specified circumstances. (The U.S. housing allowance, which benefits only a very small percentage of those low-income families who qualify, is not an entitlement program.)

The core idea of the housing allowance is simple: if a family makes a responsible contribution toward its own housing costs out of its income from all sources, and if it rents or owns standard and reasonable housing, the government will pay a share of the excess costs. The contribution will usually be based on family size, income, housing costs, a concept of a fair share of income to be assigned to housing, a concept of a fair cost for housing, and some minimum requirements as to the quality of the housing and the amenities it provides.

Housing allowances are an important addition to the finances of low- and moderate-income families in half the countries studied. The Swedish and French benefits make by far the most significant contribution; however, the German and British benefits, although less substantial, clearly bolster the income of single-parent families (as well as of those two-parent families with unemployed and underemployed wage earners).

The significance of the benefit is best gauged by noting how much it contributes to the incomes of the three mother-only families in the study. The Swedish housing allowance, available primarily to families with children, constitutes between 20 and 30 percent of family income. Although income-tested, its ceiling was so high that in 1979 half of all families with children qualified for and received it. Indeed, Sweden views its housing allowance as an income-tested supplement to its more modest family allowance. The French grants are smaller but do make up 15 percent of the income of mother-only families; about one-quarter of the French families with children benefit. The British and German allowances constitute a much smaller contribution to family income and benefit a much smaller group, in part because they are targeted more toward the elderly than toward families with children. Nevertheless, this allowance is an important component in the income package of mother-only families.

The experience with housing allowances in these four countries, especially in Sweden and France, is particularly interesting because the income-tested benefits are not stigmatized. The income ceiling is relatively high in each country, and a large proportion of middle-income families as well as poor families qualify for benefits. Thus most mother-only families qualify. If one adds the value of the housing allowance to the family allowance allotted a non-wage-earning mother, the total accounts for almost half of her income in France, more than a third in Sweden, and more than a quarter in Germany and the United Kingdom; for the working mother, the transfers together constitute almost 40 percent of her income in France, more than 25 percent in Sweden, and close to that in the United Kingdom and Germany. The most important consequence of such a policy, of course, is that it clearly decreases the role of social assistance in France and Sweden, affecting both the number of recipients and the role of assistance in family budgets.

In contrast to family allowances—which have a long history and are the most consistently used child benefit in all countries—and housing allowances, which also have a long-standing tradition but are less widely used, *advance maintenance payments* are a relatively new benefit. Existing as yet in only a very few countries, they are explicitly designed to provide support payments to children when one of their natural or adoptive parents is absent and fails to provide financial support or when payments are irregular or inadequate.[11] The full Swedish program title is "Advance Payment of Maintenance Allowance."

For some years social assistance has been used to help low-income families in many European countries, as it is in the United States; indeed, this system has increasingly assumed a primary role in providing support for such families. In recent years, however, dissatisfaction with this form of public assistance has grown, as has the conviction that an alternative method of providing financial help should be developed.

In some countries—Sweden, for example—a further incentive to a search for an alternative strategy has been a change in life-style of most women with children, that is, their large-scale entry into the labor force. Increasingly, government agencies recognize that child support does not arise from the need to compensate a single-parent family for the loss of the absent parent's income. The need rather lies in compensation for the loss of that parent's contribution toward the support of the child. The assumption is that except when their children are under the age of two or three, single mothers will be working and supporting themselves; however, those earnings may not adequately cover the costs of a child as well. Thus, the need for assured child support.

A changing view of women's roles, growth in the numbers of mother-only families, and increased concern about the proportion of these families receiving public assistance have led several countries to explore alternative types of income transfers. Three countries that have moved in this direction—albeit two very recently—are Sweden, Germany, and

11. For a more extensive discussion of advanced maintenance programs, see Sheila B. Kamerman and Alfred J. Kahn, "Child Support: Some International Developments," in *Parental Support Obligations*, ed. Judith Cassetty (Lexington, Mass.: Lexington Books, 1983). In addition to the three countries mentioned here, several other countries have long-standing advance maintenance programs, e.g., Austria and Denmark. France is introducing such a program in 1985.

Israel. Given that the German program began in 1980, few details are available as yet. The Israeli program, designed as an improvement on social assistance, is based on the assumptions that a single mother with a child under fourteen should not be expected to work, that mother and child should be supported by a consistently provided benefit at the poverty level, and that a public authority should assume responsibility for collecting support from the absent parent in order to offset public expenditure for the benefit. In contrast, the Swedish policy assumes labor-force participation by women (but does not require it), defines the benefit as a child entitlement, and is designed primarily to assure an adequate level of support for a child. The goal of compensating for this financial burden on the public is only secondary. In contrast to both of these programs, U.S. policy as illustrated by Title IV D of the Social Security Act has been primarily aimed at recovering money to offset public expenditures for public assistance. The Swedish program of advance maintenance payments, described briefly below, represents the most significant system for child support developed by those countries now exploring alternative ways to provide children with financial aid.

This program, established in its present form in 1964, offers tax-free, non-income-tested cash benefits equal to 40 percent of the Swedish reference wage—an indexed amount used as the basis for all social benefits. The social insurance office extends these child-support payments to single parents for each of their children under the age of eighteen. The program was instituted to prevent a child from being penalized for a parent's inability or failure to provide her or him with a maintenance allowance.

The parent seeking advance maintenance benefits, usually the mother, applies to the local social insurance office in person, by phone, or by mail. (The father is the initiator in 10–15 percent of all cases.) The person responsible for the care of the child receives payments regardless whether paternity has been established, a court order is in effect, or the court-ordered child support is lower than the benefit amount; the custodial parent's income or marital status is not taken into account. However, the custodial parent is legally required to assist in establishing the child's paternity, a fact recorded in a high percentage of cases. In effect, the benefit level represents a normative standard and is viewed as an amount equivalent to, or perhaps a little higher than, what one parent would contribute to a child's support.

Social insurance offices (the counterparts to social security offices in the United States) administer the program. In 1979 about 38 percent of the costs were offset by collections from the responsible parents, a figure expected to reach 50 percent very soon. The motive underlying the program, however, is provision of adequate support for the child, not imposition of a penalty or even a difficult burden on low-income fathers no longer living with their children's mother.

About 11 percent of all children and 53 percent of those in single-parent families are supported or partially supported by these advance maintenance payments—some 220,000 children; the others are supported through voluntary contributions of the absent parent. (In addition to the 310,128 single-parent families in Sweden—approximately 27 percent of all Swedish families with children—there are some two-parent families that receive advance maintenance payments also.) Only a very small proportion of children, including children of newly arrived immigrants, are not eligible.

Advance maintenance payments have had a substantial impact on the use of social assistance in Sweden. Social assistance accounts for only 1 percent of all social welfare expenditures and benefits 5 percent of the population at most. Less than 20 percent of all single mothers receive assistance, a number representing only 20 percent of all those collecting benefits. (Forty-five percent are males, divided evenly between middle-aged alcoholics and youths who are unemployed or substance abusers, and 23 percent are single women, mostly young.) Moreover, the benefits single mothers receive are generally small amounts provided for a very brief period to cover a temporary or transitional need or an emergency. Two-thirds are on assistance for less than three months. Furthermore, despite the substantial increase in the numbers of single-parent families, these women, like all Swedish women, are likely to work, even if only part-time.

Alternative Policies toward Mother-only Families

The link between single parenthood and poverty has been noted in U.S. census reports, international statistics, social science research, and the media. Research shows that the poverty of mother-only families largely results from changes in family composition: the birth of a child to a single woman or the loss of a father for reasons other than death. These are the circumstances that lead women to claim AFDC; only 12 percent of those making a claim do so because of a loss of earnings. Moreover, 40 percent of those who go off AFDC continue to have incomes below the poverty level, and about one-third subsequently return to the program.[12]

12. Mary Jo Bane and David T. Ellwood, "The Dynamics of Dependency: The Routes to Self-Sufficiency" (Cambridge, Mass.: Urban Systems Research and Engineering, June 1983).

Those who argue that AFDC encourages dependency—and even teenage pregnancy—are convinced that the best alternative strategy lies in changing the attitudes and behavior patterns that lead to the formation of single-parent families.[13] Perhaps so, but attitudinal and behavioral changes are not easily made through public policy; and even when achievable, they take time.[14] Certainly, the problems of teenage parenting go well beyond economic difficulties alone and suggest the need for a wide range of social interventions; but such considerations lie beyond the scope of this paper. The majority of women heading families on AFDC are not, in any case, teenagers—and while teenagers may need financial support, they could perhaps benefit more from a different type of support than now exists. The economic situation of all these families requires help and attention. The question is, How can aid be given in a way that is acceptable to the society?

Prior efforts at improving the situation of these families by reforming "welfare" in the United States have focused primarily, though unsuccessfully, on the major transfer program benefiting these families: AFDC. Many people remain convinced that modifying AFDC is the only worthwhile policy strategy. I agree, however, with those who think it highly unlikely that AFDC, even when it includes food stamps, will be reformed in such a way that it will bring a national benefit level up even to the poverty threshold.

Moreover, as women's roles have changed, AFDC itself has become an increasingly obsolete program. Established in 1935 at a time when most married women stayed home to care for their several children, AFDC was amended early in its history to enable low-income women to maintain a life-style resembling that of their middle-class peers. In recent years, however, the familial, domestic, and working roles of women have been dramatically transformed. Most married mothers are now employed outside the home; indeed, more than half of all mothers of children aged two and older were in the labor force in 1983. Thus a policy that enables poor mothers to stay at home while middle-class mothers are working seems questionable, to say the least. When their children are older, these women will be thrust into the labor force in any case, with all the problems of late-entry or reentry but without skills or training. While requiring good care, children also need positive role models and can find

13. Blanch Bernstein, "Will Welfare Dependency Be Reduced?" in *The Social Contract Revisited*, ed. D. Lee Bowden (Washington, D.C.: Urban Institute, 1984); Victor Fuchs, *How We Live* (Cambridge, Mass.: Harvard University Press, 1983).

14. For information about the recent efforts of various black leaders and national groups to address this problem within the black community, see Joint Center for Political Studies, *A Policy Framework for Racial Justice* (Washington, D.C.: Joint Center for Political Studies, 1983); Sheila Rule, "Leaders and Experts Plan to Meet to Address Ills of Black Families," *New York Times* (September 13, 1983).

them best in mothers who are not peripheral or excluded but are part of mainstream society.

Any examination of the income status of female-headed families underscores the importance of earnings if family income is to be above the poverty level. Thus, some suggest a third strategy: a focus on employment policies, and on training and educational opportunities, in order to make it possible for low-income women to obtain jobs and decent salaries. Some such efforts, ranging from supported work, to special training programs, to "workfare," have been or are being developed in the United States.[15] However, the market wages these women may earn will not always be adequate to meet family needs or to compensate for the loss of fringe benefits like Medicaid. Many low-wage jobs provide no health insurance, an absolute necessity for poor mothers and their families. Indeed, one major finding of the studies assessing the impact of AFDC policy changes was that, although women dropped from the program continued to work, a substantial proportion were without health insurance. Clearly, jobs—labor market policies or job development strategies— are an essential foundation for any policy directed at reducing the poverty of these women and children. But even if such a policy were in place (and this article cannot discuss in detail how it could be brought into effect), it would not give adequate help to all female-headed families with children. A job may be a necessary precondition for family income to be adequate, but it is not necessarily sufficient by itself for all such households, especially since many of the women who head them are in need of further education and training.

Still a fourth strategy is possible. The findings reported in this article show that several countries make far less use of "welfare"—public assistance—than does the United States. Yet they provide mother-only families with a standard of living that is much closer to the national average. Moreover, they accomplish this without creating work disincentives, and in a way that is not viewed as encouraging long-term dependency. Are there lessons here for the United States?

A Policy Agenda for the United States

Fundamental to a new U.S. policy strategy would be an acknowledgment of the dramatic change in women's roles, a view of mothers as "employable," and a commitment to assuring them job opportunities and training as needed. There are, however, other essential ingredients in a

15. "Workfare"—requiring public assistance beneficiaries to work at public tasks in order to "earn" their benefits—raises other issues, such as the morality of coercion, and the question of whether women are working for a wage or working off their AFDC benefit.

policy package if we are to reduce the poverty of women and children, eliminate the stigma of AFDC, and reduce long-term dependency on welfare. Attention must focus on assuring low-income women a place in mainstream society and guaranteeing children an adequate standard of living. The combined elements of such a policy could include the following:

1. A family or child allowance offered to all parents, regardless of income, as a universal child benefit. Although relatively modest in some countries, these allowances constitute a significant benefit for low-income families and can even be supplemented, as in France, with an additional income-tested benefit for selected types of low-income families. This is not necessarily an expensive benefit, since it can be a substitute for the tax allowances now available for dependents; such tax adjustments are worthless to families with a very low income and most advantageous to families with the highest incomes. Indeed, a child allowance in the form of a refundable child tax credit could act as a cash benefit to low-income families and a tax benefit—worth the same to all taxpayers—for those with tax liabilities. The Earned Income Tax Credit is a modest political precedent.

2. Child support, or a benefit like the Swedish advance maintenance payment, for all children with an absent parent who fails to provide support. In contrast to the current U.S. child-support program, this policy would entitle all children in single-parent families to basic support from the absent parent (father or mother) at a nationally set, uniform level. Rigorous efforts at collection from the absent parent could involve actions such as salary garnishment or attaching tax refunds in order to reduce the program's costs; however, the child would not be penalized for the parent's failure to pay.

3. A housing allowance provided on an income-tested basis as an entitlement, in contrast to the current U.S. system. The Reagan administration has already officially endorsed such a device, but the benefit I recommend would be available to many more families than have heretofore been considered. Although expensive, this benefit would recognize the worsening problem faced by young families who are unable to obtain adequate and affordable housing without some kind of help. Given the situation, some type of housing benefit will probably need to be developed in the future in any case. It makes sense to begin such a policy sooner rather than later and to phase it in gradually, beginning with current AFDC recipients who obtain jobs but still have very low incomes. The initial expenditure could replace AFDC rent payments.

4. Health insurance for single mothers who have jobs but inadequate or nonexistent fringe benefits. The need for such insurance should be obvious; there are women now who seek AFDC because they have a

greater need for its health care coverage—Medicaid—for their children than for the cash benefits.

5. Improved maternity and parenting policy, backed by the states or the federal government, that assures all women an eight-week minimum paid disability leave following childbirth and that enables either parent to take a minimum of four more months unpaid leave with full job protection.[16]

6. Improved subsidies for child care, enlarged either by raising the benefit level of the current child care tax credit and making it refundable, by increasing the federal social services grants for child care, or by combining these methods in some way. Clearly, if mothers are to work, public policy must assure the availability of adequate and affordable child care.

Mother-only families may be at risk of poverty everywhere, but I contend that policy strategies can be devised to raise their incomes—if our society views this as a desirable goal. I cannot claim that such a policy strategy would be cost-effective in the short run—although long-term savings are likely through the increased productivity of low-income women and the more positive socialization of their children. Moreover, whatever the short-term price tag of such policy initiatives, a modest start toward their enactment could be justified as an alternative to current AFDC costs. If we in the United States really want to better the condition of women and children, we may need debate over the specific components of a policy package, but we should recognize that many alternatives are clearly better than what we now have.

School of Social Work
Columbia University

16. For a discussion of this and related issues, see Sheila B. Kamerman, Alfred J. Kahn, and Paul W. Kingston, *Maternity Policies and Working Women* (New York: Columbia University Press, 1983).

The "Woman Question" in Cuba: An Analysis of Material Constraints on Its Solution

Muriel Nazzari

At the turn of the century European socialists believed that the advent of a socialist society would solve what they called the "woman question." Women would gain equality before the law; they would enter socially useful production on a par with men; private domestic economy would be transformed into a public enterprise through the socialization of housework and child care; and the personal subjection of women to men would end.[1] The Soviet Union, the Eastern European nations, and the People's Republic of China have all proclaimed these goals, yet they have fallen short of fully realizing them.[2]

Participants in the Cuban Revolution shared the belief that socialism would bring about complete equality between the sexes. As early as 1959, Fidel Castro spoke about the need to free women from domestic slavery so that they could participate widely in production to the benefit of women themselves and the Revolution.[3] Over the next twenty years the government increased women's educational opportunities and labor force participation while providing more and more services to lighten domestic chores for those who worked outside the home. In the early seventies it went one step farther than any other socialist nation by

I wish to thank Emilia da Costa, Silvia Arrom, David Montgomery, Peter Winn, Frank Roosevelt, and the Women's History Study Group of the Institute for Research in History for comments on earlier drafts of this essay.

1. *The Woman Question: Selections from the Writings of Karl Marx, Frederick Engels, V. I. Lenin, Joseph Stalin* (New York: International Publishers Co., 1951).

2. Gail W. Lapidus, *Women in Soviet Society: Equality, Development and Social Change* (Berkeley and Los Angeles: University of California Press, 1978); Batya Weinbaum, "Women in Transition to Socialism: Perspectives on the Chinese Case," *Review of Radical Political Economics* 8, no. 1 (Spring 1976): 34–58.

3. Fidel Castro, "Speech to the Women" (Havana, 1959), p. 9.

enacting the Cuban Family Code, which makes husband and wife equally responsible for housework and child care.[4]

Despite these positive developments, the consensus in Cuba today is that full equality for women has yet to be achieved. A factor frequently invoked to explain this state of affairs is the persistence of prejudice and machismo in Cuban society. According to one scholar, these attitudes remain because of the inevitable time lag between structural and ideological change.[5] Important though ideological change may be for achieving women's equality, this paper concentrates instead on the material constraints that prevent Cuban society from attaining this goal. The changing position of women will be analyzed in the context of the larger struggle surrounding the economic strategies adopted during Cuba's transition from capitalism to socialism. I will argue that the Cuban Revolution's full adoption in the early seventies of a system of distribution based on material incentives and the requirement that enterprises show a profit perpetuates women's inequality in the home and in the work force.

My argument rests on the fact that child rearing requires both labor and resources. Marxist-feminist theory has stressed the social importance of women's labor for reproducing the work force, both generationally (through biological reproduction and the socialization of children) and on a day-to-day basis (through housework and emotional nurturance).[6] If we assume that the labor involved in the daily care of a worker (housework) is a given in any society and could conceivably be performed by workers for themselves, then the variable that determines women's position in the home and society is generational reproduction, that is, childbearing and child rearing. This follows the trend of current feminist thought, which recognizes that reproductive labor is implicated in women's oppression.

I take this argument one step further, however. Women's position is determined not only by the institutional arrangements that apportion the labor of child rearing to women but also by the institutions that determine how children gain access to means of subsistence. In developed industrial societies, both capitalist and socialist, most children receive their means of subsistence from the wages of one or both parents. Wage labor, however, cannot usually be performed simultaneously with the labor necessary to raise children. The resulting contradiction historically led to a specific division of labor within the family, the father working outside the home for a wage, the mother doing housework.

4. Marjorie King, "Cuba's Attack on Women's Second Shift, 1974–1976," in *Women in Latin America: An Anthology from Latin American Perspectives,* ed. Eleanor Leacock et al. (Riverside, Calif.: Latin American Perspectives, 1979).

5. Lourdes Casal, "Revolution and Conciencia: Women in Cuba," in *Women, War and Revolution,* ed. Carol Berkin and Clara M. Lovett (New York: Holmes & Meier, 1980).

6. For example, see Isabel Larguia and John Dumoulin, "Aspects of the Condition of Women's Labor," *N.A.C.L.A.'s Latin America Empire Report* 9, no. 6 (September 1975): 2–13.

The theoretical socialist answer to the woman question was to change this division of labor by socializing child care and housework so that married women and mothers could engage in production on an equal basis with men.[7] In practice, socialist countries have thus far found it impossible to eliminate all aspects of privatized household and family maintenance. Cuba has sought to compensate for this shortcoming by passing a law requiring men to share housework and child care.

My analysis of the Cuban case makes it seem evident that both socialist strategies (the socialization of domestic chores and child care and the equal apportionment of the remaining tasks between husband and wife) are necessary but not sufficient conditions for achieving full equality between women and men. Although both address the issue of the allocation of labor for child rearing, neither considers the implications of the fact that raising children also requires access to resources. A full solution to the woman question must therefore address the issue not only of the labor needed to raise children but also of the income needed to raise children. Power relations within the family can be affected by whether that income comes from the father, the mother, both parents, or society as a whole. The issue of systems of distribution therefore has a direct impact on Cuba's attempts to solve the woman question.

The Choice of Systems of Distribution in Cuba

The Cuban Revolution moved quickly toward the implementation of a socialist society. In the early sixties it effected a general redistribution of income by raising wages while lowering rents and prices. Meanwhile, it nationalized all means of production except for small peasant holdings and small businesses. To manage the nationalized productive units, the new government had to develop and institute nationwide systems of management and choose a system of distribution of goods, services, and income. Because the Revolution was committed to guaranteed employment for all, it also had to design a system of work incentives to replace the fear of unemployment that motivates workers in capitalist economies.

The problem of work incentives in a socialist society is linked to the choice of a system of distribution. In capitalist economies, income distribution is carried out principally through the wage and through the profit that accrues from ownership of the means of production. In socialist economies, private ownership of the means of production is largely abolished, and private profit disappears as a source of income.

7. A review of the problems socialist countries have encountered trying to implement this solution can be found in Elisabeth J. Croll, "Women in Rural Production and Reproduction in the Soviet Union, China, Cuba and Tanzania: Socialist Development Experiences," *Signs: Journal of Women in Culture and Society* 7, no. 2 (Winter 1981): 361–74.

When Marx envisioned this ideal society he proposed that distribution be carried out by the formula: "From each according to his ability, to each according to his need." He called this the communist system of distribution. Under this system people would be expected to work to contribute to society, but not for wages, because goods and services would not be bought or sold, and needs would be met as they arose. Marx believed it would be impossible to implement a communist system of distribution during the transitional stage from capitalism to socialism. For a time, distribution would have to follow a different formula: "From each according to his ability, to each according to his work." This formula is called the socialist system of distribution, and under it needs would primarily be met through remuneration for work, that is, through the wage.[8] After the triumph of the Cuban Revolution, the question was whether it would be possible to use a combination of both the socialist and the communist systems of distribution.

During the early sixties there were ideological struggles within the Cuban Communist party over this issue as well as the related issue of incentives—a problem embedded in the formula of distribution according to need.[9] In all historical eras people have worked to satisfy their needs, either directly through access to the means of production or indirectly through wage labor. But if a socialist society satisfies needs independently from work, what will induce people to labor? The Cuban Revolution never completely abandoned the wage as a system of distribution or a work incentive. Nevertheless, throughout the sixties the Revolution emphasized moral over material incentives and promoted nonwage volunteer labor.

During that period Castro expressed the belief that Cuba could utilize both systems of distribution simultaneously. In 1966 he declared that as soon as possible society must use its resources to provide for all essential needs, including health, housing, adequate nutrition, physical and mental education, and cultural development. The Revolution was already providing free education, health care, sports, recreation, and meals in schools and workplaces. He added that the government intended to supply housing and day care without charge as soon as possible.

In the same speech Castro discussed the problem of family dependents. Should the earning power of a son determine how an elderly parent lives, or would it not be preferable for society as a whole to ensure that the old have all they require? In the case of children, he contended that the "shoes and clothing they receive, as well as their toys, should not

8. Castro explained both systems to the Thirteenth Congress of the Confederation of Cuban Workers. See "XIII CTC Congress: A History Making Event," *Cuba Review* 4, no. 1 (July 1974): 15–25.

9. See Bertram Silverman, *Man and Socialism in Cuba* (New York: Atheneum Publishers, 1971).

depend on whether the mother has ten children and can do little work, but rather on the needs of the child as a human being."[10]

These statements indicate that Castro envisioned a society in which the means to satisfy basic needs would be freely available to everyone and children and old people would receive their subsistence from society itself rather than depend on relatives' wages for support. Although this ideal solution was never fully implemented in Cuba, much of the initial redistribution after the Revolution was evidently carried out according to need, unrelated to recipients' work in production.

Initial Effects of the Cuban Revolution on Women

Many Cuban women have claimed that women were the greatest beneficiaries of the Revolution. Are they right in their assessment? Did women gain more from the Revolution than men?

Differences in the ways women and men were affected by the Revolution can be traced to their traditional roles. Most Cuban women were housewives, not wage workers. The initial measures of redistribution brought about a change in their living and working conditions, but the class lines that divided Cuban women caused them to experience these changes in very different ways.

Middle- and upper-class women experienced a loss, since they shared with their male relatives a reduction of income. The nationalization of productive enterprises and banks abolished dividends at the same time as lower rents decreased landlords' profits. Many emigrated, but of those who remained in Cuba, women experienced greater hardships than men. Men from these classes retained their status because their skills as entrepreneurs and professionals were valuable to the Revolution. In contrast, the status of middle- and upper-class women (except for those who were themselves professionals) had formerly been defined by the large amount of leisure they enjoyed, which was a function of their ability to avoid performing menial labor by hiring others to do domestic chores. After the Revolution, these women lost servants, chauffeurs, and nurses.

Conditions for lower-class housewives, on the other hand, improved dramatically during the first five years. All the initial measures of redistribution resulted in positive changes within the lower-class home, with the most spectacular differences evident in rural areas where pre-revolutionary poverty had been greatest. The Agrarian Reform eliminated rural rents and evictions by giving tenants, sharecroppers, and squatters free title to the land they were farming. All large estates were

10. Martin Kenner and James Petras, eds., *Fidel Castro Speaks* (New York: Grove Press, 1969), p. 213.

nationalized and transformed into collective farms to be worked by landless agricultural workers, resulting in permanent incomes and adequate housing for the remaining rural families.[11] The Urban Reform slashed rents and electricity and telephone rates by half. These redistributive measures meant a 15–30 percent rise in wages, which increased the purchasing power of the poor at the same time that prices for other essentials were being lowered.[12]

Lower-class housewives could feed and clothe their families better. Consumption of the foods that a majority of Cubans had rarely eaten before, such as milk, eggs, and meat, soared. Until production could be increased to meet the expanded purchasing power, rationing was instituted to guarantee everyone a certain amount of these products. At the same time, better clothing became available through a program that brought young women to Havana from all over Cuba to learn to sew. The first thousand took free sewing machines back to their rural homes; each committed herself to teach at least ten other women how to cut and stitch.[13]

During this early period housing was also upgraded. Urban housing was redistributed by transforming large old residences abandoned by their former owners into apartments. New buildings were constructed for the agricultural collectives, latrines were added to existing rural dwellings, cement replaced dirt floors, and many people had running water and electricity for the first time. New roads in rural areas made buses available to previously isolated families.[14]

The most spectacular accomplishments of the Cuban Revolution—the literacy campaign and the institution of free education and health care for all—also had an effect on the working conditions of lower-class housewives. Education revolutionized both immediate opportunities and future expectations for them and their children. Free health care combined with lessons in hygiene and an improved standard of living to yield a decline in the infant mortality rate from 43.6 per one thousand live births in 1962 to 19.4 in 1979.[15] By the early seventies, 98 percent of all childbirths were medically attended.[16] Polio, diphtheria, and malaria were eradicated, and life expectancy rose to seventy years. Since women were the ones who traditionally cared for the ill, they especially benefited from these improvements in health.

11. Edward Boorstein, *The Economic Transformation of Cuba* (New York: Monthly Review Press, 1968), pp. 42–54, 78–79.

12. Archibald R. M. Ritter, *The Economic Development of Revolutionary Cuba* (New York: Praeger Publishers, 1974), p. 107.

13. Laurette Séjourné, ed., *La mujer cubana en el quehacer de la historia* (Mexico, D.F.: Siglo Veintiuno, 1980), pp. 124–33.

14. Ibid., pp. 121, 128.

15. Fidel Castro in *Granma Review* (March 16, 1980).

16. *Economia y desarrollo*, September–October 1974, p. 198.

Much of the early redistribution in Cuba was undoubtedly effected through the formula "to each according to his need." Rural inhabitants were not given cement floors because they had money to pay for them, nor were they allocated housing because their individual jobs were important. Rather, people learned to sew and read and received health care solely because they needed these skills and services. Yet not all distribution was carried out according to this formula. During the same period, a large portion of people's needs was still met through the wage. The improved purchasing power of the wage, however, was not due to wage earners' efforts or productivity but to deliberate policies framed by the Revolution in accordance with the formula of distribution according to need.

This lavish initial redistribution was only made possible by drawing on existing reserves such as nationalized land and capital, formerly unused resources in equipment and land, and underutilized sectors of the labor force like women and the unemployed.[17] But these reserves were not inexhaustible. To achieve economic growth, hard work and increased productivity became necessary.

Economic Growth and Work Incentives

To meet these economic imperatives, in the mid-sixties the Revolution adopted a mixture of moral and material incentives and experimented with different strategies for growth. One strategy involved industrialization through import substitution and agricultural diversification. By 1963 a crisis in the balance of payments prompted a shift in economic policy. From 1964 to 1970, the government returned to sugar production as the principal source of foreign exchange, stressing investment in production for export and the acquisition of capital goods at the expense of the production of consumer goods.[18] Meanwhile, services such as education, health care, public telephones, sports, and child care continued to be furnished at no cost. The income gap between workers with the highest wages and those with the lowest narrowed, as did the gap between urban and rural incomes.[19]

By the end of the decade the combination of ample wages and free services with rationing and the restricted production of consumer goods put money in people's pockets but gave them nowhere to spend it. The wage no longer functioned as an incentive to work when there was not enough to buy and many goods and services were provided at no cost. Absenteeism at work reached a high point.

17. Boorstein, pp. 81–83.
18. Ritter, pp. 128–270.
19. Jorge I. Dominguez, *Cuba: Order and Revolution* (Cambridge, Mass.: Harvard University Press, Belknap Press, 1978), pp. 227–28.

At the same time, economic problems were multiplying, leading to an increased awareness of general inefficiency and low productivity. In response to these problems, massive readjustments of Cuba's social, economic, and political structures took place after 1970, culminating in 1975 with the First Congress of the Communist Party. This restructuring addressed several areas of concern. A deflationary monetary policy corrected the imbalance between money in circulation and the amount of available consumer goods. A reorganization of the managerial system and the substitution of material for moral incentives responded to the problems of low productivity and inefficiency. Union reforms, moves to strengthen and broaden the Communist Party, and the creation of People's Power (the new government administrative system) sought to structure channels for carrying negative feedback to the central planning bodies.[20]

All these measures increased the efficiency of Cuba's planned socialist society, but the first two (the monetary policy and the new system of management) involved a change from a commitment to carry out as much distribution as possible according to need to an ever greater reliance on the socialist formula. Distribution became principally tied to the wage, and enterprises were expected to show a profit. Since the wage, material incentives, and production for exchange are also the mainstays of capitalist societies, these measures represented a decision not to go as far in revolutionizing society as initially planned.

This was a conscious decision. The Thirteenth Congress of the Confederation of Cuban Workers, which took place in 1973, extensively debated the two systems of distribution and the issue of moral versus material incentives. Castro maintained that the development of productive forces had been hindered because Cuba had been too idealistic in the use of moral incentives and distribution according to need. The Congress concluded that Cuba must adopt distribution according to work, since the productive forces would have to develop much further to reach the stage in which all distribution could successfully be carried out according to need.[21]

In order to analyze the effects of these policy decisions on the condition of women in Cuba, we will compare the situation of women in the labor force and the home before and after the shift in systems of distribution.

Women in the Work Force, 1959–69

Because the Batista regime left a legacy of seven hundred thousand unemployed and three hundred thousand underemployed men, one of

20. Ritter, p. 250; Dominguez, pp. 243–49, 271–79, 306–40.
21. Castro (n. 8 above).

the first goals of the Revolution became full male employment. By 1964 this goal had been achieved, and it affected not only the men involved but also the women and children who depended on the men's wages.

Despite the priority placed on achieving full male employment during the first five years, the Revolution did not entirely ignore the issue of women's participation in the work force. Instead, it concentrated on women who were already working by providing child care and other services to assist them. Night schools and boarding schools were set up for the large number of women who had been domestic servants or prostitutes at the time of the Revolution. These institutions functioned until the women learned new jobs, becoming typists, secretaries, bank tellers, and bus drivers.[22]

Though the Revolution did not immediately incorporate all women into paid work, it created the Federation of Cuban Women to mobilize them for building the new society. The federation organized day-care centers and started schools to train day-care workers, formed sanitary brigades to supplement professional medical care, and became the backbone of the campaign to eliminate illiteracy.[23]

Women's participation in voluntary organizations required their liberation from the patriarchal norms that had traditionally confined them to the home. Individual men often resented this change. One woman recalled, "It was husbands who were most limiting, and the rest of the family, too, because they were used to seeing woman as the center of the home, the one who solved all problems, and they didn't understand that women could solve problems outside the home, too."[24] Going from the home to the street, from solving the problems of a family to resolving issues in the larger community, profoundly altered women's lives and perceptions of themselves.

As soon as full male employment was achieved, a demand for women in the work force developed. In May 1966, Castro called for the addition of a million women to the labor force, remarking that, if each woman created a thousand pesos of value per year, a billion pesos of wealth would be produced by women annually. And he indicated that the government was building more and more nurseries and school cafeterias to make it easier for women to work outside the home.[25]

Yet only nine months later, Castro's emphasis had shifted. Women were still needed in production, but the Revolution was finding it difficult to provide the thousands of facilities that would make it possible for a million women to work. He pointed out that, to liberate women from all the activities hindering their incorporation into the work force,

22. Ramiro Pavon, "El empleo femenino en Cuba," *Universidad de Santiago,* December 1975, p. 123.

23. Ministerio de Justicia, *La mujer en Cuba socialista* (Havana: Editorial Orbe, 1977), pp. 20–42.

24. Séjourné, ed. (n. 13 above), p. 193, my translation.

25. Kenner and Petras, eds. (n. 10 above), p. 207.

society had to create a material base. In other words, Cuba had to develop economically.

This means that, at the same time Castro was asking women to work, he was also informing them of material constraints that prevented the government from providing the costly social services that would free them for wage labor. When government planners had to decide between alternative investments, day-care centers frequently came in second. Castro noted that the establishment of day-care centers was slowest in regions where the greatest amount of road and building construction was underway. Nevertheless, this speech was a rousing call to women. In it Castro claimed that the most revolutionary aspect of Cuba's transformation was the revolution taking place in Cuban women.[26]

During the rest of the decade the Federation of Cuban Women responded valiantly to his appeal. It mobilized thousands of women for volunteer work, especially in agriculture, culminating in the 41 million hours of volunteer labor women contributed to the sugarcane harvest of 1970. Meanwhile, the federation continued to pursue its objective of incorporating one hundred thousand women per year into the paid work force and conducted a search for women to run the countless small businesses nationalized in 1968.

By the early seventies, however, it was obvious that recruiting women into wage work was an uphill effort. Seventy-six percent of the women who joined the labor force in 1969 left their jobs before the year was out.[27] As the Cuban Revolution modified its policies to address inefficiency and low productivity, analysts began to explore the causes behind women's impermanent tenure in paid occupations.

Diagnoses and Solutions

In 1974 the Federation of Cuban Women reported that high turnover among women workers could be attributed largely to "the pressure from housework and family members; the lack of economic incentive; and the need for better services to aid working women."[28] The federation also organized a survey to investigate why there were so few women leaders in government. In the trial run of People's Power held in the province of Matanzas, women constituted only 7.6 percent of the candidates and 3 percent of those elected. Both male and female respondents to the survey believed that if women had not been nominated, had

---

26. *Bohemia* (December 16, 1966). Day-care centers continued to be built, providing three meals a day and laundering clothes worn at the center. There were 433 centers in 1970 and 782 in 1978 (Federation of Cuban Women, *La mujer cubana, 1975–1979* [Federation of Cuban Women, Havana, n.d., mimeographed], p. 10).

27. Ministerio de Justicia (n. 23 above), pp. 252–57.

28. Ibid., p. 252, my translation.

refused nomination, or simply were not elected, it was due to family responsibilities.[29]

These disturbing trends at the national level posed the question of whether the problems that prevented women from participating in government were the same as those that kept women from joining or remaining in the labor force. Another study was conducted comparing the free time available to working women with that available to working men and nonworking women. It found that housework occupied nine hours and fourteen minutes of the daily time budget for housewives, four hours and forty-four minutes for working women, but only thirty-eight minutes for working men. In the words of the study's authors, "The time society and especially women dedicate to housework is at the center of all discussion having to do with the struggle toward women's full equality."[30]

I would argue, in contrast, that the issue in the struggle for women's equality is not housework per se but child care and the additional housework the presence of children requires. In this respect the research mentioned above has a serious defect, since it averages time spent performing housework and child care without establishing how many women in the sample had children. A survey of mothers alone, as opposed to women in general, would have revealed much less free time. Thus the "family problems" cited to explain why few women were nominated or elected to People's Power in Matanzas must have referred not to housework, which can usually be postponed, but to child care, which cannot.

In response to these and other studies, the federation made many suggestions that were later implemented to help correct the problems women experienced. Day care was restricted to children of working mothers. Those children were also given priority access to boarding schools and to day schools that served meals. Stores lengthened their business hours so women could shop after work, and a plan was devised to give working women precedence at food markets. Employed women received better laundry services, some provided at the workplace.[31] These measures helped, but they did not eliminate women's double work shift. The conclusion ultimately reached by Cubans was that men and women must share housework and child care. As one woman worker argued in one of the many popular debates about the Family Code, "If they're going to incorporate us into the work force, they're

29. Primer Congreso del Partido Comunista, *Sobre el pleno ejercicio de la igualdad de la mujer,* 3d thesis, p. 5.

30. Marta Trigo Marabotto, ed., *Investigaciones científicas de la demanda en Cuba* (Havana: Editorial Orbe, 1979), pp. 96–101, esp. p. 101, my translation.

31. Carollee Benglesdorf and Alice Hageman, "Emerging from Underdevelopment," in *Capitalist Patriarchy and the Case for Socialist Feminism,* ed. Zillah Eisenstein (New York: Monthly Review Press, 1979).

going to have to incorporate themselves into the home, and that's all there is to it."[32] In 1975 this belief was made law with the adoption of the Family Code that gave women and men equal rights and responsibilities within the family.

This law can be seen as a change in the locus of the solution to the woman question. The solution first attempted, socializing child care and housework, tried to move women toward equality by transferring their family duties to social institutions without disturbing men's lives or roles.[33] Cuban economists calculated that for every three women who joined the work force, a fourth must be employed in institutions supplying supportive services to facilitate their incorporation.[34] The great cost of this solution meant that it had to compete with other investment needs in the national budget, especially those that would more obviously aid economic development. The Family Code, on the other hand, provided a solution to the woman question that did not need to come out of the national budget. It would take place within the home without affecting the rest of society. It did, nevertheless, require a change in individual men's lives, and men resisted.[35] However, as we shall see, other factors operating in the Cuban context indicate that the difficulties encountered in achieving equality between men and women within the family cannot be attributed solely to men's recalcitrance.

Inequality within the Home

To discover what factors make the equality proclaimed by the Family Code difficult to achieve, we must analyze the situation of wives and mothers. Housewives constituted three-fifths of the adult women outside the work force in 1972, and married women were only 18 percent of women employed.[36] A possible conclusion to draw from this data would be that housework and child care discouraged married women from taking paid employment. Yet the same set of data shows that the largest category in the female labor force was divorced women (43 percent, followed by single women, 30 percent, and ending with widows, 9 percent). Since divorced women are just as likely as married women to have children to care for, the variable determining their incorporation into the work force must have been divorce itself. Conversely, the variable permitting married women to remain outside the work force must have been access to a husband's wage. Under a system of distribution accord-

32. Margaret Randall, *Afterword* (Toronto: Women's Press, 1974).
33. As suggested by Edmund Dahlstrom, *The Changing Roles of Men and Women* (Boston: Beacon Press, 1971), p. 175.
34. Pavon (n. 22 above), p. 115.
35. Megaly Sanchez, "Rights and Duties Go Together," *Cuba Review* 4, no. 2:13–14.
36. Juceplan, *Aspectos demográficos de la fuerza laboral femenina en Cuba* (Havana, 1974), pp. 32, 44.

ing to work, the needs of the wageless housewife are met only through her husband's labor, reinforcing his power and her dependence.

The dependence of children and the elderly also continued under the socialist system of distribution. The Family Code held parents rather than society responsible for the support of minors.[37] This section of the new law provoked no objection when the code was debated throughout Cuba, possibly because similar statutes prevail in most modern nations. But tying the fulfillment of children's needs to the wages of their parents directly contradicted Castro's 1966 statement that a child's subsistence should be determined solely by the "needs of the child as a human being." The Family Code also established the responsibility of workers to support parents or siblings in need, contrary to Castro's suggestion that the income of the elderly should not depend on the earning power of relatives.[38] In this sense the Family Code itself was a step away from distribution according to need toward distribution according to work.

While the Family Code was being elaborated and discussed in the early seventies, the Cuban Revolution was making important economic changes related to the full implementation of the socialist formula for distribution. The government instituted price increases that were explicitly intended to reduce the amount of money in circulation and to act as an incentive to individual productivity.[39] The goal of abolishing house rents was postponed indefinitely. Prices for long-distance transportation, cigarettes, beer, rum, restaurant meals, cinemas, and consumer durables rose. Free public telephones were abolished, and people were now charged for canteen meals, water, and electricity.[40] By 1977 day care was no longer free, forcing mothers to bear part of the cost of providing the conditions that enabled them to work.

In the face of higher prices and fewer free services, the nonworking mother's increasing dependence on her husband's wage might lead her to avoid pressing him to share housework and child care. Whether the working mother would do so would depend on the degree of parity between her wage and her spouse's. If the husband's income were much greater, making the well-being of the children more heavily dependent on the father's wage than the mother's, a woman might perform the extra labor associated with child care so as not to hinder her husband's productivity. This would allow him to work overtime, join the Communist Party, or be elected to People's Power as ways to augment his earning capacity. Unless the wages of husband and wife were equal, we would therefore expect a system of distribution tied to the wage to

37. Ministry of Justice, *Family Code* (Havana: Editorial Orbe, 1975), articles 33, 122.

38. Ibid., articles 122, 123.

39. Dominguez (n. 19 above), p. 170.

40. Carmelo Mesa-Lago, *Cuba in the 1970's* (Albuquerque: University of New Mexico Press, 1974), pp. 42–48.

exacerbate inequalities between men and women in the home. What is the current situation in Cuba?

Women in the Work Force, 1970–80

It is not at all evident whether there is a gap between the national average wages of male and female workers in Cuba. Cuban law establishes that men and women must be paid an equal wage for equal work, and no statistics are compiled comparing men's and women's earnings. Yet the General Wage Reform of April 1980 shows a difference between the minimum wage set for office and service employees, $85 per month, and that of industrial workers, $93.39 per month.[41] In 1979 only 21.9 percent of the female work force held industrial jobs, while 66.5 percent were in service occupations.[42] We can conclude that, at least at the level of minimum wage work, women's average wage is lower than men's due to the concentration of female labor in the service sector. This is partially confirmed by data on day-care workers, an exclusively female occupational group, who were the lowest-paid workers in 1973, receiving only 77 percent of the national average wage.[43]

Yet the fact that women are overrepresented in the service sector does not necessarily mean that women as a whole earn less than men, since there are also many female professionals. For example, in 1977, 66 percent of the employees at the Ministry of Public Health were women. Professionals were 39 percent of all workers in that ministry, and of these, 75 percent were women. Women constituted 5 percent of the superior personnel who formulate overall plans and policies for public health, 20 percent of upper-level administrators, 33 percent of the doctors, 95 percent of the nurses, 82 percent of the paramedics, and 75 percent of community assistants.[44] In 1979 professionals and technicians constituted 27 percent of the entire female work force. If we add the 4.7 percent who were managerial personnel, we find that over 30 percent of all women employed in Cuba are technicians, professionals, or managers.[45] This high proportion of women in better-paid positions means there may not be a gap between the national average wages of men and women.

There is, however, a general inequality between Cuban men and women that proceeds from the way the constitutional principle of guaranteed employment has been interpreted. In practice, only males

41. *Granma Review* (April 6, 1980).
42. Calculated from a table in *La mujer cubana, 1975–1979* (n. 26 above), p. 9.
43. Dominguez (n. 19 above), p. 501.
44. Federation of Cuban Women (n. 26 above), pp. 16–17.
45. Statistics presented to the Third Congress of the Federation of Cuban Women (see *Direct from Cuba,* March 15, 1980).

and female heads of household are guaranteed jobs. The antiloafing law, passed in the early seventies, makes work compulsory for all males (but not females) over seventeen who are not students or military personnel. As a result of these policies, women in Cuba are used as a labor reserve.

Categorization as a labor reserve has had different effects for women under each system of distribution. During the sixties when Cuban women provided much unpaid voluntary labor, the lack of a wage was not such a disadvantage because a large number of needs were met at no cost. In contrast, once the satisfaction of needs became principally tied to the wage, to go without a wage for volunteer work or to have difficulty finding employment had more serious consequences.

Being part of the labor reserve results in lower wages for some working women in Cuba. This is certainly the case for female cyclical contract workers in agriculture. Although contracts protect these women from uncertain employment, and the women also receive full maternity benefits even when childbirth occurs outside the work period,[46] their wage and pension rights are apportioned according to work accomplished.[47] Because they work only part of the year as seasonal laborers, their annual income and pension rights will necessarily be smaller than those of male counterparts who work year-round.

There are also indications of a lack of sufficient employment for Cuban women. An important function of the Federation of Cuban Women is to coordinate information about job vacancies for female applicants. In 1980, even women trained as technicians were reported to be having difficulty finding jobs.[48]

When full male employment is viewed against the shortage of jobs for women, it appears that women are hired only as needed. This is confirmed by Vilma Espin, who notes that the proportion of women in the work force grew from 23 percent in 1974 to 30 percent in 1979 but adds that expansion of the female labor force will not be able to continue at this pace because women's participation in employment depends on the "requirements of the economic development of the nation."[49] Linking women's job opportunities to national economic needs adds an insecurity to the lives of Cuban women that Cuban men, with guaranteed employment, do not experience.

There are also negative consequences for women that follow from the new system of management adopted in the seventies, which established that enterprises must show a profit by producing over and above inputs. This profit is different from profit in capitalist societies, which goes to shareholders and owners. In Cuba, since all enterprises belong to the state, the largest share of the profit goes to the national

46. Ministerio de Justicia (n. 23 above), p. 130.
47. Vilma Espin in *Granma Review* (March 7, 1980).
48. Ibid.
49. Ibid., my translation.

budget by way of a large circulation tax. The remaining profit is distributed by the workers' collective of each enterprise for three purposes: (1)
to improve the technical and productive capacity of the enterprise; (2) to
improve the sociocultural level of employees; and (3) to provide material
and monetary rewards to individual workers, including management, in
proportion to results achieved.[50] But an emphasis on profit includes a
concern with cost. Under the new system of economic management, any
extra expense entailed in the employment of women would logically
result in prejudice against hiring them. There is evidence of both the
cost and the discrimination.

The first expenditure enterprises employing women encounter is
tied to the maternity law. This excellent law provides that pregnant
women receive a fully paid leave of six weeks before and twelve weeks
following childbirth. However, the employing enterprise must under-
write the total cost of this leave.[51] It is safe to assume that, given the
choice between hiring women who might become pregnant and hiring
men, any enterprise required to show a profit would prefer to hire men.

The most constant cost of employing women workers lies in their
higher absentee rate, which is due to family obligations. In his 1980
speech to the Federation of Cuban Women, Castro remarked that a
certain amount of absenteeism has now practically been legalized so that
women can perform duties they cannot carry out after hours, such as
taking children to the doctor.[52] Castro's comments confirm that, despite
the Family Code, men have not assumed family responsibilities that
interfere with their wage labor. This may be partly due to resistance in
the workplace. If we accept the existence of a cost to the enterprise in
women's conflicting duties at work and at home, it becomes evident that
it would require major readjustments in the workplace if males, 70 percent of the work force, were to perform an equal share of domestic tasks.
These conflicting responsibilities continue to be identified as "women's
problems."

In the early seventies the Revolution created the Feminine Front to
provide an "organized channel through which women workers' needs
are made known to the entire workplace, to be solved by the entire
workplace."[53] But having women workers' needs addressed by the
workplace signifies yet another cost to the enterprise. In practice, we
would expect to find a tendency for businesses to avoid or reduce the
extra expenses inherent in solving the "problems" of women workers.
This reality may have prompted the Federation of Cuban Women to

50. Fidel Castro, *Report of the Central Committee of the Communist Party of Cuba to the First
Party Congress* (Havana, 1977), p. 159; Raul Martell, *La empresa socialista* (Havana: Editorial
Orbe, 1978).

51. Ministerio de Justicia (n. 23 above), pp. 120–32.

52. Castro (n. 15 above).

53. *Cuba Review* 4, no. 2 (September 1974): 27–28.

recommend in 1975 that enterprises employing women hire sufficient personnel to compensate for absences caused by maternity leaves, vacations, and illnesses of the worker or her family; otherwise, female co-workers end up absorbing the added work load.[54] Attempts to put this recommendation into practice would certainly conflict with the need to lower costs and show a profit under the system of management now in effect.

There is ample evidence of ongoing discrimination against hiring women. For example, a report to the Second Congress of the Federation in 1974 reads, "Managers sometimes refuse to employ female labor, because this forces them to increase the number of substitutes with the consequent growth of the staff, which affects the evaluation of productivity."[55] Another account describes the prejudice that leads managers to choose men to occupy jobs instead of women and documents how women are denied political and administrative promotions to avoid subsequent difficulties related to their family responsibilities.[56] In 1980, Vilma Espin denounced the persistence of this prejudice.[57] But denunciations alone cannot be effective as long as such prejudice has a material basis in the actual cost to the enterprise of finding solutions to the "problems" of women workers.

Conclusion

Material constraints to the solution of the woman question in Cuba originate in the drive for socialist accumulation and the development of the country's productive forces. These concerns have led the Revolution to make policy decisions that preserve women's inequality in the labor force, perpetuate the personal dependence of women on men, and thus work against the equal sharing of housework and child care decreed by the Family Code.

The Cuban constitutional guarantee of employment for all has, in practice, been transformed into guaranteed male employment, backed by a law making work compulsory for men. Underlying these measures is the assumption that adult women will be supported by their husbands or other male relatives. In accordance with this premise, the government feels free to use women for seasonal agricultural labor and as a labor reserve. Though efficient at the national level, at the individual level these practices reinforce male power at women's expense.

The Cuban Revolution's current endorsement of the socialist system

54. Primer Congreso del Partido Comunista (n. 29 above), p. 7.
55. *Memories: Second Congress of the Cuban Women's Federation* (Havana: Editorial Orbe, 1975), p. 4.
56. Primer Congreso del Partido Comunista (n. 29 above), p. 5.
57. Vilma Espin (n. 47 above).

of distribution and material incentives also contributes to women's continued subordination. Distribution through the wage, combined with higher prices and fewer free goods or services, makes wageless or lower-paid wives more dependent on their husbands than they were during the period when distribution according to need was also in effect. For mothers this dependence is compounded by concern for the well-being of their children. The requirement that enterprises show a profit contributes to discrimination in hiring because women's needs increase operating expenses. Since they constitute a labor reserve and cannot always find employment, individual women who realize they may not be economically self-sufficient all their lives will rely primarily on relationships with men for financial support. The degree to which women's access to resources is more limited than men's in an economy where distribution is tied to the wage and children rely on parental support thus constitutes a material barrier to any final solution of the woman question.

Because the socialist formula for distribution based on material incentives has had negative effects for women in Cuba, women would seem to have an even greater stake than men in the eventual implementation of a communist system of distribution. Such a system would allow people to work according to their abilities and reward them on the basis of their needs. Household maintenance and child care would be counted as work. Inequalities would disappear between manual and intellectual labor, between service providers and industrial workers, between individuals who raise children and those who do not, and between women and men. This ideal society appears to be far in the future.

In the meantime the Cuban national budget could subsidize maternity leaves and other expenses related to women's employment in the paid labor force. At a national level, plans could be made to restructure enterprises so that men can assume their share of family responsibilities. Lessening the individual mother's dependence on her husband's wage would also involve carrying out what Fidel Castro envisioned in 1966: society as a whole must provide the means of subsistence for children, so that not only parents but all workers share in their support.

Department of History
Yale University

Bank Loans to the Poor in Bombay: Do Women Benefit?

Jana Everett and Mira Savara

Under what conditions, if any, can development programs improve the material welfare and increase the power of poor Third World women? What kinds of programs can bring about such changes? These are among the questions raised by scholars of women and development. Although poor women have become a target group for development planners, there is little published research on the ways economic programs have affected women or on the nature of their participation as beneficiaries. In this article we examine women's involvement in one development program: a lending scheme for the poor in India. After reviewing selected debates in the development literature, we address four issues: (*a*) Do women get their fair share of loans earmarked for the poor? (*b*) Does bank credit increase women's power and improve their material welfare? (*c*) What types of relationships exist between banks and women borrowers? (*d*) Are bank loans to poor women a productive use of financial resources?

Working in Bombay, we studied women's participation in one of the nationalized banks' lending programs directed at the "weaker sections" (a term designating the poor): the Differential Rate of Interest (DRI) scheme, under which banks lend 1 percent of the previous year's advances to the poor at the concessional rate of 4 percent.[1] These are

Jana Everett's fieldwork was made possible by a grant from the American Institute of Indian Studies. A longer version of this study is available from the Research Unit on Women's Studies, Shreemati Nathibai Damodar Thackersey (SNDT) Women's University, Vithaldas Vidya Vihar, Juhu Road, Santa Cruz (West), Bombay 400049, India.

1. The usual interest rate ranged from 12.5 to 16 percent during 1979–82. The majority of banks were nationalized in 1969, and DRI was approved in 1971. Although the

intended as business loans for the self-employed to help them meet their needs for fixed and working capital. The Indian government recognizes that the modern industrial sector can absorb only a tiny fraction of the labor force. The DRI scheme is one of the poverty-focused strategies adopted by the government to generate employment, increase productivity, and reduce poverty by providing capital to the self-employed in trading, production, and service activities. Over the last decade researchers have documented the deteriorating socioeconomic conditions of the masses of Indian women: the declining sex ratio, women's decreasing labor force participation, and the increasing literacy gap between men and women.[2] Since self-employment is the most common income-generating activity among urban women in India, it is important to investigate whether they have access to DRI loans and, if they do, whether they benefit from this program.[3]

Provision of Credit to Self-employed Women in the Third World

Potential of Poverty-focused Strategies

Liberal and Marxist development scholars have debated the potential of poverty-focused strategies, such as providing credit to the self-employed poor. As Ray Bromley states, "Fundamentally, these debates are between liberal, neoclassical evolutionary views that policies can be formulated to bring 'the benefits of development' to the poor, and radical neo-Marxist views . . . that only . . . [structural] change can improve the situation of the poor in Third World countries."[4] According to the liberal

---

scope of this program is woefully inadequate in light of the size of the poor population, it has grown from 230,000 accounts and Rs 10.06 crores (1 crore = 10 million) outstanding in 1973, its first full year of operation, to 2,253,000 accounts and Rs 158.14 crores outstanding in 1980 (Reserve Bank of India, *Report on Currency and Finance*, vol. 1, *Economic Review, 1980–81* [Bombay: Government of India, 1981], p. 127). DRI loans are limited to Rs 1,500 for working capital and Rs 5,000 for fixed capital. In urban areas DRI borrowers must have annual family incomes not exceeding Rs 3,000. (At the time of our research Rs 10 = US$1.00.)

2. Committee on the Status of Women in India, *Towards Equality* (New Delhi: Ministry of Education and Social Welfare, 1974); Vina Mazumdar and Kumud Sharma, "Women's Studies: New Perceptions and the Challenges," *Economic and Political Weekly* 14, no. 3 (January 20, 1979): 113–20.

3. See Andrea Menefee Singh and Alfred de Souza, *The Urban Poor Slum and Pavement Dwellers in the Major Cities of India* (New Delhi: Manohar Publications, 1980), pp. 93ff. According to the 1981 census, nearly 24 percent of the Indian population resides in urban areas. One study that critically examines programs to improve urban women's employment is Maithreyi Krishna Raj, *Approaches to Self Reliance for Women* (Bombay: SNDT, 1980).

4. "Introduction—the Urban Informal Sector: Why Is It Worth Discussing?" *World Development* 6, no. 9/10 (1978): 1033–39, 1035.

perspective that emerged in the 1970s, the urban poor are engaged in the "informal sector" of the economy, and their poverty results from the discrimination this sector experiences in access to credit, raw materials, and markets.[5] Liberal development scholars believe that "the informal sector has potential for dynamic evolutionary growth" and that there is "considerable scope for expanding the productive use of resources."[6] They urge governments to provide credit to the self-employed and are optimistic that this will improve the situation of the poor and contribute to overall economic growth.

Marxist development scholars usually argue that such strategies will not work because the so-called informal sector is controlled by and linked to the overall capitalist mode of production. The resulting dependency relationship sharply circumscribes the potential for capital accumulation within the informal sector. Marxists conclude that poverty-focused policies (*a*) help some at the expense of the majority, (*b*) indirectly subsidize capitalists by enlarging the supply of cheap goods and services for the working class (thus reducing upward pressure on factory wages), and (*c*) lead to benefits being appropriated by the politically and economically powerful.[7] Such policies do not attack the centers of power and privilege, Marxists argue, and thus have limited potential for improving the lives of the poor.

In the last few years some liberal and Marxist scholars have rethought their arguments. Low repayment rates in Third World rural credit programs have led liberal scholars to be pessimistic about the productivity of poverty-focused strategies.[8] Paul Streeten, for example, now advocates a welfare approach—"meeting basic needs"—rather than providing investment resources to the poor. In a recent article, Streeten

5. The informal sector refers to income-generating activity that does not involve a formal wage contract. It is a residual category created by the absence of characteristics of the "formal sector": economic activity that is capital intensive, large scale, and publicly or corporately owned, regulated, and unionized. It encompasses a large number of disparate phenomena—petty trading, production and service activities that usually involve self-employment, and contract labor and outwork that are disguised wage employment. Scholars have criticized the theoretical adequacy of the formal/informal distinction, but the term "informal sector" remains useful for describing much of the income-generating activity in the Third World.

6. International Labour Office (ILO), *Employment Incomes and Equality* (Geneva: ILO, 1972), p. 505; Hollis Chenery et al., *Redistribution with Growth* (London: Oxford University Press, 1974), pp. xvii–xviii.

7. Caroline O. N. Moser, "Informal Sector or Petty Commodity Production: Dualism or Dependence in Urban Development," *World Development* 6, no. 9/10 (1978): 1041–64; Ray Bromley and Chris Gerry, eds., *Casual Work and Poverty in Third World Cities* (New York: John Wiley & Sons, 1979).

8. Michael Lipton, "Agricultural Finance and Rural Credit in Poor Countries," in *Recent Issues in World Development: A Collection of Survey Articles*, ed. Paul P. Streeten and Richard Jolly (New York: Pergamon Press, 1981), pp. 201–11.

implies that "basic needs" is a better way to improve the material welfare of the poor because of resistance by Third World elites to "redistribution with growth" and because the poor do not necessarily use additional income wisely.[9]

As production-/investment-oriented programs for the poor have been deemphasized by some liberal development scholars, they have gained some support among certain Marxist scholars who argue that policies to improve the income of the self-employed could help improve the material welfare of the entire working class by preventing wages from falling further in a labor surplus situation.[10] The position of these scholars on poverty-focused strategies tends to be shaped by whether they think the short-term benefits will facilitate or compromise the long-term betterment of the poor.

Approaches to the Problems of Poor Women

Women and development scholars present two different approaches to the problems of poor women in the Third World.[11] According to the liberal thinkers, the problems stem fundamentally from discriminatory development policies. Women, for example, lack access to bank credit, which would likely improve women's income and productive use of resources. The liberal approach tends to be pragmatic and policy oriented, characterized by the (usually unstated) assumption that "the compromises inherent in working with existing institutions are . . . a necessary trade-off in order to influence those institutions and thus to expand or redirect resources to women."[12] The Marxist approach identifies the hierarchical structure of accumulation and power as the fundamental cause of the problems of poor women in the Third World. According to this approach, bank credit is unlikely to result in an improvement in women's income or productive use of resources. Any benefits are likely to be appropriated by the economically and politically powerful. Only

9. Paul Streeten, *Development Perspectives* (London: Macmillan Press, 1981), pp. 334ff.

10. Manfred Bienefeld, "The Informal Sector and Women's Oppression," and Nirmala Banerjee, "The Weakest Link," *Bulletin of the Institute of Development Studies* 12, no. 3 (July 1981): 8–13, 36–40.

11. This distinction is made for heuristic purposes only. The work of an individual scholar may encompass both approaches at different times or in different contexts. An example of a liberal approach is Mayra Buvinić, "Women's Issues in Third World Poverty: A Policy Analysis," in *Women and Poverty in the Third World*, ed. Mayra Buvinić, Margaret A. Lycette, and William Paul McGreevey (Baltimore: Johns Hopkins University Press, 1983), pp. 14–31. An example of a Marxist approach is Lourdes Benería and Gita Sen, "Accumulation, Reproduction, and Women's Role in Economic Development: Boserup Revisited," *Signs: Journal of Women in Culture and Society* 7, no. 2 (Winter 1981): 279–98.

12. Kathleen A. Staudt and Jane Jaquette, "Women and Development," *Women and Politics* 2, no. 4 (1982): 1–6, 2.

through the elimination of class and gender hierarchies will poor women improve their welfare and increase their power. These scholars are engaged in a reformulation of Marxist theory so that it will more adequately address class and gender relations in peripheral capitalist countries. They usually do not address concrete policy issues in any detail.

Even those scholars optimistic about the potential of poverty-focused strategies are aware that the poor in general and poor women in particular often do not benefit from such programs. Although they use different terms, Marxist and liberal thinkers point to the structure of power in Third World societies as a major obstacle. Mayra Buvinić states, "Productivity programs in general tend to be easily monopolized by the more powerful people in the community, and the likelihood this may happen to programs for poor women increases because virtually all other groups in the community are powerful relative to poor women."[13] Two different (although not mutually exclusive) recommendations have been offered as ways of maximizing the benefits poor women obtain from poverty-focused strategies in stratified societies. The first is that poor women should be organized, the second that women-only interventions should be designed.

Importance of Organization

Many scholars have argued that only when the poor are organized will they realize benefits from poverty-focused strategies. For example, Lourdes Benería and Gita Sen argue that "a 'basic needs' strategy . . . could benefit women if it were energized by the self-organization of poor women."[14] Samuel Paul and Ashok Subramanian suggest that "the stronger the participation of poor beneficiaries or their organizations in the planning and implementation, the higher the benefits will flow to the weaker sections."[15]

Other scholars, however, remain skeptical about the prospects for organizing the poor. Atul Kohli labels as a "liberal fallacy" the idea that "the numerical weight of the lower class can be transformed into an effective political power aimed at incremental redistribution of economic resources." He argues that "inequalities of power are 'prior' to the 'political.' . . . [They are] a function of the position various groups occupy in the

---

13. Buvinić, pp. 25–26.

14. Lourdes Benería and Gita Sen, "Class and Gender Inequalities and Women's Role in Economic Development—Theoretical and Practical Implications," *Feminist Studies* 8, no. 1 (Spring 1982): 156–76, 173.

15. Samuel Paul and Ashok Subramanian, "Development Programmes for the Poor: Do Strategies Make a Difference?" *Economic and Political Weekly* 18, no. 10 (March 5, 1983): 349–58.

division of labor."[16] Joan Nelson identifies a number of obstacles to horizontal patterns of mobilization among the poor.[17] She concludes that the
poor tend to be incorporated into the system, if at all, through patron-
client relationships. Peter Cleaves discusses the dangers of organization—
co-optation, on the one hand, and increased repression, on the other.[18]
Kathleen Staudt points out that it is unrealistic to count on women's
organizations to empower poor women, as such organizations are likely to
be dominated by elite women insensitive to the economic needs of the
poor.[19]

Women-specific Interventions

In policy-oriented literature on women and development, scholars
have debated the relative merits of designing specific women's programs
or integrating women into general programs. Some of the arguments
advanced against women-only programs are that they typically focus on
health, welfare, and the domestic sphere and so do little to increase the
earning power of women. Furthermore, when such programs address
income-generating activities, they lack the expertise (in management,
marketing, etc.) to be successful.[20] Maria Mies concludes that women-
specific programs impose the Western concept of "housewife" on Third
World women.[21] According to Buvinić, policies with this orientation "lead
to the exclusion of women from development programs operated by the
mainstream development agencies that provide a significant proportion
of development funds." She argues that a better alternative is an "anti-
poverty strategy that justifies assistance to poor women in terms of economic growth rather than welfare and that is embodied in projects to raise
women's economic productivity and income."[22]

Although most researchers in this area acknowledge that the above
criticisms are valid, some point out that Third World women say they

16. Atul Kohli, "Democracy, Economic Growth and Inequality in India's Development," *World Politics* 32, no. 4 (July 1980): 623–36, 624, 631.

17. Joan M. Nelson, *Access to Power Politics and the Urban Poor in Developing Nations*
(Princeton, N.J.: Princeton University Press, 1979).

18. Peter S. Cleaves, "Implementation amidst Scarcity and Apathy: Political Power
and Policy Design," *Politics and Policy Implementation in the Third World*, ed. Merilee S. Grindle
(Princeton, N.J.: Princeton University Press, 1980), pp. 281–303.

19. Kathleen A. Staudt, "Sex, Ethnic, and Class Consciousness in Western Kenya,"
Comparative Politics 14, no. 2 (1982): 149–67.

20. Barbara Rogers, *The Domestication of Women: Discrimination in Developing Societies*
(New York: St. Martin's Press, 1979).

21. Maria Mies, "The Dynamics of the Sexual Division of Labor and Integration of
Rural Women into the World Market," in *Women and Development*, ed. Lourdes Benería (New
York: Praeger Publishers, 1982), pp. 1–28.

22. Buvinić, p. 25.

want women-specific programs. According to Ilsa Schuster, these include "education and training by women experts for existing employment opportunities, innovations designed by women experts sensitive to domestic requirements of women, special aid for women's self-help groups, and increased involvement of women's organizations."[23]

Even though Buvinić is highly critical of the welfare orientation in women-only programs, she, along with other scholars, acknowledges the need for "women-specific interventions": "The monopolizable aspects of productivity projects should be reduced by designing women-only interventions. This does not imply women-only projects but women-only components within larger projects. One example of this would be the establishment of a credit line for women only."[24] But would a welfare orientation be associated with such interventions, and would this compromise the economic development goals of the project? Buvinić and other researchers who have surveyed the literature on women and credit base their suggestions in large measure on the successful programs of the Self-Employed Women's Association (SEWA) of Ahmedabad, India.[25] Specific policy recommendations include "the establishment of women's cooperatives and banks as intermediary programs to mobilize capital for women's productive activities . . . [and] women-specific credit programs in appropriate cases where male/female interactions are socially limited, or where women may feel the need to operate in a program not dominated by men."[26]

Research Findings

We examined DRI accounts in selected branches of two public sector banks in Bombay. Out of the roughly 16,000 DRI loans outstanding throughout Bombay in 1982, bank A had about 6,000 accounts and bank B 1,800.[27] The two banks organized weaker-section lending services in

23. Ilsa Schuster, "Review Article: Recent Research on Women in Development," *Journal of Development Studies* 18, no. 4 (July 1982): 511–35, 531.

24. Buvinić, p. 30.

25. On SEWA, see Devaki Jain, *Women's Quest for Power* (Bombay: Vikas Publishing House, 1980); and Jennefer Sebstad, *Struggle and Development among Self-employed Women: A Report on the Self-employed Women's Association, Ahmedabad, India* (Washington, D.C.: Agency for International Development [USAID], 1982).

26. Ilsa Schumacher, Jennefer Sebstad, and Mayra Buvinić, *Limits to Productivity: Improving Women's Access to Technology and Credit* (Washington, D.C.: USAID, 1980), p. 54.

27. From July to October, 1982, we interviewed officers at the head or zone offices of fifteen public sector banks, the staff at two branches of bank A and four branches of bank B, various intermediaries connected with the bank programs, and seventy-five women borrowers. Our primary data on weaker-section loans came from branch records. At bank A records on DRI and other weaker-section loans (for retail trade, small business, and self-

different ways. Bank A centralized these services in four branches we refer to as Weaker Section Advancement Departments (WSADs), which had specialized procedures and employees assigned to do investigation, collection, and assistance work in the slums. We examined a random sample of the approximately 3,000 loans advanced to two Bombay WSADs in 1979. In bank B, weaker-section lending services were available in the bank's eighty-five Bombay branches but were utilized mainly in branches located in working-class neighborhoods. At bank B there were simplified forms for weaker-section borrowers, but no staff there specialized in weaker-section accounts or outreach. We examined the records of all 212 DRI loans advanced in 1980 by the four branches of bank B with the largest numbers of such accounts.

Most of the women borrowers studied had obtained loans for working capital in one of six informal sector businesses. Two of these, broom making and glassmaking, involved production and trading activities. The broom makers fashioned brooms and baskets out of a particular kind of grass from the jungles of Karnataka, the state to the south of Maharashtra, where Bombay is located. The women sold the brooms, called *jaroos*, to lower-class households with dirt floors and the baskets to wholesale markets. The glassmakers bought used bottles, cut off their tops, and filed and washed them. Then they glued the tops back on as stems and painted designs on the glasses, which they sold on the street. The makers of hand-rolled Indian cigarettes, called *bidi*, were involved solely in production activities and could be categorized as "outworkers" since merchants supplied the raw materials and bought the finished products. Two of the businesses involved trading activities. The vegetable vendors bought produce at the wholesale market and sold the vegetables on the street. The utensil barterers bought stainless steel cooking utensils and traded them to middle-class housewives. Instead of taking cash payments from the housewives, they exchanged the utensils for old clothes, which they sold to merchants. The *khannawallis* (food providers) were involved in a service activity—cooking meals for the male workers who came to Bombay without their families. These women fed from fifteen to fifty workers for a fixed amount of money each month. Each worker would get two meals a day—one eaten in the *khannawalli's* home and one sent to the factory during his work shift.

---

employed at 12 percent interest) were consolidated. At branch A1 we examined a 10 percent random sample of loans (297) disbursed in 1979. At branch A2 we examined a 20 percent random sample of loans (108) disbursed in 1979. In this article we discuss only the DRI loans in our samples from these branches (224 at branch A1 and 73 at A2). At bank B, DRI records were kept separately. Records on 1979 loans were unavailable. We examined all DRI loans disbursed at branches B1, B2, B3, and B4 in 1980. We spoke with the women borrowers in Hindi, conducting interviews in their homes, at bank offices, or at the residence or office of an intermediary.

The women borrowers were from low-status communities. The broom makers were from a former nomadic tribe, and many of the vegetable vendors, utensil barterers, and glassmakers were from the scheduled castes (a legal term referring to ex-untouchables, groups at the bottom of the Hindu caste hierarchy). Most of the *bidi* makers were Muslim, and most of the *khannawallis* were Hindu. There were variations in the average income generated by the different activities.[28] There were also variations in the borrowers' household economies. All were poor, but they were not the poorest of the poor (pavement dwellers and other individuals without ration cards proving Bombay residency).

Women's Access to Loans

We found that, although women constituted the majority of borrowers in the Bombay branches studied, they received smaller loans than men did. In bank A, 80 percent of the DRI loans were to women, who received only 77 percent of the money advanced. In bank B, 72 percent of the DRI loans were to women; they received 64 percent of the money advanced. Average loan amounts at bank A were Rs 780 for women and Rs 952 for men; at bank B they were Rs 911 for women and Rs 1318 for men.

We expected that women would receive smaller loans than men would, in keeping with the existing disparities between male and female incomes. Women borrowers in our study received smaller loans mainly because they were concentrated in economic activities that the bankers assessed as requiring less working capital. There are several possible reasons why there were more women than men in our sample:[29] (*a*) women are concentrated in the least remunerative areas of self-employment and thus are most eligible for DRI loans; (*b*) self-employed women are more likely to have male family members who draw a regular wage than are self-employed men (bankers may be more willing to sanction DRI loans to women with access to male wages); and (*c*) bankers tend to believe that lower-class men drink and gamble away their money.

28. In table 1 are rough estimates (based on interviews) of the income generated by the various activities and the average loan amounts obtained by women in the different occupations.

29. Since Indian banks do not collect gender disaggregated data, and since there are no existing national studies of DRI, it is impossible to estimate on a national basis the percentage of DRI borrowers who are female. Anecdotal evidence suggests women constitute a very small percentage of DRI borrowers in rural areas. One study estimated women to be 5 percent of the DRI borrowers in urban areas of Punjab and Haryana states in North India (Pushpa Sundar, "Credit and Finance Needs of Women Workers" [New Delhi, 1980, mimeographed]).

Impact of Loans

According to our interviews, most of the women borrowers used at least some of the bank loan to repay moneylenders. Almost all of the women had taken loans against their gold ornaments from money-lenders at rates ranging from 12 to 25 percent per month.[30] These interest rates prevented them from ever getting out of debt, as payments only covered interest and never reduced the principal. Often the bank loans enabled women to escape a relationship of dependence with a merchant. One of the possible consequences of buying on credit from a merchant or of piling up debts with a moneylender was sexual harassment. The leader of an organization of *khannawallis* told us:

> One of the women got heavily into debt with one supplier. He told her, "Your amount outstanding has grown to this amount and I see no way you can pay it back. I won't be able to sell you anything on credit any longer. But I do know one way you could pay it back." She resisted for a few days but finally began to have relations with him. When she finally got her [bank] loan, she repaid him in full, and told him that this was the end of everything. I think this situation exists [widely], but the women are reluctant to talk about it.

The women who were able to invest the loan proceeds in their businesses did so in several ways. Some began buying materials from wholesalers instead of retailers. This saved both money and time, and the women felt they got more attention from merchants when they paid in cash instead of on credit. Others made improvements in their homes (putting in stone floors, building lofts and furniture for their kitchens). Since the home was also the work site, this created better working condi-

Table 1

Income and Loan Amounts by Women's Occupation

	Average Daily Net Income, 1982 (Rs)	Usual Loan Amount, 1979–80 (Rs)
Broom making	4–5	500
Bidi making	7–8	500
Utensil vending	10–15	500–1000
Vegetable vending	5–20	200–1000
Glassmaking	10	500
Khannawalli	15–20	1500

30. Singh and de Souza (n. 3 above) report that studies show almost half of slum households are in debt to moneylenders and merchants.

tions. A *bidi* worker told us, "I have been wanting to put a stone floor in my house for many years instead of the mud. Less time [now] goes in cleaning."

It is difficult to determine whether bank loans improved these women's incomes, let alone to determine whether any improvements increased the women's power and affected their material welfare. The few existing Indian studies on this subject, as well as our interviews, indicate that there have been small increases in income. But most of the borrowers remained below the poverty line.[31] Anecdotal evidence from our interviews suggests that women thought bank loans increased the respect they received from family and community members. Several women reported that for the first time they felt they were "somebody" because the banks had given them loans. Their increased self-confidence in some cases led to assertive behavior. A *khannawalli* said, "Previously my husband used to beat me up regularly. Now I tell him, you can't come home and beat me up. I have to do [my work] well or else I won't be able to repay the banks. I have also thrown him out of the house when he refused to stop shouting."

Relationships between Banks and Borrowers

We found that, contrary to the banks' assertions, borrowers usually approached banks indirectly, through an intermediary. This seemed to be the case more often for women than for men, perhaps because women were more often illiterate and hesitant to approach the banks directly. They turned to someone they knew and trusted, someone from their community who could help them get a loan. Intermediaries were of three types: individuals (such as politicians, slum leaders, or raw materials suppliers) whom the banks referred to as "social workers"; the Backward Classes Corporation (BCC), a state government agency;[32] and women's organizations that worked primarily with *khannawallis*. These interme-

---

31. Available studies are limited by their methodology (none are representative nationwide samples, and all try to assess the impact of loans by asking borrowers about their incomes before and after the loan). Three studies that do discuss women borrowers are State Bank of India, *Impact of Bank Credit on Weaker Sections: A Report Based on Eight Case Studies* (Bombay: State Bank of India, 1978); R. B. L. Agrawal, "Concessional Finance: Do Weaker Sections Benefit?" *Economic Times* (Bombay) (November 10, 1981; August 16, 1982); Bank of India, *Promotion of Self-Employment through Bank Finance: A Case Study of DRI Scheme for Slum Dwellers in Madras* (Bombay: Bank of India, 1981).

32. The BCC acts as a liaison between the banks and "backward-class" borrowers and administers certain financial subsidies and grants to backward-class borrowers. A BCC official estimated that there were 17 million backward-class individuals in Maharashtra (27 percent of the population). "Backward classes" consist of scheduled castes and tribes, neo-Buddhists (scheduled castes who have converted to Buddhism), excriminal tribes, and nomadic tribes recognized by the state government.

diaries recruited prospective borrowers, took some or all of the responsibility for investigation, and played a role in other aspects of the loan transaction and in recovery. In all cases, however, it was the individual borrower who applied for the loan and to whom the loan was disbursed.

Both banks A and B used intermediaries. Those associated with the centralized system of bank A dealt with larger numbers of borrowers than those associated with the decentralized system of bank B did. Even though bank A's cash collectors (who were men) went into the slums, they depended on a social worker or women's organization to contact a particular borrower. The BCC investigated prospective borrowers from the backward classes, and its staff was composed of backward class members, but it resembled the banks more than it did the community-based intermediaries. Thus the BCC itself often had to rely on slum leaders to locate prospective borrowers. To illustrate some of the similarities and differences among the various intermediaries we will describe one of the social workers and one of the women's organizations.

M was the social worker who helped 2,000 broom makers (90 percent of them women) obtain DRI loans from bank A. He was a member of the *panch* (council) of the broom maker community that was located in several slums in the Santa Cruz area of Bombay. His entire family made and sold brooms. M became an intermediary in 1978 after the bank had grown dissatisfied with the performance of another intermediary. Between 1978 and 1980, M established a business of supplying raw material to other broom makers. He received a bank loan of Rs 9,500, but this covered only part of his costs.

The Annapurna Mahila Mandal, a women's organization named after the goddess of food and led by Prema Purao, has helped approximately 6,000 *khannawallis* obtain bank loans since 1976. Purao had been a trade union organizer for the Communist Party of India (CPI) for over twenty-five years. She became aware of the problems of the *khannawallis* during a textile strike in 1973. As she recalled, "These women continued to feed the workers despite the fact that the workers could not pay. The *khannawallis* would pawn their jewelry, even their utensils, to feed the workers. I realized that these women were enabling the workers to continue their struggle. And I realized that as trade unionists we had never looked into the problems of these women." Purao's husband, a CPI activist and bank union leader, thought of the possibility of bank loans for the *khannawallis*. Purao approached bank A and obtained their agreement. The organization she set up was based on neighborhood groups of fifteen women. Women secured individual loans, which were guaranteed by the group and the organization. For the bank this meant increased assurance of repayment. For the women this meant breaking out of an isolated existence and meeting regularly with other women doing the same work. The organization grew to include eleven local centers, each composed of a number of neighborhood groups. The groups elected leaders who formed the local committees and elected members to an executive committee. More recently, the Annapurna Mahila Mandal also helped its members obtain loans from bank B.

Both social worker M and the Annapurna Mahila Mandal did some of the bank's work. They investigated prospective borrowers and accompanied the cash collectors on their rounds, and they kept lists of borrowers, their photos and loan numbers, and some type of repayment records. Annapurna charged its members for the services performed; the fees covered organizational expenses and contributed to a fund established for building a women's center. It was likely that M also extracted fees for his services, but he would not admit this. He may have hiked up the prices of his raw materials and forced the borrowers to buy from him. But the lending program was clearly good for his business. The broom makers usually bought grass from him on credit (his records showed no interest was charged), and so the bank loans enabled the broom makers to repay their loans to him.

Although it resembled the other intermediaries in certain ways, the Annapurna Mahila Mandal had distinctive features that were developed to suit the *khannawallis*. The group system created social pressure for repayment. There was also a compulsory 200-rupee savings deposit taken out of loan proceeds, which was used for repayment if a borrower fell behind. Annapurna facilitated recovery by having the cash collector spend a day in each local center once a month. Furthermore, leadership opportunities were available to individual *khannawallis*. And Annapurna activities extended beyond the task of operating a lending program. There were regular group meetings where business problems (e.g., boarders skipping without paying) or personal problems (wife beating) could be raised. Several trips were organized to enable members to visit other regions of India. Finally, Annapurna was in the process of establishing a women's center to provide health, educational, and vocational services for its members.

Evaluating the Loan Program

Policymakers, scholars, and bankers in India disagree about the extent to which DRI is (or ever could be) a productive use of financial resources because repayment rates have been so low. This question becomes even more important as the Indian government seeks to increase the share of bank credit extended to the weaker sections (10 percent by 1985). A full discussion of whether weaker-section loans contribute to overall capital accumulation lies outside the scope of this article. Nevertheless it is important to point out that if loans are not repaid they are in effect one-shot grants, which cannot be recycled to additional weaker-section borrowers. Thus repayment rates can be used to evaluate the loans as a productive use of financial resources.

The percentage of overdue DRI loans in the branches studied was high (from 13 to 55 percent), but not as high as in the nation as a whole (70 percent).[33] What accounts for the variation in repayment rates observed? We looked at three variables that we thought might affect repayment: the type of service delivery system, the economic circumstances of the borrowers, and the type of intermediary involved.

Based on the branches we studied, centralization of DRI lending did not seem to have much effect on repayment (table 2). There was more variation within centralized and decentralized delivery systems than between the two systems. In the two branches of bank A, increased size seemed to be associated with a low repayment rate. We estimated that 13 percent of the approximately 350 DRI loans disbursed in 1979 by bank A2 were overdue; among the approximately 2,200 loans disbursed by bank A1 we estimated 47 percent overdue. The large number of accounts handled by A1 may have created an unmanageable situation. In the four branches of bank B examined, the effort exerted in recovery seemed to be associated with the percentage of overdue loans. In determining repayment rates, however, who the DRI borrowers were and who brought them to the banks seemed to be more important than the characteristics of the banks themselves: the worst repayment rates occurred at the branches that primarily lent to the poorest slum dwellers recruited by social workers.

There are at least two important dimensions to the economic circumstances of DRI borrowers. One is the income-generating potential of the borrower's particular business. The other is the nature of the borrower's household economy—the number of earners in the household and the stability and level of their earnings. In our study, differences in repayment rates between two groups of borrowers showed that economic circumstances could be very significant. The broom makers had the largest proportion of overdue loans (66 percent) and were in the most precarious circumstances of all the groups. They were plagued by a high degree of risk in their business, low prices for their products, and the absence of a cushion provided by a household member with a formal sector job. The *khannawallis* were in the least precarious position and had the lowest proportion of overdue loans (10–29 percent).

Our data did not indicate whether a relationship existed between repayment rates and the nature of the household economy. But we were

33. Reserve Bank of India, *Report on Currency and Finance*, vol. 1 of *Economic Review* (Bombay: Government of India, 1980), p. 125. We calculated the percentage overdue on the basis of the amount sanctioned (balance divided by amount sanctioned). All of the loans should have been paid off by the time we collected the data.

Table 2

Overdue DRI Loans by Bank Branch and Sex of Borrower

	N		Amount Loaned (Rs)		Amount Overdue (Rs)		% Overdue	
	Men	Women	Men	Women	Men	Women	Men	Women
A1	57	167	54,950	92,800	18,985	51,125	35	55
A2*	...	72	...	93,700	...	12,430	...	13
B1	17	58	12,135	29,900	5,575	17,700	46	59
B2	12	14	13,950	17,000	6,115	2,084	44	12
B3	28	14	49,000	6,400	18,778	3,679	38	58
B4*	...	66	...	85,700	...	24,773	...	29

SOURCE.—Compiled from bank branch records. A1 based on a 10 percent sample, 1979. A2 based on a 20 percent sample, 1979. B based on loans sanctioned in 1980.
* There were too few male borrowers in these branches to make a meaningful comparison.

able to look at the association between repayment and the income-generating potential of the various businesses, using loan amount as an indirect indicator of a business's capacity to generate income. We examined women borrowers' overdue loans in all four branches of bank B, categorized by the size of the loan. Our results indicate that the overdue rate was 55 percent for loans under Rs 1,000, 22 percent for loans in the Rs 1,000–1,499 range, and 34 percent for loans Rs 1,500 and above (see table 3). These findings supported the proposition that economic activities with the lowest income-generating capacity (the practitioners of which thus received the smallest loans) were associated with the highest overdue rate. However, we did not find a clear pattern of decreasing overdue rates as loan size increased.

We also tried to assess the impact of different intermediaries on repayment levels. Social workers and the BCC developed only vertical ties with individual borrowers, while women's organizations also encouraged horizontal ties among women. We expected that horizontal mobilization patterns would be associated with higher repayment levels, and we found this to be the case in our data (see table 4). Borrowers recruited by social workers M, N, and Y and by the BCC had low repayment levels, while borrowers recruited by the women's organizations had high rates of repayment. Those recruited by social worker K were between these two extremes.[34] Differences among the three types of intermediaries affected the repayment rates of their borrowers. The social workers knew the

Table 3

Women's Overdue DRI Loans at Bank B by Loan Amount (Rs)

	N	Total Loaned (Rs)	Total Overdue (Rs)	% Overdue
0–999	73	35,100	19,186	55
1,000–1,499	48	48,400	10,445	22
1,500–	31	55,500	18,639	34
Total	152	139,000	48,270	35

Source.—Compiled from bank B branch records. Figures based on DRI loans sanctioned by the four branches in 1980.

34. Social worker N worked with glassmakers, utensil barterers, and vegetable vendors in the Kurla slums. He was a dockworker who lived nearby. Y was a former taxi driver living in Dharavi slum who had obtained loans for *bidi* makers and utensil barterers. He admitted taking money for his services and was an activist for Congress (I), the party of the late Prime Minister Indira Gandhi. K lived in one of the original fishing villages of Bombay. He worked as an officer in a public sector company and said he liked to help his poorer neighbors. The second women's organization was established by Saroj Chandras, a school principal and a Bharatiya Janata Party activist. It operated out of the Child Welfare Society (SVK), which she ran.

borrowers, but they lacked the organizational structure and technical expertise to maintain a high recovery rate when the number of borrowers became large. The BCC had organization and expertise, but its staff was unfamiliar with the slum communities and thus ineffective in recovering money. The women's organizations created the necessary organizational structures and personal relationships with borrowers that contributed to high repayment rates. In addition, only such organizations allowed women to work with women borrowers.

The two sets of variables, however—the economic circumstances of the borrowers and the type of intermediary—were closely correlated, making it difficult to disentangle the effects of each on repayment levels. The women's organizations worked with the *khannawallis*, who had the more remunerative businesses and were more likely to have husbands or sons with formal sector jobs. The borrowers recruited by the social workers (with the exception of K) and by the BCC tended to be in less remunerative businesses and were less likely to have household members in stable jobs. It seems to us that economic circumstances were the more crucial of the two sets of variables, as they determine the amount of surplus available for loan repayment. However, women's organizations were able to decrease overdue rates by creating group pressure to repay, by developing innovative repayment procedures, and by adopting a more complete approach to the needs and problems of the self-employed. This can be seen by comparing the *khannawallis* who were women's organization members with those recruited by social worker K. *Khannawalli* over-

Table 4

Women's Overdue Loans by Borrower's Occupation and Loan Intermediary

Occupation and Intermediary	N	Amount Loaned (Rs)	% Overdue
Broom makers:			
Social worker M (bank A1)	84	42,000	66
Various occupations:			
BCC (bank B1)	64	33,535	59
Utensil vendors and glassmakers:			
Social worker N (bank A1)	26	13,000	46
Bidi makers:			
Social worker Y (bank A1)	28	14,000	42
Khannawallis:			
Social worker K (bank B4)	65	84,200	29
SVK women's organization (bank C1)	43	64,500	14
Annapurna Mahila Mandal (bank A2)	92	145,900	10

SOURCE.—Compiled from records of bank branches and intermediaries. A1 based on a 10 percent sample, 1979. A2 based on a 20 percent sample, 1979. B1 and B4 based on all loans sanctioned in 1980. C1 was a branch of another nationalized bank in Bombay; the loans were those overdue as of December 1981 that were disbursed in June of the same year.

dues ranged from 10 percent among Annapurna Mahila Mandal members and 14 percent among members of another women's organization (Shishu Vikas Kendra) to 29 percent among those recruited by social worker K.

Conclusion

Our case study suggests that, much of the time, poverty-focused strategies merely provide channels through which new ties of dependence and exploitation are established. For example, one women told us about her experience with DRI: "The banks do not realize that we need money most often in time of crisis and . . . for purposes of survival. Yes, I understand that banks give money for work only, but what happens is something like this. At times of crisis when we need money immediately, we borrow from a moneylender. We have to go there because who knows when the bank loan will come. Then when the bank loan does get sanctioned, we repay the moneylender." Under these conditions borrowers were unable to invest loan proceeds into their businesses. One of the social workers pointed out to us that in this way DRI served to increase rather than decrease the business of the moneylenders. Most of the women borrowers obtained loans through patron-client relationships with social workers who were traditional community leaders, self-made brokers, or ward bosses in urban political machines. Although these patterns of vertical mobilization certainly limit the benefits women obtain, they do enable the banks to reach the urban poor.

Banks and other government bureaucracies are not well equipped to handle poverty-focused strategies. Personnel policies contribute to the problem. Performance in weaker-section lending is not a central factor in promotion, so bank staff do not always take this work seriously. In the branches we studied there were no women working with the primarily female DRI borrowers. In addition, certain aspects of the DRI program reduce incentives for bank personnel to recover loans.[35] In order to meet the needs of the self-employed poor, bank loans should be sanctioned on a regular basis, in a timely manner, and in amounts large enough to cover business expenses and outstanding debts.

Our study illustrates that organization of the self-employed can make a difference. The women's organizations (*a*) enable borrowers to realize benefits from the lending programs, (*b*) serve as a pressure group to keep

35. These include the concessional rate of 4 percent, the fact that 90 percent of the DRI loan is guaranteed by the government's Deposit Insurance and Credit Guarantee Corporation, and the limit on DRI funds to 1 percent of the loans advanced in the previous year. In our opinion, the poor borrowers would be better served in a well-administered program with more loans at interest rates high enough to cover costs.

the government honest in efforts to reach the self-employed, (c) aid banks in recovery, and (d) address other problems of self-employed women. Still, co-optation has occurred—for example, in situations where women's organizations have turned out their membership for a demonstration or have operated as a vote bank.

We see weaker-section lending as both offering opportunities for and endangering the empowerment and welfare of poor women. Loan programs can aid grass-roots organizational development among poor women, which may contribute to their economic and political advancement.[36] Although group loyalty based on availability of money does not necessarily produce lasting organizations, in this case the establishment of neighborhood borrower groups has enabled women to develop a sense of collectivity and to discuss a variety of issues.

Our study suggests that women-specific interventions are beneficial at the grass-roots level but not, or not to the same extent, at the bureaucratic level. The key to success appears to be grass-roots women's organizations. This is not to imply that anyone could embark on such an undertaking. The existing organizations in three Indian cities are run by competent, energetic women with long histories of involvement with urban poor. The challenge remains to organize the vast majority of poor self-employed Indian women who so far do not have access to development programs and services.

In summary, we have found that programs targeted for self-employed poor women may actually benefit various intermediaries as much as (or more than) they benefit the women themselves. This is because development programs do not eliminate the hierarchical structure in which poor women exist. More program benefits flow to poor women when they are mobilized as members of grass-roots organizations. Such organizations, in turn, may help challenge the hierarchical structure itself.

Department of Political Science
University of Colorado at Denver (Everett)

Bombay, India (Savara)

36. The most well known of such organizations are SEWA (see n. 25 above) in Ahmedabad and Working Women's Forum in Madras (See Hilde Jeffers, "Organizing Petty Traders and Producers: A Case of Working Women's Forum, Madras" [M.A. thesis, University of California, Berkeley, 1982]).

Woman-headed Households and Poverty: Insights from Kenya

Mari H. Clark

Over the past four decades the number of households headed by women has increased worldwide. The great majority of these households are impoverished. Scholars have characterized poor woman-headed households as an expression of social pathology, as the outcome of cultural diffusion, as a survival strategy of the poor in capitalist economies, and, in the United States, as a legacy of black slavery.[1] Underlying these characterizations are value judgments about woman-headed households and the forces that shape them. Recognizing woman-headed households as a social form is inherently value laden for Western scholars because it calls into question basic Western assumptions about "natural" (and universal) forms for family structure and gender relations.[2]

I would like to extend special thanks to the following scholars who provided valuable critical comments on earlier drafts of this report: Michael Bamberger, Robert Daniels, Isabel Nieves, Nadia Youssef, and the anonymous *Signs* reviewer. This report is based in part on a lengthier report prepared for the World Bank, "Economic Strategies and Support Networks of the Poor in Kenya," World Bank Urban Development Department Technical Reports (Washington, D.C., 1984). The development of this article was also assisted by a grant from the Duke–University of North Carolina at Chapel Hill Women's Studies Research Center.

1. Mayra Buvinić. "Women's Issues in Third World Poverty: A Policy Analysis," in *Women and Poverty in the Third World*, ed. Mayra Buvinić, Margaret A. Lycette, and William Paul McGreevy (Baltimore: Johns Hopkins University Press, 1983), pp. 14–31.

2. For further discussion, see Mari Clark, "Variations on Themes of Male and Female: Reflections on Gender Bias in Rural Greece," *Women's Studies* 10, no. 2 (1983): 117–34.

To understand the form and functions of and reasons for the increasing numbers of woman-headed households worldwide, we must systematically untangle threads of evidence from the fabric of Western bias. This will advance social theory and enable development of programs that provide more adequately for the special needs of women who head households. Scholars of Afro-American family structure and of women and poverty in the Third World have made major progress toward these ends.[3] They have identified important universal constraints on women who head households, exposed the way in which scholars' units of analysis mask the presence of woman-headed households, and demonstrated the importance of recognizing different types of female household heads.

This report builds on and contributes to this literature. It shows how cultural and intracultural variation influences the form and function of woman-headed households and how such variation can significantly affect household needs and access to resources. It also details the economic strategies of women who head households in Kenya.

Scholarship on Poverty and Woman-headed Households

The negative effects of economic development on Third World women have long been recognized. More recently, plans for development projects have included women's concerns, particularly during the current United Nations Decade for Women. Yet the positive outcomes of such plans have been limited. Women continue to be overrepresented among the poor—particularly women who head households and support children.[4]

Most recent scholarship assumes that the increasing number of woman-headed households is associated with economic marginality. Such scholarship emerges from two different but complementary research perspectives: the system-oriented perspective and the actor-oriented perspective. System-oriented approaches view the woman-headed household as a product of larger sociostructural factors that range from the level of the family to that of world systems. For example, Nadia Youssef and Carol Hetler identify such factors as economic conditions that in-

3. Rae Lesser Blumberg, "The Political Economy of the Mother-Child Family: A Cross-societal View," in *Beyond the Nuclear Family*, ed. Luis Lucero (Beverly Hills, Calif.: Sage Publications, 1977), pp. 99–163; Carol Stack, *All Our Kin: Strategies for Survival in a Black Community* (New York: Harper & Row, 1974); Buvinić; Mayra Buvinić, Nadia Youssef, and Barbara von Elm, "Women-headed Households: The Ignored Factor in Development Planning" (Washington, D.C.: International Center for Research on Women, 1978); Nadia Youssef and Carol Hetler, "Rural Households Headed by Women: A Priority Issue for Policy Concern" (Geneva: International Labour Office, 1982, typescript).

4. Buvinić.

crease the economic marginality of men, extensive male labor migration, and the diminishing role of traditional family-based support systems.[5]

Many of the system-oriented studies rely on quantitative analyses of aggregate census and other survey data to test hypotheses about causal and conditional variables affecting the occurrence, persistence, and form of woman-headed households. This approach, however, cannot discern the interactional and individual processes by which women form and maintain these households. Such studies also tend to infer individual reasoning from aggregate data.

The actor-oriented approach views woman-headed households as the response of individual women to economic marginality. For example, Carol Stack shows how women in a poor Chicago community modify household composition in response to changing economic conditions throughout a wide network of kin and kinlike individuals.[6]

Many of the actor-oriented studies are based on long-term, in-depth ethnographic studies of few cases. This approach provides rich detail regarding individual- and household-level behavior in specific cultural contexts over time. But such studies tend to generalize about universal social and cultural processes on the basis of a small number of cases. They often discuss informal economic exchanges and adaptations in household composition without specifying the number of resources or persons involved.

Clearly, we need studies that combine the strengths of the actor-oriented and the system-oriented approaches to assure that research findings are valid and broadly applicable. While we should identify the factors that characterize all or most women who head households, we must also identify variations specific to particular types of women who head households in particular settings.

In discussing woman-headed households we need to recognize the bias inherent in conceptualizing units of analysis such as "household" and "head of household." Such bias has masked the presence of woman-headed households in census data and in ethnographic research. Because many Western scholars have seen the nuclear family as universal, they have confused family structure with household composition and have assumed residential unit, kinship unit, and domestic functions to be one and the same.[7] Their discussions generally ignore the network of kin and kinlike relations within which household activities occur.

Many scholars have also assumed, following Western economic theory, that households are basic decision-making units that maximize

5. Youssef and Hetler.

6. Stack.

7. Donald Bender, "A Refinement of the Concept of Household: Family Co-residence and Domestic Functions," *American Anthropologist* 69, no. 5 (October 1967): 493–504; Sylvia Yanagisako, "Family and Household: Analysis of Domestic Groups," *Annual Review of Anthropology* 8 (1979): 161–205.

household utility. But these scholars ignore differences in interests within the household, inequality in resource allocation based on age and gender, and separate management of certain resources by husbands and wives. All of these factors significantly affect economic behavior.[8]

Scholars often take as a given that a husband will be the major breadwinner and head of household. In sub-Saharan Africa, however, where women traditionally do most of the cultivating, women rather than men are often recognized as the primary providers for their children. Furthermore, brothers and other adult male kin—not just husbands— play an important economic and social role in women's lives.

Many scholars base definitions of woman-headed households on the assumption that husbands are normally heads of households. They define woman-headed households by the absence of a husband. Indeed, de facto female-headed households are usually identified by temporary but long-term absence of a husband. De jure female-headed households are defined by the lack of a primary adult male. These distinctions fail to specify the socioeconomic functions that distinguish heads of households regardless of gender, such as the provision and management of resources.

In addition to residential status, Youssef and Hetler propose that status as primary economic provider is a necessary criterion for identifying the head of a household.[9] Recognizing that the wider kin network influences household economic affairs leads to another important criterion: status as manager of household resources such as land, labor, and goods. It is possible that a man's kinsmen will manage his household resources in his absence, as occurs in some areas of western Kenya.[10] It is also possible that a male may be present in the household but not serve as primary provider or manager. All three criteria are necessary to identify the head of household.

Background on Kenya

To interpret the Kenyan data, one must reckon with the historical, social, economic, cultural, and demographic factors that have influenced the occurrence and the form of woman-headed households there. The

8. Buvinić; Nancy Folbre, "Household Production in the Philippines: A Non-neoclassical Approach," *Economic Development and Cultural Change* 32, no. 2 (1984): 303–30. Some recent studies offer more effective units of analysis. See Isabel Nieves, "Household Arrangements and Multiple Jobs in San Salvador," *Signs: Journal of Women in Culture and Society* 5, no. 1 (1979): 134–42; Yanagisako.

9. Youssef and Hetler.

10. Marc Ross and Thomas Weisner, "The Rural-Urban Network in Kenya: Some General Implications," *American Ethnologist* 4, no. 2 (1977): 359–75; Joyce Moock, "The Content and Maintenance of Social Ties between Urban Migrants and Their Home-based Support Groups: The Maragoli Case," *African Urban Studies* 3 (Winter 1978): 15–31.

colonial era initiated Kenya's dependency role in the world economy. To provide laborers for European estates and plantations, in the first decade of the 1900s colonial administrators initiated hut taxes, forcing many Kenyan men into wage labor. The construction of the Mombasa-Uganda railway facilitated the migration of male laborers. At the same time, Europeans provided housing only for male workers and discouraged men from bringing their families to the estates or towns. Men were also drawn out of the rural subsistence economy through military conscription during the two world wars.

This established a pattern of male labor migration and female farm management that was compatible with traditional separation of male and female social and economic spheres and with women's traditional role as cultivators. Today an estimated 88 percent of Kenyan women reside in rural areas.[11] Many male urban laborers send remittances to wives and parents in rural areas. There is a great deal of day-to-day fluctuation in the composition of households as a result of visiting, job seeking, and schooling. All these conditions create strong ties between rural and urban areas, as does the relatively recent growth of cities in Kenya.[12]

During the colonial era men had and today continue to have more opportunities than women for employment and education. They generally register land in their own names. Individual land ownership in turn provides men with greater access to credit since they can use land as collateral. These changes have diminished or eliminated women's traditional access to resources needed to support themselves and their children and have failed to offer alternatives.

In Kenya, where women rarely inherit land and have minimal access to other means of self-support, rural mothers look to their children to care for them in old age. Eight is commonly considered an ideal number of children, even though an extremely high rate of population growth is undermining Kenya's economic development. The 4 percent annual rate of natural increase is the greatest recorded for a single country to date, and Kenyan rural population densities are among the highest in Africa.[13]

Kenya's population is culturally diverse as a result of African population movements through the Rift Valley; European, Asian, and African intrusions; and regional differences in ecology that have affected patterns of subsistence and social organization. No one ethnic group

11. Audrey Chapman Smock, "Women's Economic Roles," in *Papers on the Kenyan Economy: Performance, Problems and Policies*, ed. Tony Killick (London: Heinemann Educational Books, 1981).

12. With the exception of the coastal trading towns such as Mombasa, cities in Kenya are products of the colonial experience, built as administrative and trading centers for Europeans.

13. Frank Mott and Susan Mott, "Kenya's Record Population Growth: A Dilemma for Development," *Population Bulletin*, vol. 35, no. 3 (1980).

accounts for even half of the population. The six largest of thirty major African linguistic and cultural groups in Kenya are the Kikuyu, traditionally located in Central Province; the Kamba, traditionally located in Machakos District; the Luhyia and the Luo, traditionally located in Western Province; the Kalenjin, traditionally located along the Rift Valley; and the Swahili-speaking groups, traditionally located in Coastal Province. Cultural differences, historical factors (such as proximity to the colonial administration), and geographical factors (such as uneven distribution of natural resources) account for the varied responses of these groups to economic changes in Kenya, including the variations among them in the prevalence of woman-headed households.

Household Heads and Poverty in Kenya

Existing data on the occurrence of woman-headed households in Kenya are limited. Different surveys conducted at different times using different sample populations are difficult to compare. An estimated 29 percent of the 1.7 million households in Kenya are headed by women.[14] In some low-income areas such as Mathare Valley in Nairobi, woman-headed households constitute as much as 60–80 percent of all households.[15] In other countries that provide statistical data on household headship, the occurrence of woman-headed households ranges from 5 to 31 percent.[16] Kenya's statistics, then, are at the high end of that range.

In Kenya there are four socially and economically significant types of household heads: (1) resident married men, (2) absentee married men whose resources are managed by male kin, (3) married women who practice subsistence agriculture and manage household resources in the absence of migrant spouses, and (4) women alone who have no permanent connection with a primary adult male.[17]

There are significant differences among these four types of households: they occur at different rates in rural and urban areas; the number of people living in them varies; they have differential access to resources and income; and they are impoverished to greater and lesser degrees. Households headed by resident men are found in both rural and urban settings. Of the four types, they generally house the largest number of people; survey data collected by the Central Bureau of Statistics in 1978

14. Smock.

15. Nici Nelson, "Female-centered Families: Changing Patterns of Marriage and Family among Buzaa Brewers of Mathare Valley," *African Urban Studies* 3 (Winter 1978): 85–104.

16. Youssef and Hetler.

17. Robert Daniels, Department of Anthropology, University of North Carolina at Chapel Hill, personal communication, 1984.

indicated that households headed by resident and absent married men averaged 6.78 members in contrast to the 4.19 members among those headed by women alone. The average number of workers resident is largest in households headed by married men and smallest in households headed by women alone.

A greater proportion of the households headed by married men are in areas suitable for high-value cash crops than is the case for households headed by women with absent husbands or by women alone. Married men who head households also have greatest access to off-farm employment, which is an important source of income for small-scale agricultural households. In 1978, 26 percent of the married male household heads, 22 percent of the married female household heads, and only 7 percent of the women heading households alone received at least 300 Kenya shillings (about twenty-three U.S. dollars) per month from off-farm employment.[18] A study in Taveta District (Coastal Province) showed better nutrition among children in households headed by men than among those in woman-headed households in the same areas.[19]

Households headed by absentee males are a rural phenomenon associated with male labor migration to urban areas such as Nairobi and Mombasa and to rapidly growing secondary towns. Resource management by the migrants' kinsmen appears to be most common among the Luo and Luhyia, who have strong ties within lineages.[20] Households headed by women with absent spouses also occur in rural areas and are associated with the migration of male laborers. In such households, wives rather than lineage members manage household resources. This pattern seems to be most common among the Kikuyu.[21] In practice, however, there is not always a sharp distinction between households that are headed by absentee men and those headed by women whose spouses are away, given individual differences and varied degrees of involvement of extended kin in household management.

Households headed by women alone are sharply distinguished from the other categories by their smaller size, minimal access to resources, and greater poverty. They occur in both rural and urban areas. Such household heads include widows who often support children, separated women, and women in changing consensual unions with men who contribute little to the household. Few never-married women head households

18. Carolyn Barnes, "Differentiation by Sex among Small-Scale Farming Households in Kenya," *Rural Africana*, no. 15/16 (Winter/Spring 1983), pp. 41–63.

19. Patrick Fleuret and Ned Greeley, *The Kenya Social and Institutional Profile* (Nairobi: U.S. Agency for International Development, Kenya Program Office, 1982).

20. Moock (n. 10 above); Ross and Weisner (n. 10 above); David Parkin, *The Cultural Definition of Political Response: Lineal Destiny among the Luo* (London: Academic Press, 1978).

21. Susan Abbott, "Full-Time Farmers and Week-end Wives: An Analysis of Altering Conjugal Roles," *Journal of Marriage and the Family* 38, no. 1 (February 1976): 165–74.

because it is difficult for a woman to acquire land, though there are a few who have had the benefit of good education and are pursuing professional careers in health, social services, and education.

Widowhood contributes significantly to the formation of female-headed households not only because women generally live longer than men but also because they tend to marry men three to ten years their senior.[22] Widows often have limited opportunity to remarry.[23] Traditionally they were absorbed into extended families, but as resources diminish in response to population increases, fewer families are able to provide such assistance.[24] Sometimes rural widows care for grandchildren whose parents live in the city.

Cultural Variation among Woman-headed Households in Kenya

In Kenya, contemporary patterns of woman-headed households appear to have antecedents in traditional social organization that distinguish them from such households in other parts of the world. Despite great cultural diversity, most traditional Kenyan societies were based on domestic units that consisted of a woman and her children supervised by a polygynous male. Each wife was allocated rights to use and manage land and cattle in order to provide for herself and her children. Often termed the "house-property complex," this pattern of resource allocation passed rights to land and cattle from a man to his sons via the "house" of the son's mother. This pattern sharply contrasts with traditional Latin American peasant society, where the extended family was the basic social, economic, and residential unit in which labor and resources were pooled and decision making occurred.

The Kenyan pattern of separate management of domestic units by co-wives provides a model for contemporary woman-headed households. What appears to be distinctive about contemporary female-headed domestic units, particularly those headed by women alone, is that they frequently are detached from the larger male-supervised kinship units. The extent of this detachment varies among ethnic groups and between rural and urban areas.

Ethnographic studies suggest that urban Kenyan women are manipulating elements of traditional codes and thus creating new social forms to help them get along in the marginal world in which they live. For example, women in Mathare Valley often send their children to the rural area

22. Mott and Mott, p. 9.
23. Betty Potash, "Some Aspects of Marital Stability in a Rural Luo Community," *Africa* 48, no. 4 (1978): 380–97.
24. Barnes.

to live with their grandmother, periodically forwarding remittances for child support. In this way city women continue to fulfill the traditional role of provider for their children through urban employment rather than subsistence agriculture.[25]

Woman marriage may be another somewhat infrequent adaptation of a traditional social form to serve contemporary women's needs. Among the Nandi (a Kalenjin group) and some other polygynous groups in Kenya and other parts of Africa, a woman can acquire a wife by paying bridewealth to the bride's kinsmen. Regina Oboler found that 3 percent of the households in one rural Nandi community were headed by female "husbands," which represents an increase in the rate of woman marriage. Woman marriage offers a woman past child-bearing age a young partner not only to help with domestic and farm chores but to reinforce her claims to land by providing the possibility of male heirs.[26]

Although there seems to be some continuity between current patterns of woman-headed households and traditional social structures, research also suggests that the increase in numbers of woman-headed households may reflect fundamental changes in husband-wife relationships. Carolyn Barnes's analysis of national survey data, collected in 1978 in Kenya's small-scale farming sector, suggests that "no precise division of adult labor by sex currently occurs in the crop and livestock activities. The designation of masculine and feminine tasks in agriculture has become blurred in the crop-producing regions of Kenya." Barnes attributes this change to (1) reduced livestock production and more intensive land use due to the individualization of land, which restricted the amount of land per household; (2) sale of farm products to meet household needs for cash; (3) reduced farm labor among children, who are increasingly attending school; and (4) fewer men working on farms because of off-farm employment. Despite the blurring of farm tasks, women continue to perform all household maintenance and child-care tasks. Barnes states that "the dominant economic force operating at the household level today is the ever-increasing need for cash to provide for basic needs." She suggests that as much as 60 percent of smallholders' basic needs require cash expenditures, particularly such items as tea, sugar, school fees and uniforms for children, water use, transportation to health facilities, and food to supplement crops grown on the holding.[27]

In urban areas male-female relationships also appear to be changing.

25. Nelson (n. 15 above).

26. Regina Oboler, "Is the Female Husband a Man: Woman/Woman Marriage among the Nandi of Kenya," *Ethnology* 14, no. 1 (1980): 69–88, and *Women, Power, and Economic Change: The Nandi of Kenya* (Stanford, Calif.: Stanford University Press, 1985).

27. Barnes; see also Mette Monsted, "The Changing Division of Labor within Rural Families in Kenya," Working Paper (Copenhagen: Center for Development Research, 1977), p. 7.

Nici Nelson argues that women in Mathare Valley gain little economic security from marriage because of irregular employment and high unemployment. Many women prefer "town husbands" (consensual unions) rather than "real husbands" (customary or civil marriage) because a town husband cannot control a woman's life and earnings, whereas a real husband can. When a woman has a town husband and rents or owns her own house, it is the man who must pack his belongings and leave when their relationship ends.[28]

Socioeconomic changes have affected the traditional house-property complex differently in different areas. There is considerable variation among regions in Kenya in the percentage of woman-headed households: Coastal Province, 27 percent; Central Province, 19 percent; Western Province, Kakamega District, 40 percent; and Maragoli District, 45 percent.[29] Part of these variations may be the result of different researchers' criteria for identifying woman-headed households. However, the evidence suggests that ethnic and socio-structural differences influence the formation and maintenance of woman-headed households. For example, in Kariobangi, a predominantly Luo low-income settlement in Nairobi, only 6 percent of the households are headed by women,[30] while in Mathare Valley, a largely Kikuyu settlement, 60–80 percent are.[31]

In urban settings there appear to be fewer Luo and Luhyia woman-headed households than Kikuyu woman-headed households. Kikuyu women apparently play a greater role in the management of household resources than do Luhyia women. Thomas Weisner and Susan Abbott contrast Luhyia and Kikuyu urban market women, noting that a strong patrilineal structure limits the independence and enterprise of Luhyia women, while a weaker patrilineal structure places fewer constraints on Kikuyu women.[32] Nelson similarly notes the active role Kikuyu women play in Mathare Valley community affairs, including participation in the traditionally male council of elders.[33] Research to date suggests that patrilineal and ethnic-group ties among Luo and Luhyia men are much

28. Nelson; see also Janet Bujra, "Women Entrepreneurs in Early Nairobi," *Canadian Journal of Anthropological Studies* 9, no. 2 (1975): 213–34, 227.

29. Smock (n. 11 above).

30. Thomas Weisner, "Kariobangi: The Case History of a Squatter Re-settlement Scheme in Kenya," in *A Century of Change in East Africa*, ed. William Arens (Chicago: Aldine Publishing Co., 1976).

31. Nelson.

32. Thomas Weisner and Susan Abbott, "Modernization, Urbanization, and Stress: A Controlled Comparison from East Africa," *Journal of Anthropological Studies* 35, no. 4 (1977): 421–51.

33. Nici Nelson, "Women Must Help Each Other: The Operation of Personal Networks among Buzaa Brewers in Mathare Valley, Kenya," in *Women United, Women Divided: Comparative Studies of Ten Contemporary Cultures*, ed. Ann Caplan and Janet Bujra (Bloomington: Indiana University Press, 1979), pp. 88–89.

stronger and provide a more powerful social control over women's behavior than those of the Kikuyu do. Even Luo women working in the formal sector more passively accept their husbands' decisions than do Kikuyu women.[34]

Some woman-headed households also appear in the Islamic community, which, in low-income neighborhoods in Nairobi, has provided social identity and support for widows and unmarried, divorced, and abandoned women who have broken ties with rural areas.[35] On the predominantly Islamic island of Atu, off the Kenyan coast, there is a high rate of marital instability. Many women gain considerable income from prostitution in the nearby coastal town of Mombasa. They invest these profits in houses, which, according to Islamic law, they can own separately from the land on which the houses stand. This is significant because women do not inherit land by Islamic law and thus have difficulty acquiring it. Women on Atu prefer temporary unions with men, while aspiring to build more permanent domestic units composed of female kin.[36]

Economic Strategies among Women Who Head Households in Kenya

In Kenya and other parts of the Third World, women who head households generally lack formal education; have a greater than average need for child care; have limited access to employment, social services, productive resources, capital, credit, land and cattle; and have smaller supportive kinship networks. To improve their situation, women can employ a variety of strategies: (1) informal social support networks; (2) flexible household composition; (3) multiple sources of income; and (4) unauthorized land use (squatting).

The major function of informal social support networks is the reciprocal exchange of cash, goods, and services to meet daily and emergency needs.[37] Such networks take a variety of forms in Kenya. Those most used by women who head households include close kin, neighbors, extended kin, and workmates. Close kin networks most significant to women seem to be those that involve a woman's family of origin. Women who head households thus may rely on mother-daughter cooperation, residential proximity of sisters, or three-generation households of mother, daugh-

34. Shirley Buzzard, "Women's Status and Employment in Kisumu, Kenya" (Ph.D. diss., American University, 1982), p. 98.

35. Bujra.

36. Janet Bujra, "Production, Property, Prostitution, and Sexual Politics in Atu," *Cahiers d'etudes africaines* 12, no. 65 (1977): 13–39.

37. On reciprocal exchange, see Larisa Lomnitz, *Networks and Marginality: Life in a Mexican Shanty Town* (New York: Academic Press, 1977).

ters, and granddaughters.[38] Neighborhood networks may overlap with social links based on kinship, ethnic, or religious relationships. Existing research suggests that neighborhood networks are more significant for Kenyan women than for men.[39]

In daily practice, the distinction between close and extended kin is not always a sharp one. The high rate of labor migration often means that more distantly related people are the ones with whom a person interacts on a daily basis. Rural-urban networks between urban migrants and people in the countryside include a variety of kin ranging from parents, siblings, and spouses to distant cousins and nephews. These networks appear to be strongest in the ethnic groups such as the Luo and Luhyia where the emphasis on the patrilineage and associated geneology makes it easier to find some kinship link between any two people of the same ethnicity.[40] But because extended kin connections tend to follow male lines, such networks primarily serve the needs of men rather than those of women.

Workmate networks can also be important for women. In rural areas and in some urban areas, workmates are also neighbors. For example, Nelson describes the "effective networks" in Mathare Valley, where roughly 75 percent of the women brew beer illegally.[41] Some women's work ties are not residentially based. Achola Pala Okeyo, for example, describes market-women's groups among the Luo that provide traveling companions and cooperate in trading.[42] However, workmate networks appear to have greatest significance for men.

Changing household composition—particularly in response to unemployment, landlessness, famine, and other emergencies—is another strategy employed by poor women in Kenya. There are five typical patterns of adjustment. First, women may foster children or send their own children to be fostered, often to rural grandmothers. In addition to freeing mothers from child-care responsibilities and providing grandmothers with cash remittances, sending a child to the rural areas often provides additional labor for a widow who also heads a household.[43] Second, rural and urban households can expand to incorporate adults on

38. Nelson, "Female-centered Families," p. 96.

39. See Maria Muller, *Actions and Interactions: Social Relationships in a Low Income Housing Estate in Kitale, Kenya* (Leiden: Africa-Studicentrum Stationsplein, 1975); Parkin (n. 20 above), p. 71; and Nelson, "Women Must Help Each Other."

40. David Parkin, "Migration, Settlement and the Politics of Unemployment," in *Town and Country in Central and East Africa*, ed. David Parkin (London: Oxford University Press, 1975), pp. 3–44.

41. Nelson, "Women Must Help Each Other," p. 80.

42. Achola Pala Okeyo, "Women in Household Economy: Managing Household Roles," *Studies in Family Planning* 10, no. 11/12 (November/December 1979): 337–43, 340; and see Buzzard, p. 186.

43. Nelson, "Female-centered Families," pp. 92–94.

a temporary basis. In urban areas, this often occurs when migrants, particularly men, are looking for employment. Third, women sometimes form households composed of nonkin, particularly other women.[44] Fourth, household composition can be modified by taking in boarders. Paying boarders can supplement household income on a more regular basis than many of the other activities in which poor women can engage.[45] Finally, woman marriage, discussed earlier, is another strategy by which women can increase their access to important resources.

Women who head households in Kenya also cope with poverty by diversifying their source of income. Their strategies include (1) renting rooms; (2) self-employment in the informal sector; (3) wage labor; (4) income transfers from adult kin; and (5) economic contributions from children.

If a woman owns a house in the city in Kenya, she is assured a reliable income because the demand for urban housing is high. In the past, renting rooms to male migrant laborers was one of the only sources of income for an urban woman other than prostitution. In fact, for many poor women, houses have been and continue to be a more dependable basis for security in old age than marriage is.[46] A woman can invest more easily in a house than in land because land generally is acquired through husbands or sons.

Self-employment in what is commonly called the informal sector is another common source of income for poor women who head households, particularly in urban areas. According to Nelson this includes providing entertainment (running unlicensed bars, brewing and selling beer, selling sexual favors), engaging in commerce (selling food or charcoal), and providing other personal services (doing laundry, performing female circumcision, practicing traditional medicine).[47] Some rural women are also involved in petty-commodity production of goods and services, although in the countryside men are more likely to be involved in such nonfarm activities.[48]

44. Christine Obbo, *African Women: Their Struggle for Economic Independence* (London: Zed Press, 1980), pp. 114–16.

45. Hunter Morrison, "Popular Housing Systems in Mombasa and Nairobi, Kenya," *Ekistics* 38, no. 227 (1974): 277–80.

46. See, e.g., Bujra, "Women Entrepreneurs in Early Nairobi" (n. 28 above), and "Production, Property, Prostitution, and Sexual Politics in Atu" (n. 36 above).

47. Nici Nelson, "How Men and Women Get By: The Sexual Division of Labor in the Informal Sector of a Nairobi Squatter Settlement," in *Casual Work and Poverty in Third World Cities*, ed. Ray Bromley and Chris Gerry (Chichester: John Wiley & Sons, 1979), pp. 283–302.

48. Republic of Kenya, Central Bureau of Statistics, "Nonfarm Activities in Rural Kenyan Households," *Perspectives*, vol. 2, no. 2 (1977); Ian Livingston, *Rural Development, Employment and Incomes in Kenya* (Addis Abbaba: International Labour Office, 1981), sec. 6. p. 25.

Poor women also use their sexuality to support their children and improve their social status by becoming concubines or lovers for wealthy men, by entering into consensual unions, by working as "good-time girls" in bars, or by becoming prostitutes of various sorts.[49] Since the colonial period commercial sex has been an important way for poor, uneducated women to earn money. In colonial Nairobi, for example, the high ratio of men to women gave prostitutes an opportunity to accumulate savings and invest them in buildings and business. And, unlike their European counterparts, prostitutes in Kenya have always acted as their own agents rather than working for madams or pimps.[50]

There is considerable debate about the utility of informal sector employment for poor women in Kenya. Sharon Stichter argues that it is rarely an adequate substitute for a full-time job.[51] Janet Bujra suggests that petty-commodity producers rarely rise above the poverty level because they must operate in a highly competitive market that caters to people with low incomes and is ultimately dependent on the formal sector for capital.[52] Those who emphasize the positive aspects of informal sector employment hold that it continues to absorb poor laborers. Nelson suggests that, despite the unpredictable income associated with beer brewing, women in Mathare Valley continue to do it because they have few alternatives. She also notes that brewing beer brings higher profits than working as a barmaid or domestic servant does. In addition, beer can be brewed and sold at home and thus combined with child-care responsibilities.[53]

Formal sector employment opportunities are limited for poor, uneducated women who head households. According to Audrey Chapman Smock, "Traditions of active involvement in agriculture have not translated into norms of female labor force participation in the modern sector." She suggests that this results from women's primary obligation to the family farm as well as from lower rates of literacy and lower levels of education among women and employer preference for male workers.[54] There are some wage-labor opportunities for the rural poor in agriculture—picking tea or coffee on large estates or working in small industries such as creameries. However, Rural Integrated Survey data show that, in

49. See J. Mugo Gachui, "Anatomy of Prostitutes and Prostitution in Nairobi," Institute of Development Studies Working Paper no. 113 (Nairobi: University of Nairobi, 1973); and Obbo (n. 44 above).

50. Luise White, "Women's Domestic Labor in Colonial Kenya: Prostitution in Nairobi, 1909–1950," Boston University African Studies Center Working Paper no. 30 (Boston: Boston University, 1980).

51. Sharon Stichter, "Women in the Labor Force in Kenya: Problems and Prospects" (paper presented at the Wellesley College Conference on Women and Development, 1976).

52. Janet Bujra, "Proletarianization and the Informal Economy: A Case Study from Nairobi," *African Urban Studies* 3 (Winter 1978): 47–66.

53. Nelson, "How Men and Women Get By," p. 300.

54. Smock (n. 11 above), p. 223.

1974–75, less than 5 percent of the female farm inhabitants were wage laborers, in contrast to 29 percent of their male counterparts.[55]

Survey data also indicate that income transfers are significant sources of income for some women who head households.[56] Analyzing 1974–75 data, Smock found that rural female household heads received larger remittances from relatives than did their male counterparts.[57] Comparable data on urban women are not available at present. Existing research suggests that urban female household heads are not likely to receive substantial transfers from rural kin because they have broken those ties or because their rural kin lack money to send them. The women who head urban households are more likely to send remittances to parents, particularly those fostering children for them.[58]

Children who live with their mothers sometimes make economic contributions to the household. Patrick Fleuret and Ned Greeley note that children help support rural families in Kenya, providing farm labor, performing household tasks, caring for other children, and assisting in food preparation. They suggest that children's contributions may be particularly important in woman-headed households or those where women spend time in cash-earning activities.[59] According to the scant research data available, it appears that the economic role of children in urban areas is very limited and the cost of raising them is greater. Shirley Buzzard states that children in town require better clothing and more supervision than those on the farm.[60] On the other hand, Jemimah Wainaina's study of parking boys in Nairobi suggests that some of the boys share earnings with their mothers.[61] Nelson notes that in Mathare Valley children play an important role in warning mothers about the arrival of police intent on raiding beer-brewing activities.[62]

A final economic strategy employed by poor women is unauthorized land use or squatting. By squatting, poor women can construct simple housing that they could not afford to rent. Squatter settlements have accompanied the growth of cities in Kenya since the early 1890s, as has the demolition of such settlements by authorities.[63] Dwellings in squatter

55. Ibid., p. 221.

56. James Knowles and Richard Anker, "An Analysis of Income Transfer in a Developing Country: The Case of Kenya," *Journal of Development Economics* 8, no. 2 (April 1981): 205–26.

57. Smock, p. 222.

58. Nelson, "Female-centered Families" (n. 15 above), p. 93.

59. Fleuret and Greeley (n. 19 above), p. 153.

60. Buzzard (n. 34 above), p. 100.

61. Jemimah Wainaina, "The Parking Boys of Nairobi," *African Journal of Sociology* 1, no. 1/2 (1981): 7–45.

62. Nelson, "Women Must Help Each Other" (n. 33 above), p. 96.

63. Weisner (n. 30 above), p. 77; Christine Obbo, "Women's Careers in Low Income Areas," in Parkin, ed. (n. 40 above), p. 288; Nelson, "How Men and Women Get By" (n. 47 above).

settlements are simple structures that represent small financial loss when an area is demolished.[64]

Conclusions and Policy Implications

From the preceding discussion it is clear that we must identify the needs specific to different types of female-headed households in Kenya and the particular constraints on women who head households that differentiate them from other poor women and poor people in general.[65] In so doing we find that rural women alone who head households and support children emerge as those most in need of assistance. A study of poverty in Kenya indicated that the poorest people are rural small-holders. The poorest of these are women.[66] An estimated one- to two-hundred thousand rural households headed by women alone with children are economically at risk. Case studies suggest that this "at-risk" group may include 30–50 percent of all woman-headed households in Kenya.[67]

It is also clear that we must recognize cultural and ethnic variation in the form and function of woman-headed households. We need comparative research that combines the quantitative strengths of the system-oriented approach with the qualitative strengths of the actor-oriented approach. We should pursue a number of research questions. What are the major differences among woman-headed households cross-culturally? How do these differences influence the numbers of women who head households and the economic well-being of those households? Is the increase in the number of female-headed households predominantly the result of economic marginality, or do other factors, such as traditional social patterns and economic opportunities, also account for the increase? Research on higher-income professional women who head households would shed light on this last question. Are there any constant patterns cross-culturally in the way that ethnic differences affect the formation and maintenance of woman-headed households?

We must also consider cultural and ethnic differences when designing programs and policies befitting female-headed households, particularly differences that affect access to and use of material and human resources. We should build on the valuable set of recommendations for

64. Morrison (n. 45 above). On squatting, see also Phillip P. Mbithi and C. Barnes, *Spontaneous Settlement Problems in Kenya* (Nairobi: East Africa Literature Bureau, 1975), pp. 1–2.
65. On universal constraints faced by rural women who head households, see Youssef and Hetler (n. 3 above).
66. Paul Collier and Deepak Lal, "Poverty and Growth in Kenya," World Bank Staff Working Paper no. 399 (Washington, D.C.: World Bank, 1980).
67. Fleuret and Greeley, p. 35.

policy-oriented research proposed by Youssef and Hetler, comparing the needs of the various types of women who head households in both urban and rural settings and in the context of different modes of production such as farming, herding, fishing, and trading. We should also compare household composition among households headed by women, particularly with regard to the number of dependents resident.

Finally, it is important to understand the economic strategies and social networks now maintaining woman-headed households in order to avoid developing programs that would undermine them. Evidence of considerable variation among woman-headed households serves as a warning against general policies that do not take into account specific local needs. Researchers must make practical recommendations about the types of assistance most likely to fill those needs without disrupting productive social relationships and sources of income. Far too often research reports do not include the kind of practical guidance that can help in implementing successful development projects.

Department of Anthropology
University of North Carolina at Chapel Hill

The Paradox of Women's Poverty: Wage-earning Women and Economic Transformation

Joan Smith

Two recent developments have contributed significantly to the growth of women's poverty in the United States. First, more women than ever before must depend exclusively on their own earnings or on welfare payments as the major source of support for themselves and their families. The number of women heading households with children under eighteen doubled between 1970 and 1980. By 1981 close to one-fifth of all families with minor children were headed by women, who were more than three times as likely to have incomes below the poverty line than were their male counterparts.[1] Second, most available new jobs offer workers little chance to climb out of poverty. The vast majority of these positions are in the rapidly expanding service sector of the economy and are occupied primarily by women.

This article examines the relationship between the increase in the number of women who must enter paid employment and the growth of the service sector. Although these developments are responses to some-

My deep appreciation is once more owed to Robert Jaccaud, Virginia Close, and Mimi Curphy of the Dartmouth College Library as well as to two anonymous readers for their assistance.

1. Department of Commerce, Bureau of the Census, *Household and Family Characteristics*, ser. P-20, no. 271 (Washington, D.C.: Government Printing Office, March 1981), p. 7; Commission on Civil Rights, *A Growing Crisis: Disadvantaged Women and Their Children*, Clearinghouse Publication no. 78 (Washington, D.C.: Government Printing Office, May 1983), p. 8. According to one report, if the current trend continues, the poverty population will be composed solely of women and their children by about the year 2000 (see National Advisory Council on Economic Opportunity, *Final Report: The American Promise: Equal Justice and Economic Opportunity* [Washington, D.C.: Government Printing Office, 1981]).

what different circumstances, the two have combined to create a paradoxical situation for U.S. women today. Women's labor has been the major contributor to employment growth in the most rapidly expanding sector of the economy, yet the experience of women wage workers continues to be that of the most marginally employed. Although central to economic expansion, they still receive the lowest pay and are subject to the least desirable employment practices.

The people who employ these women face another side of this contradiction. The fastest growing sectors in the private economy have been able to expand as rapidly as they have almost exclusively because women have been willing to take work that is less than desirable. Historically, such willingness stems from women's economic dependency and traditional exclusion from paid work; yet it is precisely these conditions that are seriously eroded once women become permanent members of the labor force.

The first section of this article examines the character of the service sector, its phenomenal growth, and its operating premises. While this sector resembles others in the private economy in that it must extract profits at a rate acceptable to investors, it employs unique strategies to accomplish that end. These strategies, inherent in the development and structure of service establishments, affect the entire economy—most particularly the female labor force—since they necessarily entail the creation of low-wage, intermittent, and part-time work.

The second section describes the unprecedented rise in women's paid employment over the past ten years. A substantial portion of that unexpected growth is explained by the decreased number of women who depend permanently and entirely on men for their support: women increasingly do not marry or marry later in life; they are also divorcing much more frequently. In addition, married women are far less likely to engage themselves exclusively in housekeeping and child rearing. Nevertheless, and despite women's vastly increased participation in the labor force, the nature of jobs offered them in the growing service sector is shaped by the presumption that women still have access to sufficient support beyond their own earnings and are at best only partially committed to wage labor.

The Growth of Services

Without question, service establishments have come to dominate economic activities in the United States over the past thirty years. The IBM plant may be more impressive than the local McDonald's, but the local McDonald's and other such service-sector establishments are absorbing more of total personal expenditures than any other sector in the

domestic economy. Between 1950 and 1980 spending on services increased almost twelve times, more than twice the increase for durable-
goods spending and half again the rate of growth in total private spending. Although the proportion of private expenditures on durable goods
remained near constant during the period, by 1980 nearly half of every
dollar of personal expenditures was slated for services, up from just a
third in 1950.[2]

Paralleling this increase was the growth in the sector's overall output.
In 1950 service-sector establishments produced slightly more than 47
percent of the total gross national product (GNP); by 1980 that share had
increased to almost 55 percent. In contrast, goods-producing firms wit-
nessed a decrease from approximately 37 percent to less than 32 percent.
Between 1950 and 1980, the gross product of the service sector grew by
200 percent, outpacing the growth in total GNP by 43 percent.[3]

These shifts have been accompanied by a constant differential in the
rate of return in the form of gross product—a differential that favors
service-sector firms. In 1974, for every dollar invested in wages, salaries,
and capital goods, the manufacturing sector realized $1.50 in the value of
its gross product; by 1980 that had increased to $1.60. In the service
sector, a dollar investment goes a good deal further: in 1974 it returned
$1.92 in gross product, in 1981 $2.06.[4]

Though notorious for low productivity, many establishments within
the service sector rival the traditional manufacturing industries in achieving high sales in proportion to the number of workers they employ. For
example, the food chain of Safeway Stores had approximately the same
number of employees as did U.S. Steel in 1980 but 17 percent more sales
dollars per employee than the industrial giant. Moreover, Safeway
accomplished this sales record with three and a half times fewer assets per
employee than U.S. Steel. Kroeger food stores reached close to the same
employee sales as Ford, but Ford had nearly four times as many assets
involved in every dollar of sales per employee. For every dollar of sales
per employee among the twenty-five largest industrial firms listed by
Forbes, including the two major U.S. oil companies, the average asset per
employee was eighty-seven cents; in contrast, the average for the twenty-
four largest retail establishments was just thirty-six cents.[5]

2. "National Income and Product Accounts," *Business Statistics* (October 1980), pp.
245–46; *Economic Indicators* (January 1960), p. 5, (January 1968), p. 5, (December 1981),
p. 4.

3. Council of Economic Advisors, *Economic Report of the President* (Washington, D.C.:
Government Printing Office, 1982), p. 245.

4. Ibid., pp. 258–59; and Department of Commerce, Bureau of the Census, *Statistical
Abstract of the United States, 1981* (Washington, D.C.: Government Printing Office, 1981),
p. 545.

5. *Forbes* (May 11, 1981), p. 299. It would be well to recall that the labor/capital ratio
characteristic of manufacturing firms was not a technological inevitability but the outcome

This very low capital-to-labor ratio is one of the principal characteristics, perhaps the identifying one, of service establishments, and their employment practices are absolutely shaped by this factor and by the kind of business environment within which they operate. The two together—labor intensity and operating environment—are therefore crucial for the majority of women wage workers. Before considering how these factors affect employment practices, however, one must examine the phenomenal growth in the number of workers subject to these practices. Between 1970 and 1980 service-sector establishments absorbed close 86 percent of all private sector employment growth in the country. Nearly all of that new employment—80 percent—went to just two of its subsectors, retail trade and business and personal services (see table 1). Had the service sector offered the same type of jobs as those offered in the sectors it was rapidly displacing as the major national employer, the effect on the economy in general and on workers in particular would have been a good deal less consequential. But most service-sector employment stands in sharp contrast to that in other sectors of the private economy.

The wage differential between service-sector work and manufacturing, traditionally large, widened dramatically between 1970 and 1980. In 1970, for every dollar manufacturing employees earned in weekly pay, workers in retail trade earned sixty-two cents; by 1980 retail workers earned fifty-one cents for every dollar paid to manufacturing workers. In

Table 1

Private-Sector Nonagricultural Employees by Industry

	Number of Employees (Thousands)		
	1970	1980	% Change
Goods-producing industries	23,578	20,361	−13.6
Service-producing industries	34,748	48,632	40.0
Transportation and utilities	4,515	5,156	14.2
Wholesale trade	3,993	5,281	32.2
Retail trade	11,047	15,292	38.4
Finance, insurance, and real estate	3,645	5,162	41.6
Business and personal services	11,548	17,741	53.6
Total	58,326	68,993	18.3

SOURCE.—*Employment and Earnings*, vol. 29, no. 7 (July 1982), table B1.

of specific New Deal and Fair Deal compromises between labor and capital (see James O'Connor, *The Fiscal Crisis of the State* [New York: St. Martin's Press, 1973], p. 22). The growth of the service sector could be considered an outcome of that compromise, especially since the sector's low level of unionization exempted it from the constraints imposed by the agreements.

general merchandise stores—stores like those occupying the largest spaces in local shopping malls—the ratio declined from fifty-seven to forty-eight cents for every dollar in weekly earnings in manufacturing; in eating and drinking places, from forty-three to thirty-three cents. In personal services, the ratio went from seventy-three to sixty-six cents for every dollar. Even the prestigious financial establishment's relative wage rates have deteriorated from eighty-four to seventy-two cents for every dollar paid in weekly manufacturing wages (see table 2).[6]

Besides differing significantly from manufacturing firms in their wage rates, service-sector establishments have a considerably greater capacity to sustain relatively high labor turnover. In January 1978, for example, close to 30 percent of the 91 million workers on the job in all sectors held positions that they had not held the year before; service industries were the major contributor to this instability (see table 3).[7] Between 1970 and 1976 the average quarterly turnover rate for manufacturing establishments was 1.1 percent. By contrast, the general merchandising sector had a rate of 3.2 percent, eating and drinking places 4.4 percent.[8]

The contrast in employment practices is even greater. Not only do employees in the service sector have twice the turnover rate of those in manufacturing, but they also have a substantially higher rate of part-time employment (see table 4). By 1977, close to 37 percent of those employed in retail and wholesale trade worked less than thirty-five hours per week, whereas a decade earlier the figure was only 29 percent.[9] Comparable increases in part-time work can be found in all service-sector establishments. For example, although the total number of persons working in food stores increased by 21 percent between 1958 and 1975, the total

6. A reviewer quite properly notes that a major part of the wage increases in manufacturing during the 1970s and thus the relative decline in service-sector wages was due to the strength of unions in manufacturing. Indeed that was the case, which supports my two major points here. First, social and political conditions, rather than conditions endemic to the kind of work they do, account for women's relatively low wage levels. Second, precisely these conditions are undermined when women become central to major economic processes. Now that "women's work" increasingly is the new form of labor, unions are increasingly trying to organize them. In that context the recent attacks on unions can be seen as a feminist issue, whether or not the membership of any particular union is composed of women.

7. Edward S. Sekscenski, "Job Tenure Declines as Work Force Changes," *Monthly Labor Review* 103, no. 12 (December 1979): 48–50.

8. See table D2 in the following issues of *Employment and Earnings*, a monthly publication of the U.S. Department of Labor, Bureau of Labor Statistics: vol. 17, no. 1 (July 1970); vol. 18, no. 1 (July 1971); vol. 19, no. 1 (July 1972); vol. 20, no. 1 (July 1973); vol. 21, no. 1 (July 1974); vol. 22, no. 1 (July 1975); vol. 23, no. 1 (July 1976).

9. Barbara Coltman Job, "Employment and Pay Trends in Retail Trade," *Monthly Labor Review* 103, no. 3 (March 1980): 40–43.

Table 2

Average Weekly Earnings of Private-Sector Nonsupervisory Workers

	1970		1980		
	Average Weekly Earnings ($)	% of Average Weekly Manufacturing Earnings	Average Weekly Earnings ($)	% of Average Weekly Manufacturing Earnings	% Change
Manufacturing industries	133.73	...	288.62	...	115.8
Retail establishments	82.47	62	146.89	51	64.4
General merchandise stores	75.84	57	139.18	48	63.3
Food stores	87.48	65	195.00	68	122.9
Eating and drinking places	57.72	43	96.31	33	66.9
Financial, insurance, and real estate firms	112.98	84	209.24	72	85.2
Business and personal services	97.98	73	190.71	66	94.6
Average	120.16		235.10		95.7

Source.—Employment and Earnings, vol. 17, no. 9 (March 1971), table C2, vol. 28, no. 3 (March 1981), table C2.

number of hours worked rose less than 1 percent. Despite greatly extended weekly shopping hours, the average number of hours worked per week by nonsupervisory personnel in the retail food industry decreased by 11 percent between 1958 and 1975.[10] Although operating hours escalated substantially, the average work week in eating and drinking establishments declined from 36.6 hours in 1968 to 28.0 hours in 1976.[11]

All the developments associated with growth in the service sector—substantial rise in employment, increases in operating hours accompanied by decreases in full-time work, and higher-than-average rate of employee turnover along with considerably lower-than-average wages—are not just the unplanned outcome of typical employment practices but are fundamentally tied to the two conditions of operation mentioned above that sharply distinguish service-sector establishments from their counterparts in the rest of the economy.[12]

The first of these conditions is the low capital-to-labor ratio found among service firms. Not only is the amount of capital equipment per

Table 3

Job Tenure of Private-Sector Wage and Salary Workers, by Industry, January 1978

	Median Years on Current Job
Manufacturing	4.3
Transportation and utilities	4.9
Retail and wholesale trade	2.0
Financial, insurance, and real estate firms	3.1
Business and personal services	3.0
Average	3.75

SOURCE.—Edward Sekscenski, "Job Tenure Declines as Work Force Changes," *Monthly Labor Review* 103, no. 12 (December 1979): 48–50.

10. John L. Carey and Phyllis Flohr Otto, "Output per Unit of Labor Input in the Retail Food Industry," *Monthly Labor Review* 100, no. 1 (January 1977): 42–47.

11. Richard B. Carnes and Horst Brand, "Productivity and New Technology in Eating and Drinking Places," *Monthly Labor Review* 100, no. 9 (September 1977): 9–15.

12. A common explanation for all these changes in labor practices associated with the growth of the service sector is the somewhat novel process of actually decommodifying labor. The work is reorganized so that the customers themselves perform part of it for free, thus reducing owners' overall wage costs: direct dialing long-distance calls, pumping gas, bookkeeping when banking, acting as their own waiters and waitresses, or packing their own produce. Notice that, although the redesign of the work is gender neutral, women perform the lion's share of this new unpaid work. The following articles describe (and applaud) this redesign: Theodore Levitt, "The Industrialization of Service," *Harvard Business Review* 54, no. 5 (September–October 1976): 63–73; Richard B. Chase, "Where Does the Customer Fit in a Service Operation?" *Harvard Business Review* 56, no. 6 (November–December 1978): 137; and Christopher H. Lovelock and Robert F. Young, "Look to Consumers to Increase Productivity," *Harvard Business Review* 57, no. 3 (May–June 1979): 168–78.

employee in the service sector considerably less than in manufacturing, but the disparity has been growing substantially. Similarly, the amount of total investment per employee (though greater in 1960) is now considerably less in the service sector than in manufacturing firms (see table 5). Because service-sector establishments are highly labor intensive, expanded production rests less on productivity growth (increases in units of output per units of labor) than on absolute increases in the labor force itself.

The second distinguishing feature of service-sector establishments is the highly competitive nature of their business environment. In contrast to the manufacturing giants, which enjoy virtual oligopolistic control over markets, even the largest service-sector firms face far more severe price competition.[13]

The first condition, a relatively high dependence on labor for increased output, leads to a general rise in overall wage costs. The potential impact of this tendency is heightened by the second condition: a greater imperative to cut wages in reaction to relatively stronger-than-average downward pressures on prices (relative, that is, to manufacturing firms). These two distinguishing conditions within which service-sector establishments must operate—a highly labor-intensive work process and a highly competitive business environment—have fundamentally shaped that sector's development and daily operations. Such operating conditions

Table 4

Extent of Part-Time Employment in the Private Sector, May 1977

	Total Number of Employees (Thousands)	% Part-Time
Goods-producing industries	25,527	17.1
Mining	781	17.4
Construction	4,508	20.4
Manufacturing	20,238	16.3
Service-producing industries	47,971	29.4
Transportation and utilities	5,437	19.7
Retail and wholesale trade	16,448	36.8
Financial, insurance, and real estate firms	4,509	19.9
Business and personal services	21,577	31.2
Total	78,441	25.4

Source.—William V. Deutermann, Jr., and Scott Campbell Brown, "Voluntary Part-Time Workers: A Growing Part of the Labor Force," *Monthly Labor Review* 12, no. 6 (June 1978): 3–10.

13. James O'Connor, "Competitive Capital and Monopoly Capital," in *The Capitalist State*, ed. Richard Edwards et al., 2d ed. (Englewood Cliffs, N.J.: Prentice-Hall, Inc., 1978), pp. 91–109.

Table 5

Investment in Manufacturing and Nonmanufacturing Sectors

	Total Business Capital per Employee (1972 $)			Capital Equipment Investment per Employee (1972 $)		
	Manufacturing	Non-manufacturing	Ratio	Manufacturing	Non-manufacturing	Ratio
1960	15,534	17,167	1.10	8,012	6,662	.83
1965	16,444	17,564	1.07	8,739	6,604	.75
1970	19,121	18,656	.97	10,757	7,641	.71
1975	23,339	20,822	.89	14,055	9,017	.65
1980	25,425	20,953	.82	16,720	9,486	.57

Source.—Calculated from data given in Department of Commerce, Bureau of the Census, *Statistical Abstract of the United States, 1981* (Washington, D.C.: Government Printing Office, 1981), table 924; and *Employment and Earnings*, vol. 28, no. 1 (June 1982), table B1.

strongly encourage employment practices that allow overall wage reductions and increases in the size of the labor force simultaneously. Further, these practices necessarily include rapid expansion and contraction of the labor force to match fluctuations in demand. While each of these practices would naturally be advantageous to any firm, they have become indispensable for the vast majority of service-sector firms precisely because of their distinctive operating constraints.

As a direct result of such employment practices, then, labor costs have decreased over the past decade while the labor force absorbed by service-sector establishments has vastly increased. Part-time workers constitute a steadily increasing portion of the labor force and are frequently found in firms open twenty-four hours a day; an increasing number of workers float in and out of jobs depending on seasonal demands. The irony is that the increase in such employment practices signals a vastly increased dependence on a wage labor force that, paradoxically, must be treated in all other respects as though it was entirely dispensable. In short, the contemporary economy has moved to center stage a labor force that must be continually endowed with marginal characteristics.

Creating the Poverty of Working Women

This paradoxical situation was facilitated by the unprecedented number of women willing to enter the ranks of paid labor. Between 1970 and 1980 there were over 13 million of them, the greatest increase in the history of the U.S. labor force (see table 6). This phenomenal growth in women's paid employment accounts for more than half of the increase in employment in each of the major industrial sectors throughout the decade—even though women constituted no more than half the labor force in each sector. Women contributed over three-quarters of the increase in financial, real estate, and insurance firms and more than 60 percent in both the service-producing and retail food store industries.[14] This trend toward increased wage work clearly challenged stereotypic assumptions about women's labor and encouraged many women to rearrange their daily patterns of living.

In 1980 the number of adult women exclusively engaged in the routine activities of keeping house was close to 10 million less than one would have projected given 1970 figures—a momentous shift in social arrangements.[15] Fewer women married—in 1980 there were 5.2 million fewer married women than 1970 marriage rates would have indicated—

14. *Employment and Earnings*, vol. 28, no. 9 (March 1981), tables B1, B2.
15. *Employment and Earnings*, vol. 18, no. 7 (January 1971), tables A1, A3, A5, A23, vol. 28, no. 7 (January 1981), tables A1, A2, B5, B2.

and a substantially greater number of married women worked for wages. By 1980 2.8 million more married women were in the active labor force than could have been expected according to 1970 conditions. By March of 1980, according to Labor Department figures, half of all married women living with their husbands were either actively seeking work or actually working for wages. More startling is what happened to the two groups of women between thirty-five and forty-four and between twenty and twenty-four: their employment rate exceeded that of women in similar age groups in 1970 by almost 60 percent.[16]

All of these factors represent a drastic redesign in the fabric of women's lives. In one brief ten-year period, expectations firmly held (although perhaps less firmly realized in practice) were radically altered.[17] The question is, Where did women go for jobs, and how were economic arrangements affected by the sudden appearance of so many new workers on the market?

Table 6

Labor Force Activities of U.S. Women, 1970–80

	1970 (%)	1980 (%)
Females over 16:		
Employed or seeking work in the labor force	43.3	51.5
Working exclusively in the household	47.9	36.6
Engaged in other activities*	8.8	11.9
Total	100.0	100.0
	($N = 72,774,000$)	($N = 86,604,000$)
Employed women:		
Working full-time	72.1	71.4
Working part-time	27.9	28.6
Total	100.0	100.0
	($N = 29,666,000$)	($N = 41,283,000$)
Married women:		
Working full-time for wages	23.8	28.8
Working part-time for wages	9.2	11.6
Not working for wages	67.0	59.6
Total	100.0	100.0
	($N = 47,900,000$)	($N = 51,800,000$)

SOURCE.—*Employment and Earnings*, vol. 18, no. 7 (January 1971), tables A1, A3, A5, A23, vol. 28, no. 7 (January 1981), tables A1, A2, B5, B2.

*Students, military personnel, institutionalized women, etc.

16. Beverly L. Johnson and Elizabeth Waldman, "Marital and Family Patterns of the Labor Force," *Monthly Labor Review* 104, no. 10 (October 1981): 36–37.

17. For a study of how these expectations structured women's work experiences in the early part of the century, see Leslie Tentler, *Wage Earning Women* (New York: Oxford University Press, 1979).

There is no direct way to measure exactly where each new woman worker went when she found paid employment. (There is no way to identify precisely which women expanded the labor force beyond the size predicted by 1970 rates of employment; such a category of women is an analytical rather than an empirical one.) Indirectly, though, the vastly disproportionate growth of some industries relative to others suggests the kinds of new jobs responsible for absorbing this altogether new source of labor.

Between 1970 and 1980 the service sector grew by close to 14 million jobs—a 31 percent growth in the sector's share of the labor market. Close to 4.5 million more jobs appeared here than would have been the case had the service sector merely maintained its 1970 share of total private employment in the nation. Close to 75 percent of that unexpected new employment was provided by women new to the paid labor force.[18]

Consider, for example, the expansion of retail trade. In 1970 this sector was a major employer of women: 46 percent of its total labor force was female. Yet when it added employment beyond just its 1970 share—in short, when it added approximately 2.2 million unexpected jobs—women took close to three-quarters of them. The same pattern persists in all of the subsectors of service industries. Although women made up 52 percent of the 1970 labor force in financial, real estate, and insurance firms, they contributed 87 percent of the disproportionate growth those firms enjoyed in the decade. All of the disproportionate growth in advertising was contributed by women's unexpected employment. In business services women contributed close to 57 percent of the disproportionate growth, although they had constituted just 34 percent of that sector in 1970. Even in the male-dominated engineering subsector, women's unexpected increase in employment accounted for more than 30 percent of the sector's disproportionate growth. Similarly, in legal services, women provided 82 percent of the unexpected growth in the decade between 1970 and 1980.[19]

In summary, two kinds of growth took place between 1970 and 1980. One is simply the absolute increase in employment of women and the corresponding absolute growth in the firms that employed them. The other is the relative growth that represents significant shifts in the dominance of particular kinds of economic activities and the disproportionate growth in women's employment that accommodated those shifts.

To be sure, the economy grew between 1970 and 1980, and despite rising levels of unemployment, more people were employed in 1980, relative to the population, than in 1970. But these new employees found work in altogether different sorts of industries. There was a significant

18. Calculated from data in *Employment and Earnings*, vol. 18, no. 9 (March 1971), tables B2, B3, vol. 28, no. 9 (March 1981), tables B2, B3.
19. Ibid.

shift in what people could expect to do because of the significant shift in how profits are generated. A new emphasis, at least domestically, has been placed on generating profits through a relative decrease in domestic goods production and a relative increase in what have been regarded until very recently as merely ancillary services.[20]

Women have been the principal facilitators of this fundamental change in the nature of the U.S. economy. And, as we have seen, the availability of that new pool of labor signals a vast rearrangement in the traditional social institutions that are part of women's lives. Two developments—more women working and fewer women marrying—contributed decisively to the growth of the labor force between 1970 and 1980. Whether there is a causal link between these two events is not at issue here. What is at issue is that, unlike the economic climates in other periods, today's economic climate has been transformed by a considerably different kind of labor force. This labor force, although central to key economic developments, is treated as if its work is only marginal to those developments.

In an earlier time, working outside the home was for most women a stopgap between youth and maturity. It was the exceptional woman who found in paid employment the authority conferred on full-fledged members of the labor force. According to reigning ideologies—and women's experiences led them to accept these ideologies—women could expect to find recognition and respect only through a domestic role. Anything that interrupted that role was viewed as, at best, an aberration, a temporary measure rather than a lifetime commitment.[21]

The kinds of jobs available to women in a predominantly sex-

20. One reader suggested that a second transformation is taking place as well. Capital investment in manufacturing has shifted from productivity-increasing investment to wage-decreasing investment; plant and equipment move to low-wage, nonunionized areas. I would also add that when runaway shops move overseas there appears in labor force data for the United States a relative increase in service-producing jobs at the expense of those in manufacturing. This happens for two reasons, one real and the other more illusionary. The decrease in domestic manufacturing jobs automatically causes a relative increase in service jobs quite independent of their absolute growth. Second, however, the increased business activities associated with exporting jobs overseas lead to increases in some service-producing jobs in the United States—banking and other financial activities, legal and other business services, recreational services, and the like—all of which cannot be as conveniently moved overseas.

21. Tentler puts the matter this way: "As unskilled workers, women were often described as timid, ignorant, and easily manipulated. But in the home they worked with skill and assurance, in control of the job and coequal with the judges of their work—family members and other women in the neighborhood . . .; housekeeping and mothering, if done well, assured a woman high status in her small world" (p. 16). While this account is a highly romanticized version of the life of working-class housewives, it testifies to the ideology surrounding their domestic activities and the set of expectations working-class women were expected to hold about their domestic roles.

segregated labor force were altogether consistent with these expectations: they were the most temporary, the most dispensable, the worst paying, and the least associated with skill and achievement in the public sphere of production. Economic dependence on men was a proper corollary of being only marginally important to major economic processes. And yet women—and especially married women, that traditionally most marginal group of all wage workers—have now become the principal source of energy necessary for the recent recomposition of economic activities.

As they moved so massively into the ranks of paid labor, women had to rearrange their lives in ways that were different from the traditional stereotype. Part of those rearrangements had to include a rethinking of expectations concerning relations to men. In short, a crack widened in the apparently sturdy wall of economic dependency. Women had to give up the idea that they were properly dependent on men for their sole support. And yet the nature of the jobs they were offered during the decade was totally incompatible with the eradication of economic dependence.

Consider, for example, the issue of part-time employment. A dramatic increase in the proportion of part-time work to all forms of work in an economy is undoubtedly both a sign and an effect of relatively important changes in the labor process itself, quite independent of the characteristics of part-time workers. By 1980 close to a quarter of all jobs in the private sector were part-time—an unprecedented 68 percent increase in the rate of part-time work since 1970.[22] In short, there is little doubt that some profound transformations took place in the organization of work to permit such a drastic shift of available jobs away from full-time and toward part-time work.

Despite what amounts to a structural change in the organization of work, the argument is frequently advanced that the increase in part-time jobs reflects the workers' preference rather than changes in the labor process itself. According to this reasoning, part-time work has increased because women are the new employees and because they prefer part-time work, given their domestic responsibilities. Indeed men took considerably fewer of the disproportionately large numbers of part-time jobs to appear between 1970 and 1980: 1.6 million went to men as compared to slightly more than 3 million that went to women. Countering this argument, though, is the fact that men and women increased their part-time work almost at the same rate. Of the total number of women who worked part-time in 1980, 25.8 percent would not have been expected had the 1970 rates for women merely been maintained. Of the total number of men working part-time in 1980, 24.8 percent would not have been expected, given 1970 rates for men (see table 7). In short, both men and

22. *Employment and Earnings*, vol. 17, no. 7 (January 1971), tables A23, A24, vol. 28, no. 7 (January 1981), tables 8, 35.

women demonstrated equally a substantial growth in the degree to which they accepted part-time work. This strongly suggests that the growth in overall part-time labor, rather than rising from putative gender-based preferences, resulted from changes in the form and content of available work.

Nevertheless, men apparently have an upper limit on the degree to which they will engage in part-time work, a limit considerably lower than women's. Women are both socially and culturally assumed to be in a position to accept less than full-time work. Between 1970 and 1980, of the close to 6 million women who went into the labor force unexpectedly (that is, women who represent the disproportionate increase in women's labor force participation rate), 51 percent received only part-time work. Very surprisingly, however, married women alone cannot account for this growth. Of the 2.8 million married women who, in joining the work force, exceeded 1970 work force participation rates, just 28 percent took part-time work; of the women workers who did not live with husbands and entered the labor force at a rate that exceeded 1970 levels, however, 73 percent had taken part-time work by 1980.[23]

In sum, the degree to which work has ceased to be a matter of full-time employment cannot be explained exclusively by changes in work preferences. Men took a considerably greater proportion of the new

Table 7

Part-Time Employment, 1980

	Workers Employed Part-Time			
	Expected by 1970 Rates (Thousands)	Unexpected by 1970 Rates (Thousands)	% Unexpected	% of Total Unexpected Part-Time Workers
Women	8,756	3,045	25.8	65.5
Married	5,204	807	13.4	17.3
Unmarried	3,552	2,238	38.6	48.2
Men	4,846	1,601	24.8	34.5
Married	1,928	116	5.7	2.5
Unmarried	2,918	1,485	33.7	32.0
Total	13,602	4,646		

SOURCE.—*Employment and Earnings*, vol. 18, no. 7 (January 1971), tables A23, A24, vol. 28, no. 7 (January 1981), tables 8, 35.

23. Ibid. While teenagers were in part responsible for some of the growth in part-time work, the greatest proportion has gone to older women. Anne McDougall Young observes that teenagers are actually suffering unemployment because they are facing "competition with adult women for part-time jobs" ("Youth Labor Force Market Turning Point in 1982," *Monthly Labor Review* 106, no. 8 [August 1982]: 29–34).

part-time work than part-time labor rates in 1970 would have led one to expect, and women who did not live with husbands took on considerably more, proportional to their 1970 rates, than did married women living with husbands. Yet, of course, it was still married women who contributed a disproportionate share of part-time labor: though they formed just 28 percent of the total 1980 labor force, they constituted 34 percent of the part-time labor force.

The capacity to shift work from full-time to part-time, to be sure, was facilitated by the increased rates of employment of married women—of that there can be no question. Nevertheless, what facilitates an economic process is not to be confused with what initiates it. The substantial growth in part-time work reflects significant changes in the pattern of work itself and the terms on which dominant economic activities take place. The stretch out in operating hours accompanied by a relative decrease in wage costs—the service sector's key strategy for increasing production—has been influenced by a vast increase in part-time personnel.

A second feature of most new jobs to appear in the private economy over the past decade is that they yield the lowest wages. The vast majority of women workers labor in precisely those occupations that pay less than the average wage. Of the 30.6 million working women in 1980, 51 percent held jobs paying less than 66 percent of an average crafts worker's wage. Close to 90 percent of the women who unexpectedly entered paid labor between 1970 and 1980 found jobs in establishments that paid on average just sixty-three cents for every dollar paid elsewhere in the private economy—a decrease of almost 23 percent in the relative wage rates paid in those sectors that are the major employers of the new women workers.[24]

Much like the growth of part-time work and periodic employment, the unprecedented movement of women into the ranks of labor within these low-wage sectors facilitates fundamental changes in the character of work. One sign of those changes is the disappearance of the so-called family wage. Two or more jobs are now required to meet family financial needs.[25] Although it is often argued that this is the result of a rapid rise of prices relative to wages, the growth of two-earner families is also an effect of substantial changes in the structure of employment: the new jobs are in

24. *Employment and Earnings*, vol. 28, no. 9 (March 1981), tables B1, C2.
25. Martha May argues in "The Historical Problem of the Family Wage: The Ford Motor Company and the Five Dollar Day" (*Feminist Studies* 8, no. 2 [Summer 1982]: 399–424) that the majority of male workers throughout the twentieth century did not receive wages sufficient to support a family without at times having to send a second member of the family into the paid labor force. Be that as it may, the labor force participation rate of married women has been constantly below that of married men, increasing only during specific periods of crisis. The major source of additional workers was, of course, children. But this source has been eradicated by a variety of new child-rearing practices, labor laws, school attendance laws, and the like.

low-wage sectors, and there has been a resulting decline in the average wage. As we have seen, virtually all the new jobs between 1970 and 1980 were in sectors that paid less than average wages. Rising prices combined with the scarcity of well-paid work requires a family to do more paid work.

Compare, for example, the wages paid in the most rapidly expanding sectors to what the Bureau of Labor Statistics (BLS) defines as the "lower living standard"—an amount established as a benchmark against which eligibility for public assistance is determined.[26] (Should a family of four fall below this income level, it qualifies for a wide variety of government support programs, including admission to public housing projects, food stamp programs, programs for the distribution of surplus government food, and Medicaid.) In 1979 close to half of all working women found themselves in industries paying an average wage less than the bare minimum set by the BLS for a family of four. The two and a half million women working in eating and drinking places in 1979 found themselves in an industry that paid the average workers $151.37 per week less than the BLS minimum for a family of four. Another million and a half women worked in an industry—general merchandising—that paid its average worker $111 less per week than the amount a family of four needed to stay alive without government assistance, according to the BLS. Even in the financial, insurance, and real estate industries, which are relatively well paid in comparison to other service-sector industries, the average worker earned in 1979 nearly $46 a week less than the BLS minimum. Because the jobs most available to women pay less than an acceptable family wage, many fully employed women who head households remain poor despite their work efforts. In 1980 fully employed women heading households had a poverty rate almost three times that of husband-and-wife households and twice that of men who headed households without a wife present.[27]

To be sure, most of the women working in these sectors were not exclusively responsible for the support of a family of four. That is not the point. The point is that those industries most responsible for employment growth pay a wage rate that absolutely requires the recipient of those wages to find additional resources in order to support a family above the poverty level. And it is this condition that is largely responsible for the "feminization of poverty." This is not an entirely novel set of circumstances; these service-sector industries have historically paid considerably less than the going rate and certainly less than a family wage. Two related developments are what is novel.

First, these low-wage industries are growing at a rate that far out-

26. For a discussion of the construction of family budgets at the BLS, see *Monthly Labor Review* 92, no. 4 (April 1969): 5.

27. Commission on Civil Rights (n. 1 above), pp. 22–23.

strips the growth of other higher-waged sectors, and, second, a considerable portion of economic activities have been transferred to them. Thus, these industries have taken on an importance far beyond that which they may have had in the past. Their characteristically low-wage levels and their less than full-time, less than all-year, work now play a role in the private economy far different from that played in an earlier period during which goods-producing firms were expanding.

What might have been taken as aberrations in more normal employment practices in an earlier period have now become the dominant patterns in the 1980s. These patterns in turn depend on the availability of a labor force prepared to continue to accept less than optimal employment. And here is the basic contradiction. The expansion of the economy over the recent decade has had as its major premise the availability of workers who will act as though they perform only marginal, inconsequential labor. Because of the social relationships and expectations that stereotyped them as nonwage workers in the past, women are expected to accept less than standard employment—employment that is frequently less than full time, considerably less stable, and substantially lower paid. Yet once this labor force is utilized as a labor force, the nonmarket conditions that shaped these expectations—conditions most frequently associated with being outside the main currents of economic development—are by definition fundamentally eroded.

Conclusion

Although the availability of women to the labor force has required a massive shift in many women's expectations—they must think of themselves as workers in addition to their other social identities—women wage earners must consider their domestic roles the most salient ones in shaping their experiences at work if they are to play their assigned parts. While this has always been the case for wage-earning women at least during the past century, something entirely new has occurred that has become the central feature for the decade's most decisive economic developments.[28] Now, rather than actually being a marginal sector of the overall labor force, women constitute upwards of 40 percent of it. Much more important than their mere numbers, however, is the fact that women constitute by far the bulk of that labor that was and is necessary to accommodate the massive shifts in employment practices that were necessary for the con-

28. See, e.g., Alice Kessler-Harris's discussion in "Stratifying by Sex: Understanding the History of Working Women," in *Labor Market Segmentation*, ed. Richard C. Edwards, Michael Reich, and David M. Gordon (Lexington, Mass.: D. C. Heath & Co., 1973), pp. 217–42.

tinued profitable operation of the fastest-growing sectors of the private economy.

Had women not increased the rate at which they worked for wages, these changes in typical practices now characteristic of the private economy could not have taken place—at least in the manner they did. But this is hardly evidence that the presence of women caused such changes unless one wants to accept the untenable position that a consequence of an economic event can be equated with its cause. The growth in the number of jobs in the service sector relative to growth in other sectors and women's greater willingness (or greater need, as the case may be) to work for wages are in all likelihood two separate aspects of deeper social and economic developments over the recent and not-so-recent past.

Nevertheless, the increased rate at which women became available for wage work during the recent decade and the distinctive constraints on employment practices in the fastest-growing sectors of the economy that absorbed this new labor meant that the development of these industries, their daily operating premises, and their characteristic labor processes are all predicated on a supply of workers who are presumably involved primarily in nonmarket institutions. Therefore, to the extent that the growth and relative importance of these industries are central to the transformations in typical economic practices in the nation, the set of social arrangements characterizing women's lives as nonwage workers are incorporated into the very grounds of the economy. These social arrangements are precisely those that support the assumption that women are properly considered a cheaper and more dispensable labor force and are less dependent on their wages than are male workers.

In short, women's poverty and continued economic dependency are now the central operating premises of the most rapidly expanding sectors of the U.S. economy today and form the basis for the profound changes that have characterized that economy over the past decade.

But this situation is highly unstable. Women's earlier economic dependency arose under entirely different circumstances and was strongly related to conditions very different from those facing women today: women then either excluded themselves entirely from the more visible aspects of paid labor or faced severe social degradation.[29] Individual poverty and its companion, economic dependency on men, were the concomitants of the social conditions women were required by social convention to deal with in their daily lives. It is no surprise that necessity

---

29. Women took in boarders and lodgers, did laundry and alterations for pay, did typing, and took in others' children for pay—and thus "didn't work." Today's equivalents are the rapidly growing home industries where women once more are pressed into service without appearing to be "in" the labor force.

was transformed into a virtue. The so-called cult of true womanhood elevated such poverty and dependency to the level of a societal good.

Under contemporary conditions, all that has changed; but the economic dependency remains the same. Poverty and dependency are now the results not of women's relative exclusion from the wage labor force but of the very conditions under which women are actively incorporated into its ranks. The ideology of domesticity previously used to support the nonwaged roles of women must now be invoked to support the conditions of their waged work. But the ideology wears thin under such circumstances. Rather than being obscured behind the veil of a biological destiny that seems to be somewhat easily associated with housekeeping and child rearing, the pauperization of women and their continued dependency on either men or the state are now clearly linked to profound economic developments.

Department of Sociology
State University of New York at Binghamton

Toil and Trouble: Women Workers and Unemployment Compensation

Diana M. Pearce

Discussions of women's poverty almost inevitably concentrate on income replacement for families for whom the institution of marriage has failed. In concrete terms, that has meant maintaining a strong focus on strengthening such income transfer programs as child support and welfare. Overlooked is the way labor market institutions contribute to the creation of poverty through their failure to provide sufficient income to all workers—and particularly through their inequitable treatment of women. The majority of those women who maintain households alone work, yet a fifth of them still have incomes below the poverty level. Since over 90 percent of the women on welfare have worked or are currently working,[1] it can be said that only when both marriage and the labor market fail to provide sufficient income do mothers turn to welfare. Realizing how labor market institutions contribute to women's poverty is, then, as much a key to understanding the dynamics of the feminization of poverty as is the study of welfare.

Women, who have always had a disproportionate share of unemployment and underemployment, have nonetheless been underrepresented among recipients of unemployment benefits and services because unemployment insurance (UI) was created with male family heads and full-time workers as its intended recipients. The situation of women workers, particularly working mothers, by virtue of their patterns of labor force participation, do not fit this breadwinner model. As a result, from its very

1. Joel F. Handler and Ellen J. Hollingsworth, *The Deserving Poor: A Study of Welfare Administration* (New York: Academic Press, 1971), p. 138.

beginnings, UI has excluded many women in the labor market and forced many to accept poverty-level wages and/or welfare, thus making their position as workers even more precarious and vulnerable.

Unemployment compensation grew out of a new understanding that began to develop in the early years of this century that joblessness is sometimes an industrial phenomenon and not always the result of personal failings. In short, some jobless poor lacked employment although willing and able to work.[2] Together with other groups, such as the blind, widows, and the aged, whose lack of income was not their own making, unemployed workers thus came to be seen as a new type of the deserving poor.

This view of the unemployed regular worker as an innocent victim profoundly shaped the character of unemployment compensation. Its punishing aspects were aimed not at workers, who were victims after all, but at employers, the alleged perpetrators of poverty resulting from unemployment. From its beginnings, right up to the present, UI sought to induce owners and managers to "regularize" their employment policies by assessing the highest payments to the unemployed workers' compensation fund from those firms that laid off the highest number of workers.[3]

At the same time it was realized that if employers were to respond to this system by stabilizing employment within their establishments, many regular workers would still lose their jobs as a result of changes in consumer demand, the development of new products and processes, skill obsolescence, business failure, and general economic downturns. In these situations, not only were the workers innocent victims who suffered personally, but society as a whole was also a victim in being deprived of their skills and experience. Thus the UI program has always had as a central objective the goal of helping displaced workers maintain or regain their status in the labor market. This objective was accomplished by three programmatic forms of assistance: help in finding new jobs; training in new, more marketable skills; and income support during periods of joblessness. Each of these programs is important to the others: cushioning the impact of unemployment through income support also subsidizes a longer job search and provides time to develop new job skills, so that workers may return to employment at levels comparable to the ones that they had left. In the early years, there was great fear that the unemployed would become "unemployables." Even in the 1970s, analysts of the system were pointing out that the job search requirements of unemployment

2. U.S. Congress, House Committee on Labor, *Statement of Juliet Stuart Poyntz to the Commission to Study Social Insurance and Unemployment, Hearings in H.J. Res. 159*, 64th Cong., 1st sess., 1916, 46.

3. Daniel Nelson, *Unemployment Insurance: The American Experience, 1915–35* (Madison: University of Wisconsin Press, 1969), pp. 20ff.

compensation help keep the unemployed "in" the labor market, that is, help maintain their identity as workers.[4]

Although motivated by sympathy toward the unemployed "victim," unemployment compensation was also grounded in society's self-interest. As Juliet Stuart Poyntz stated in 1916, "When the factory shuts down the manufacturer takes care of his machinery, keeps it under shelter, oils it, and covers it up, so that it will not deteriorate. With his living machinery he does not do this. He can only turn his workers out into the street to swell the army of unemployed labor."[5] From society's point of view, unemployment compensation served the dual purpose of preserving skilled labor for later reemployment and of preventing unemployed workers from joining the rabble.

Unemployment compensation and related programs were never meant to be used by all the unemployed. In fact, in the 1930s the term "unemployed" did not refer, as it generally does today, to all who wish to work but cannot find a job. Instead, the unemployed and the programs developed for them were restricted to those who had proven themselves to be full-time, regular workers of long standing.

What about others among the poor, many of whom also found themselves without work or with too little work to support themselves and their families? In the 1930s, these unemployed were referred to as casual workers, and it was assumed that they would work regularly only if compelled to do so. The problem they presented to society was not the loss of their skills (which by definition were negligible) but rather the potential political threat they posed. For as nonworking, able-bodied paupers they might foment unrest, riots, and even revolution. For casual workers, then, the main objective of public policy was to get such workers into any job that would put them under the control and discipline of the world of work. Likewise, since their unemployment was of their own making, and since there was no societal or individual benefit to be derived from providing relatively generous support and services, help for unemployed casual workers was (and still is) stigmatizing, penurious, and punishing. The dole and work relief—or in today's parlance, welfare and workfare—are variations on the traditional programs for the pauper: the "undeserving" able-bodied but nonworking poor.

The creation of a two-tiered, highly differentiated and highly unequal income support system for these two groups of the unemployed was in no sense accidental, as table 1 demonstrates. Nor was it incremental; unemployment compensation was created "out of whole cloth" to deal with the problem of unemployment-caused poverty that early twentieth-

---

4. Raymond Munts and Irwin Garfinkel, *The Work Disincentive Effects of Unemployment Insurance* (Kalamazoo, Mich.: W. E. Upjohn Institute, 1974), p. 18.
5. *Statement of Juliet Stuart Poyntz*, p. 47.

century policymakers believed to be distinctly different in origin, effect, and cure from the problem of poverty and pauperism generally. In table 1 these differences are highlighted. On the one hand, we have unemployment compensation which was developed for a limited group of regular workers and was designed to help them and society deal with the capri-

Table 1

The Dual Welfare System: A Comparison of Programs Targeted at Workers

	Primary Sector (Unemployment Compensation)	Secondary Sector (Relief/Welfare, Work Relief/ Workfare)
Clientele	Unemployed full-time, regular workers	Jobless casual workers
Type of social threat posed by unemployment	Economic disorder: waste of skills, waste of human beings who join the "unemployables"	Sociopolitical disorder: food riots, communism, underground or illegal economy
Cause of unemployment ..	Employer layoffs, industrial cycles, economic trends (leading to skill obsolescence)	Laziness, unwillingness to work, drug addiction, worker-caused firings, voluntary unemployment
Cure for unemployment ..	Provide short-term income support; provide related services in order to subsidize job search and optimize the match between worker and job	Force recipient either to take first available job or do public work (work relief/ workfare)
Means used to limit program expenses	Pass claimant on to work relief or welfare when limited benefits are exhausted; limit eligibility to those with "proven" attachment to work force	Set extremely low benefit levels; terminate benefits if claimant is able but unwilling to accept a job; stigmatize and degrade claimants
Examples of programs, policies, and services	State employment services; extended benefit programs (as well as regular state UI); Trade Adjustment Assistance act (provides aid to workers displaced by foreign competition)	WIN (Work Incentive Program); workfare; CWEP (Community Work Experience Program); some JTPA (Job Training and Partnership act) programs; Depression work relief, e.g., PWA (Public Works Administration); workhouses

ciousness of employers as well as the vicissitudes of the economy. On the other hand, we have a relief/welfare program that stands in stark contrast to this new treatment of the jobless poor: then and now, casual workers are viewed as being instigators rather than victims of their joblessness.

Women and Unemployment Compensation

Gender was not a salient issue in the debates on unemployment compensation. Since the word "men" was used generically, references to women (and these were rare) had to be explicit. But two powerful assumptions about gender and sex roles are nonetheless apparent: first, the "regular" workers for whom the program was designed were a group largely synonymous with male breadwinners, and second, women were nonworking dependents, or if workers, were "secondary" earners, a category that had a large overlap with that of casual workers. These assumptions predisposed unemployment compensation to exclude women—especially married women—from eligibility.

Almost all state laws that provided for dependents' allowances presumed that the male worker was the principal supporter of children (and/or wife). Some policymakers would even use UI to enhance the economic predominance of the male breadwinner; thus Joseph Becker recommends that dependents' allowances should be paid as part of UI, even though such provision takes on the character of welfare: "A strong case exists for improving the position of primary beneficiaries relative to the single and secondary beneficiaries."[6]

The access of a man to unemployment compensation was determined on the basis of his proven "attachment" to the labor force, although the amount might be increased to reflect his breadwinner status. In contrast, a woman's right to benefits was as much contingent on her marital status as on her work history; being a wife was prima facie evidence that one was a casual or secondary worker. Thus one of the first denials of benefits was upheld by a state board because the woman had an employed husband and was herself well dressed.[7]

Even in recent years some analysts have suggested that married women be given less benefits and others that wives be subject to stricter tests of their "availability" for work, on the presumption that they are less

6. Joseph M. Becker, "The Adequacy of Benefits in Unemployment Insurance," in *In Aid of the Unemployed*, ed. Joseph M. Becker (Baltimore: Johns Hopkins University Press, 1965), p. 94.

7. See Margaret M. Dahm and Phyllis H. Fineshriber, "Women in the Labor Force," in *Unemployment Compensation: Studies and Research* (Washington, D.C.: National Commission on Unemployment Compensation, 1980), p. 739.

committed to working. As with all monolithic views, what is accepted as truth—father is the major breadwinner—and what is actually true are never one and the same. Yet policies, unfortunately, are often more likely to reflect the myth than the actuality. In regard to women's, particularly mothers', eligibility for UI, policies reflect the paradoxical logic that, since women should not be working, those women who do are at best casual workers and therefore do not deserve the help through UI given the serious, regular (i.e., male, breadwinning) worker.

Unemployment compensation programs no longer discriminate in law or in practice against women, whether as women or as wives or mothers. But because of the mismatch between a program explicitly designed to aid only regularly employed male heads of households and a female work force whose labor market participation patterns differ fundamentally from that model, unemployment compensation is structurally biased against women. Consequently, women find themselves disqualified as claimants or allotted reduced benefits more often than men do. As a result, women experience poverty more often because they must rely on few or no benefits; they must take a job, any job; or they must turn to the impoverishing, stigmatizing, and compulsory work of the welfare world, or some combination of these. To understand how the structure of UI contributes to women's poverty, it is necessary to look in detail at women's labor force participation patterns, highlighting the difference between their experience and that of the regular worker/male breadwinners for whom UI was designed.

Women's Labor Force Participation Patterns

Despite a dramatic increase in participation and "attachment" to the paid labor force, women—particularly minority women and those solely responsible for children—occupy a disadvantaged position in the labor force. Three forms of disadvantage are particularly relevant to unemployment compensation: the disproportionate numbers of women who work part-time, the occupational segregation and concentration experienced by women, and the higher rate of unemployment and qualitatively different unemployment experience of women workers.

Women's part-time employment.—Part-time work accounts for one out of five jobs today and is particularly important for women workers, over one-fourth of whom work part-time. The proportion increases even more during economic downturns; thus, two-thirds of all workers employed during 1981 on an involuntary part-time basis cited reductions in their scheduled working hours as the cause.[8] Nonetheless, there is a trend

---

8. Sylvia Lazos Terry, "Work Experience, Earnings, and Family Income in 1981," *Monthly Labor Review* 106 (April 1983): 13–20, esp. 18.

toward more part-time jobs primarily in occupations and industries that have traditionally hired women. While many wage-earning mothers may "voluntarily" choose to work part-time, for others the ratio between the cost of after-school or full-time day care and women's wages has made it uneconomical for them to choose full employment. Women's desire—or need—for part-time work, their availability as a skilled but low-wage work force, and the increasing demand for relatively cheap services come together to reinforce the pattern of part-time, low wage employment for many women workers.

Women's occupational segregation and isolation.—Despite dramatic increases in the number of women working and in the sectoral shifts of economy over the last four decades, women continue to be highly concentrated in a few areas of employment. Forty percent of them are still found in ten traditionally female occupations: secretary, retail trade salesworker, bookkeeper, private household worker, elementary school teacher, waitress, typist, cashier, sewer/stitcher, and registered nurse.[9] The decrease in some service-sector job categories has been matched by increases in white-collar clerical jobs, but with no net improvement in the pattern of concentration and segregation of women workers in sex-stereotyped occupational ghettos.[10] Although some of these occupations (waitress, household worker, even nurse) are typically part-time jobs, they tend to have lower-than-average levels of unemployment. Nonetheless, the wages and earnings received by women in these occupations are so low that they are an important factor in the explanation of women's poverty, both directly because they provide such low incomes and indirectly because they make it difficult for women to meet the minimum earnings qualifications required to receive employment-related benefits.

Women's unemployment patterns before the 1980s.—The increased participation of women in the labor force has been matched by an increase in the number of women unemployed, but the proportion of women among the unemployed has always been slightly higher than that among the employed. Likewise, women's unemployment rate has historically been higher than men's, with the ratio between the two ranging from 1.09 to 1.46. While, as one would expect, women's unemployment rates rise and fall with the recessions and booms of the economy, they do so less than men's, neither descending as much in good times, nor ascending as much during recessions. In fact, in 1982, during the last and most severe recession in the last half-century, men's unemployment rates exceeded those of women for the first time.[11]

9. Dahm and Fineshriber, p. 738.

10. Barbara F. Reskin, "Sex Segregation in the Workplace," in *Sex Segregation in the Workplace: Trends, Explanations, Remedies,* ed. Barbara F. Reskin (Washington, D.C.: National Academy Press, 1984), pp. 1–8.

11. Bureau of Labor Statistics, *Employment and Earnings,* vol. 30, no. 2 (February 1983), table A2, p. 17.

This apparent "improvement," however, is misleading and reveals one qualitative difference in women's unemployment. Women are much more likely than men to leave the labor force altogether during bad times, with the resulting anomaly that the more women lose their jobs, the less their unemployment rises. Therefore, even though they are in fact unemployed, they are not counted as such but described officially instead as "not in the civilian labor force." Sometimes this group of people is referred to as "discouraged workers." Although the second term is imprecise and unofficial, it is probably more accurate than the first. S. L. Terry found that of workers jobless for more than a year, three-fourths were officially "out" of the labor force; nevertheless, the overwhelming majority stated that the main reason that they did not work was the lack of job opportunities.[12] This and other evidence from census-conducted surveys, as well as from studies and demonstration projects, suggests that many jobless women workers are better described as discouraged workers than as workers out of the labor force altogether.[13]

Even among those officially classified as unemployed, women are disadvantaged by a second qualitative difference in their unemployment. While about three-fourths of the men who suffer unemployment do so through losing a job, fewer than half the unemployed women do. On the contrary, over 40 percent of female job seekers have not recently, if ever, held a job—twice the proportion of men who are new entrants or re-entrants to the labor force. In fact, about 10 percent more men than women are technically unemployed but are not actively seeking a job because they already have one: they are either on layoff or expect to begin a new job within thirty days.[14] Obviously, having had a recent job is advantageous to the unemployed person, for it not only enhances one's prospects of regaining employment, but it makes one eligible for unemployment compensation and related job-training and job-placement programs.

Irregular employment, combined with several short or long spells of unemployment, has been termed by the U.S. Commission on Civil Rights as "intermittent employment." Using a criterion of three short spells of unemployment during the year, and/or one spell of fifteen weeks or longer, the commission found that 4.0 percent of white women, 8.1 percent of black women, and 7.5 percent of Hispanic women had experienced intermittent unemployment in 1981.[15] While the average for white

12. Terry, p. 19.

13. Leonard Goodwin, *Causes and Cures of Welfare: New Evidence on the Social Psychology of the Poor* (Lexington, Mass.: Lexington Books, 1983), pp. 1ff.

14. In January 1983, e.g., there were two and a half times more men than women who were unemployed because of layoff—1,986,000 and 792,000, respectively (Bureau of Labor Statistics, *Employment and Earnings*, vol. 30, no. 2 [February 1983], table A13).

15. Commission on Civil Rights, *Unemployment and Underemployment of Blacks, Hispanics, and Women*, Clearinghouse Publication no. 74 (Washington, D.C.: Government Printing Office, November 1982).

women was less than the 5.3 percent experienced by white males, it is likely that, if one took into account spells of time outside the labor force, in addition to time officially unemployed these numbers would be considerably higher for all women.

In the late sixties women maintaining households alone had unemployment rates that resembled those of married women. But as more of the former entered the labor force—60 percent of female family heads were there in 1983—this pattern gradually changed. The unemployment rates of married men and women have converged while those of women who head households with no spouse present have become consistently higher, as well as more resistant to improvement during expansionary periods.[16] Thus in January 1983, married men and married women (spouse present) had identical unemployment rates of 8.4, while women who maintained families alone had unemployment rates of 13.6 percent.[17]

For women, particularly those heading families, these higher unemployment rates are associated with high poverty rates for two reasons. First, the income loss is less likely to be compensated by income from other family members, and second, the income loss is less likely to be made up by unemployment compensation. Married couples are better able to cushion the economic hardship of a wife's unemployment through the income of a second earner: even in mid-1982, at the depth of the recession, three-fourths of unemployed wives were in families with an employed member.[18] In contrast, the percentage of unemployed female household heads with an employed family member has never exceeded 22 percent and was about 19 percent in mid-1982.[19] While only 11 percent of married-couple families with an unemployed member were poor in 1981, 18 percent of all families who experienced unemployment lived in poverty.[20]

Part-time employment is also tied to higher levels of poverty, not only because fewer working hours yield lower earnings but also because part-time workers suffer higher levels of unemployment. The combination of part-time employment and unemployment leads to the worst poverty; Terry found that families in which both occurred had a 1981 median family income of $15,600, and over a fifth were poor.[21]

Tables 2 and 3 illustrate the consequences of these different employment patterns as they are experienced by male and female household

16. Sarah Pisetzner Klein, "Trends in Employment and Unemployment in Families," *Monthly Labor Review* 106 (December 1983): 21–25.

17. Bureau of Labor Statistics, *Employment and Earnings*, vol. 30, no. 2 (February 1983), tables A9, A10.

18. Klein, p. 24.

19. Beverly Johnson and Elizabeth Waldman, "Most Women Who Maintain Families Receive Poor Labor Market Returns," *Monthly Labor Review* 106 (December 1983): 30–34.

20. Terry (n. 8 above), p. 15.

21. Ibid., p. 18.

Table 2

Male Work Patterns and Poverty Rates, by Race/Ethnicity of Householder, 1982

	All Races/Ethnicities			White			Black			Hispanic		
	Male House-holders*	Number in Poverty	Poverty Rate	Male House-holders*	Number in Poverty	Poverty Rate	Male House-holders*	Number in Poverty	Poverty Rate	Male House-holders*	Number in Poverty	Poverty Rate
Worked in 1982: ...	41,197 (80.4)	2,143	5.8	37,394 (80.7)	2,059	7.2	2,815 (75.5)	283	10.1	2,195 (85.6)	343	3.5
Full-time, all year†	30,063 (58.7)	959	3.2	27,561 (59.5)	858	3.1	1,890 (50.7)	81	4.3	1,469 (57.3)	118	8.0
Part-time, all year†	1,482 (2.9)	132	8.9	1,257 (2.7)	111	8.8	95 (2.5)	16	16.8	66 (2.6)	18	27.2
Full- or part-time, part year‡	9,652 (18.8)	1,322	13.7	8,576 (18.5)	1,090	12.7	830 (22.3)	186	22.4	660 (25.7)	207	31.4
Did not work in 1982	10,063 (19.6)	1,646	16.4	8,945 (19.3)	1,234	13.8	913 (24.5)	335	36.7	369 (14.4)	146	39.6
Total	51,260 (100)	4,059	7.9	46,339 (100)	3,292	7.1	3,728 (100)	618	16.6	2,564 (100)	489	19.1

Source.—U.S. Bureau of the Census, Money Income and Poverty Status of Families and Persons in the United States, 1982, Current Population Reports, ser. P-60, no. 140 (Washington, D.C.: Government Printing Office, July 1983).

Note.—All figures are given in thousands. Figures in parentheses are percentages. Totals may not add up due to rounding.
*Includes men in married-couple households, as well as those who head households alone.
†All year is defined as fifty to fifty-two weeks in 1982.
‡Part year is defined as one to forty-nine weeks in 1982.

Table 3

Female Work Patterns and Poverty Rates, by Race/Ethnicity of Householder, 1982

	All Races/Ethnicities			White			Black			Hispanic		
	Female House-holders*	Number in Poverty	Poverty Rate	Female House-holders*	Number in Poverty	Poverty Rate	Female House-holders*	Number in Poverty	Poverty Rate	Female House-holders*	Number in Poverty	Poverty Rate
Worked in 1982: ...	5,649 (59.7)	1,247	22.1	4,026 (61.9)	692	17.2	1,480 (54.1)	527	35.6	389 (50.7)	122	31.3
Full-time, all year†	3,277 (34.6)	224	6.8	2,385 (36.7)	104	4.4	808 (29.5)	111	13.7	208 (27.1)	20	9.6
Part-time, all year†	469 (5.0)	141	30.1	352 (5.4)	77	21.9	107 (3.9)	58	54.2	42 (5.5)	20	47.6
Full- or part-time, part year‡	1,903 (20.1)	882	46.3	1,289 (19.8)	511	39.6	565 (20.7)	358	63.4	139 (18.1)	82	59.0
Did not work in 1982	3,820 (40.3)	2,187	57.2	2,481 (38.1)	1,120	45.2	1,254 (45.9)	1,008	80.4	378 (49.3)	303	80.2
Total	9,469 (100)	3,434	36.3	6,507 (100)	1,813	27.9	2,734 (100)	1,535	56.1	767 (100)	425	55.4

SOURCE.—U.S. Bureau of the Census, *Money Income and Poverty Status of Families and Persons in the United States, 1982*, Current Population Reports, ser. P-60, no. 140 (Washington, D.C.: Government Printing Office, July 1983).

NOTE.—All figures are given in thousands. Figures in parentheses are percentages. Totals may not add up due to rounding.

*Includes only those women heading households alone.

†All year is defined as fifty to fifty-two weeks in 1982.

‡Part year is defined as one to forty-nine weeks in 1982.

heads. First, it should be noted that the proportion of women who did not work at all was twice that of men (two-fifths vs. one-fifth), resulting in very high levels of poverty for those families, particularly for minority families. Second, among those who worked, a much smaller proportion of female household heads was able to work at full-time jobs for the entire year. The part-time and/or part-year employment pattern of women household heads contributes to a higher incidence of poverty among their families than among those of working male household heads. Among the latter, fewer than 6 percent have poverty-level incomes. Perhaps most ironically, the poverty incidence among families of white male householders who did not work at all was almost identical to that experienced by the families of black women heads of households who worked full-time for the whole year; in both cases, about one in seven of these families is poor. Black women's wages are depressed by race and sex discrimination,[22] and the impact of the white male household head's unemployment on the family's income is often cushioned by other family members' earnings, but these factors do not provide a complete explanation. Theoretically, income transfers provide an important shield against poverty for families with insufficient earnings; most of these are public transfers, including welfare, unemployment compensation, disability payments, and pensions. Although women have generally had a disproportionate share of unemployment, they have been underrepresented among recipients of unemployment compensation. As described above their patterns of labor force participation do not fit that of the regular worker/male breadwinner for whom the unemployment compensation system was designed, and as a result they receive lesser amounts or no benefits at all. I will consider next exactly how this happens. In particular, I will examine how earnings eligibility, regulations regarding "domestic quits," disqualification rules, pregnancy discrimination, sexual harassment, and requirements on availability, ability, and willingness to work are translated into a denial of benefits and/or disadvantaged status under UI for women workers.

Women Workers and UI Qualification Requirements

Earnings Eligibility

Many more people consider "going on unemployment" than in fact do. In 1979, there were 194.4 million contacts with unemployment com-

---

22. Commission on Civil Rights, *A Growing Crisis: Disadvantaged Women and Their Children*, Clearinghouse Publication no. 78 (Washington, D.C.: Government Printing Office, May 1983).

pensation offices, but only 20.2 million claims were filed. Among these claimants, over four million were found to be ineligible; almost half had either been fired or had left their last job "voluntarily," and another third were either not available or not able to work or had refused suitable work.[23] Since no records are kept on denied claims, it is not possible to know whether women or minorities are disproportionately denied benefits. The only study made so far that examines this question found that in South Carolina the number of minority and women applicants who were found to be ineligible was larger than would be expected by chance.[24]

Of course, word of such barriers as minimum earnings requirements and the exclusion of certain occupations from eligibility, whether accurate or not, may discourage many of the unemployed from applying. Thus it is necessary to look at the numbers of men as compared to the numbers of women who *would* be denied UI claims because their earnings and/or hours worked are too low, regardless of how many actually go through the application process and are denied. Because each state has its own requirements, one would have to make calculations based on more than fifty different sets of figures—if indeed the data were available by gender on both earnings distributions and UI claimants. However, a rough idea of women's disadvantage can be gauged by taking one state, Virginia, as an example. There in mid-1981, eligibility for UI required minimum earnings of $2,200 during two quarters, or about $4,400 for a steady worker on an annual basis. In 1982, nationally, over 33 percent of women workers as compared to 19 percent of men workers earned less than $4,400 annually.[25] The proportions for both sexes are probably higher in Virginia, where wages are lower, but the differential would be roughly the same. Thus by a rough estimate at least one out of three women workers (and one out of five men workers) would not meet the minimum earnings requirements in Virginia. While each state has different sets of requirements concerning both minimum earnings and minimum work time, it is probable that in most states substantially more women than men workers would find that they are ineligible on a minimum earnings basis alone.

23. National Commission on Unemployment Compensation, *Unemployment Compensation: Final Report* (Washington, D.C.: National Commission on Unemployment Compensation, July 1980), p. 46.

24. South Carolina Employment Security Commission, Research and Analysis Unit, "Monetary Validity of UI Claims: Related to Sex and Race of Claimants" (Columbia: South Carolina Employment Security Commission, March 1982).

25. U.S. Bureau of the Census, *Money Income and Poverty Status of Families and Persons in the United States, 1982*, Current Population Reports, ser. P-60, no. 140 (Washington, D.C.: Government Printing Office, 1983).

Disqualifications for Voluntary Quits

As described above, UI was set up to protect workers against unemployment that was not of their doing. Logic suggests that those workers
who quit voluntarily, or were fired because of misconduct, are not innocent victims and should therefore not be eligible for UI support. This
logic separates all unemployment into two clear-cut categories, distinguished by whether the employee or the employer caused the loss of the
job, which in turn determines whether the employee qualifies for UI
benefits. The advent of women workers in large numbers, more and more
of whom are married and/or mothers, muddied this distinction; many
women leave work because they can no longer reconcile their domestic
obligations with their work obligations. While some of these "domestic
quits," such as leaving to join a spouse in another city, are clearly the result
of the employee's initiative, others, such as changing the employee's shift
to hours in which day care is unavailable, are just as clearly the result of
employer action.[26] Nonetheless all domestic quits were specifically excluded from UI coverage by twenty-three states in 1971. The passage in
1972 by both houses of Congress of the Equal Employment Opportunity
Act, however, caused a dramatic change, and today only six states specifically forbid UI benefits to workers who have quit because of domestic
obligations. Since one study has estimated that women make up 99 percent of those disqualified because theirs is a domestic quit, this decline
might seem to be advantageous to them.[27]

Unfortunately, the situation is neither that simple nor that positive.
First, there are still about twenty-eight states that rule as ineligible any quit
that is not work-connected, thus including all domestic quits. In most
states, moreover, some types of quits, even when work-related, are
domestic in nature and thus de facto grounds for disqualification, while
others are highly circumscribed. For example, if an employee seeks a
transfer to accompany a spouse or to obtain child care, and its denial or
unavailability leads her to leave her job, virtually all states deny benefits.
In regard to other problems created by changes in job sites or hours that
are disruptive to domestic obligations, quits are considered involuntary
only if they were initiated by the employer and constitute a departure
from the original terms of employment or contract.

Even states that do not automatically disqualify anyone on the
grounds that a quit is not work-related make it difficult in practice to
qualify. For example, California and Colorado statutes do not rule out

26. There are four major types of domestic quits: leaving a job to marry, leaving to
join a spouse, leaving due to lack of child care (including care of teenagers), and leaving to
fulfill family obligations, as in the case of a family member's death or illness.

27. From Alice Wallace v. Unemployment Compensation Board of Review (1979),
quoted in Margaret M. Dahm and Phyllis Fineshriber, "Disqualifications for Quits to Meet
Family Obligations," in *Unemployment Compensation* (n. 7 above), p. 18.

problems connected with marriage, child care, and emergency domestic obligations as justifications for leaving employment, but application of the eligibility tests in those states virtually always results in disqualification. In order to qualify for unemployment compensation in other states, such as New York and Nevada, the worker must have unsuccessfully sought to make alternative arrangements for child care, family members' emergencies, and so on, before leaving her job.

Whether work-related or not, moreover, domestic quits tend to be held up to stricter scrutiny than other voluntary quits; the Pennsylvania Court took note of this difficulty, pointing out that "by effectively preventing persons who quit their jobs for domestic reasons from showing that their resignations were motivated by necessitous and compelling causes, whereas persons quitting their jobs for any other reason may so argue, the statute establishes a classification which bears no rational relationship to any legitimate State interest and hence violates the guarantee of equal protection."[28] Ironically, however, it is men who are most likely to be successful in establishing the legitimacy of domestic quits; of the dozen court cases described in detail by Margaret Dahm and Phyllis Fineshriber (selected from the forty they reviewed), the two that concerned male claimants were also the only two in which the claimant won. This was more than mere coincidence. One of the reasons is clear from the referees' reasoning in the Hawaii case. It involved a male claimant who left his job to care for his ailing mother. The decision was that "leaving work is considered to be good cause where it is for a real, substantial, or compelling reason, or a reason which would cause a reasonable and prudent worker, genuinely and sincerely desirous of maintaining employment, to take similar action."[29] In short, male workers are considered a priori to be attached to the work force and not in danger of leaving altogether even if they "voluntarily" leave a specific job. Thus the stricter scrutiny accorded domestic quit claimants is in part triggered by the gender stereotype that presumes less commitment to paid work on the part of women workers.

A second reason that male claimants are more likely to win domestic quit claims is that, as "secondary" workers, women rarely qualify for the "major or sole support" exceptions to domestic quit disqualifications. Once again, women's situation is ironic: recipients of lower wages because they work fewer hours in order to carry out familial obligations, they are further discriminated against as "secondary" workers and denied benefits.[30] Put another way, the waiver of disqualification in the case of workers who quit for domestic reasons when they are the sole or major

28. Ibid.
29. Dahm and Fineshriber, "Disqualifications for Quits to Meet Family Obligations."
30. This is similar to the process of "blaming the victim" described by William Ryan, *Blaming the Victim* (New York: Pantheon Books, 1965).

support of their families exposes the assumption hidden within the unemployment compensation system: it is designed to help male breadwinners.

Sexual Harassment

Sexual harassment can lead a woman to quit a job. Because it is "voluntary," such a quit can disqualify one from receiving UI benefits. For even though a number of states have explicitly exempted such quits from disqualification, little is known about the number of quits actually necessitated by sexual harassment. Women's unwillingness to come forward is understandable given the barriers to explaining a case. Perhaps the oddest statute is that of Illinois, in which a claimant who quits because of sexual harassment will not be disqualified if her former employer knows of the situation. (What happens if the employer is the perpetrator of the harassment is not clear.) In general, despite increased awareness about the misery caused by sexual harassment and about its legal definition as a form of sex discrimination, unknown numbers of women are forced to deal with this problem by leaving their jobs. Many choose not to state their reasons for quitting because they fear an employer's reprisals and/or because they find it difficult to document the "necessitous and compelling" nature of the sexual harassment that led to their "voluntarily" leaving the job; their silence disqualifies them from receipt of benefits. Although clearly victims in their unemployment, their exclusion from UI punishes them and not the harassers.

Pregnancy

Much of the discrimination against pregnant workers has been eliminated through the federal Pregnancy Discrimination Act. Nonetheless, many women are either misled by their employers or misinformed about their rights. Many pregnant women, forced by employer policy to take maternity leave without pay, do not realize that they are eligible for unemployment benefits as long as they are willing and able to work and available for it. They also, of course, must be given the same benefits that their employers give to any employee with a temporary disability.

Previous Work Requirements

Many women workers are at a disadvantage because of their "port of entry" to unemployment. They have been engaged in some form of work that UI does not recognize or does not cover: as homemaker, as unpaid family worker in a business or on a farm, as a student or a self-employed worker, as someone working on commission or someone in low-paid or seasonal work. Lacking recent experience in the paid labor force as well as knowledge of the job market, they are labeled as "new" or reentrant members of the labor force, which disqualifies them from both the services such as job placement and the benefits accorded the "regular" worker.

Available/Able/Willing to Work Requirements

Since one goal of unemployment compensation is to facilitate return to paid employment, a fundamental condition imposed on all UI recipients is that they must be available, able, and willing to work. This stricture is mitigated somewhat by the provision that claimants may hold out, at least for a while, for suitable work—that is, for a job commensurate with their skills, experience, and previous pay; situated within a reasonable distance; and offering reasonable working conditions. Even so, women find themselves put at a disadvantage in three ways by the "available/able/willing" to work requirement.

First, the same events that lead a woman to leave her job may make her, or be presumed to make her, unavailable for work. For example, if a woman leaves a job because her employer reassigned her to night shift hours for which she was unable to arrange child care, her resignation may place her in a category of one unavailable for employment because in many states, a claimant must be "available" to work at all hours. Limiting availability to certain hours or days of the week renders one ineligible for benefits.

Second, one of the most widespread problems faced by women workers turns on the issue of part-time employment. Although many women have worked enough hours or have earned enough during part-time employment to be eligible for unemployment compensation, they are denied benefits because their "availability" for work is limited to part-time employment. This requirement, of course, harks back to the original presumption that only full-time employees have proved their attachment to the work force, and conversely, that part-time or part-year workers have by definition a tenuous commitment to work and thus deserve "casual" (now "secondary") worker status. Whether that status is by choice, or reflects commitment to home or community, is irrelevant. Perhaps most ironic, while the UI claimant must be looking for and available for full-time work, refusal of otherwise suitable part-time work is grounds for ineligibility, as it presumably indicates a lack of willingness to work.

As with other aspects of unemployment compensation, the law is blind to the needs of workers who also have family commitments. Thus a worker can refuse a job on the "graveyard shift" because it is impossible to get public transportation at those hours or because the working conditions during that time are dangerous but not because she cannot arrange child care. A worker can refuse a job because it is too far away from his or her residence but not because it is too far away from a child's day care center.[31] The law is also quite conservative; dissatisfaction with the low wages of cafeteria workers is not deemed a good rationale for an unemployed cafeteria worker to seek other, better-paying employment, particularly if the dissatisfied worker refuses an available cafeteria job after several months of unemployment.

Women and the Distribution of UI Benefits

Given this mismatch between women's work patterns and the assumptions and requirements of unemployment compensation, it is not surprising that women's share of unemployment insurance is always less than their share of unemployment. And the gap has been widening in the 1980s; in the last decade, the proportion of unemployed women workers receiving UI has dropped from almost 60 percent to 40 percent.[32]

As a direct effect of the lower wages and smaller earnings of women workers, even those women who receive UI benefits get less than men do. Further, in 1982, while 22 percent of all male claimants receive the highest benefit bracket of $175–$199 per week, only 3 percent of the women claimants are so fortunate.[33] Although the gender difference in the median UI benefit may not seem great, on an annual basis the average women's unemployment benefit is below the poverty level for a single person, while the average man's benefit is above the poverty level for two people. Gary Burtless found that even among families receiving income from the primary-sector unemployment compensation program, those maintained by women alone are much more likely to remain poor than are families with a male head of household. While 29 percent of poor households headed by men were lifted out of poverty through the help

31. Actual cases cited in Virginia Employment Commission, *Restructuring Virginia's Unemployment Compensation System: A Program for Solvency* (Richmond: Commonwealth of Virginia, 1981).

32. See U.S. Bureau of Labor, *ES203 Report: Characteristics of the Insured Unemployed* (Washington, D.C.: Government Printing Office), tables 34 and 32.

33. See U.S. Bureau of Labor, *ETA5159 Report: Claims and Payment Activities* (Washington, D.C.: Government Printing Office), table 85, for weekly average benefit amounts by state; and Unemployment Insurance Service, "Determination of Differences Between Regular UI Claimants and FSC Beneficiaries" (Continuous Wage and Benefit History Project, Employment Training Administration, U.S. Department of Labor, February 1983), table IVB, for data on the base period earnings of regular UI claimants in Georgia, Idaho, Missouri, Nevada, New Mexico, New York, North Carolina, Pennsylvania, South Carolina, Utah, Washington, and Wisconsin.

given by UI, only 16 percent of poor households headed by women experienced the same improvement after obtaining UI.[34]

The trend in the 1980s reflects a general decrease in UI coverage; the Center for Policy and Budget Priorities estimates that only about one-third of unemployed workers were receiving unemployment compensation in 1983.[35] Thus the recent decreases in UI coverage that impinge on all unemployed workers reflect a deliberate choice not to invoke extended benefits even for those workers who can show long-term employment.[36] But women, who have always been underrepresented among UI recipients, became even more so in the 1980s, and their benefits were consistently lower than men's. Thus the last few years have seen an exacerbation of their unequal and disadvantaged status rather than an alleviation of it.

Women's Poverty and the Dual Welfare System

Unemployment compensation is one kind of transfer received by families with insufficient earned income. Together with welfare it forms a two-sector, or dual, welfare system. While each sector has its own history, benefit system, and recipient clientele, the two are not only very different but also decidedly unequal. The primary sector includes benefits that are usually, although not necessarily, work-related, such as unemployment compensation, workers compensation, and veterans pensions. These are given as a right, are considered to be "earned," and are not withheld because of lack of need. Benefit amounts are often determined by the previous levels of the recipient's—but not the family's—income, regardless of "need." One does not need to be impoverished to receive primary-sector benefits, nor is one stigmatized or left impoverished by their receipt.

Secondary-sector benefits are the direct opposite. As their receipt is usually means-tested, the family as well as the recipient must become demonstrably poor even to be eligible to receive them. Savings must be exhausted, and property reduced to the bare minimum necessary for survival. Terms of receipt and amount of the benefit change according to time, place, and the vagaries of politics. There is a constant: benefit levels are set at or below minimum standards of need and fall even lower during periods of high inflation.

34. U.S. Congress, House Committee on Ways and Means, *Testimony of Gary Burtless for the Committee on Ways and Means*, 98th Cong., 1st sess., October 18, 1983.

35. Center on Budget and Policy Priorities, "Unemployed and Unprotected: A Report on the Status of Unemployment Insurance" (Center on Budget and Policy Priorities, Washington, D.C., October 1983, mimeographed).

36. Gary Burtless, "Why Is Insured Unemployment So Low?" *Brookings Papers on Economic Activity* 1 (1983): 246.

Table 4

Primary- and Secondary-Sector Benefits and Poverty Rates of Household Heads, by Race and Sex, 1978

	All Welfare Recipients		Primary Sector*		Secondary Sector†	
	%	Poverty Rate	%	Poverty Rate	%	Poverty Rate
Male householders:‡	85.4	5.3	88.8	4.3	40.3	36.1
White	79.2	4.7	81.5	4.0	30.2	35.7
Black	6.2	11.8	7.3	7.2	10.1	36.9
Female householders:§	14.6	31.4	11.2	15.1	59.6	71.2
White	10.4	23.5	8.9	10.4	28.7	66.8
Black	4.2	50.6	2.3	32.3	30.9	75.8

SOURCE.—U.S. Bureau of the Census, *Characteristics of the Population below the Poverty Level, 1978,* Current Population Reports, ser. P-60, no. 124 (Washington, D.C.: Government Printing Office, 1978), tables 37, 38.
*Includes unemployment and workers compensation and veterans benefits.
†Includes all types of cash public assistance (AFDC, General Assistance, etc.).
‡Includes men in married-couple families, as well as those who head households alone.
§Includes only those women heading households alone.

Women, particularly minority women, are greatly underrepresented in the primary sector. While black women make up only 2 percent of the recipients of primary-sector benefits, over 60 percent of the recipients of secondary-sector benefits, primarily welfare, are women—half of them black women who head households. The effect of this skewed distribution on women's experience of poverty is apparent in table 4. While only about 5 percent of the families who received some income from the primary sector are poor, two-thirds of the families receiving income through secondary-sector transfer programs remain poor.

Conclusions

As one observer has noted, unemployment compensation is an extension of the hierarchically ordered wage system.[37] It is, therefore, a publicly subsidized fringe benefit that, like almost all fringe benefits, only goes to relatively privileged workers: male breadwinners with "regular" work patterns. Those who suffer labor market disadvantages—women and minorities—will have those disadvantages reinforced and even intensified by UI. Being denied the job-hunting time and supportive services afforded to more privileged workers, some of the less fortunate become

37. Joseph M. Becker, *Unemployment Insurance Financing: An Evaluation* (Washington, D.C.: American Enterprise Institute for Public Policy Research, 1981), p. 135.

discouraged, some impoverished, and some turn to welfare programs that give women workers even less help than UI does. The experiences of these women have a profound effect on all women workers. Inadequate protection against the loss of income through unemployment makes women workers as a class much more vulnerable to employer exploitation.

Some time ago, Harold Wilensky observed that private fringe benefits run counter to the egalitarian trends in the distribution of public transfers. The availability of private fringe benefits also undermines public support for more universal, income inequality–reducing programs.[38] The present character of unemployment compensation shows that Wilensky's argument should be modified, for UI is the worst of both worlds: it is a publicly supported set of fringe benefits that reinforces rather than decreases the inequality produced in the labor market. Moreover, the program gives precedence to the economic security and status maintenance of some of the jobless, while providing little or no support for the majority of the unemployed or their families. As long as we have income support systems that are based on distinctions—for example, between deserving and undeserving workers, or between regular workers and casual or secondary workers—we will have systems that reinforce the inequality experienced by women and minorities. Just as the court declared separate, dual systems to be inherently unequal in the field of education, we must recognize that the dual system of income support is likewise inherently unequal. Only a single and universal system of income support for the unemployed can function with real justice, and only with universal systems can we truly be a society of opportunity for all.

Center for National Policy Review
Catholic University Law School

38. Harold L. Wilensky, "The Problems and Prospects of the Welfare State," in *Industrial Society and Social Welfare*, ed. Harold L. Wilensky and Charles Lebeaux (New York: Free Press, 1965), pp. xv–xvi.

Comparable Worth:
Toward Theory and Practice
in the United States

Roslyn L. Feldberg

Poverty among women in the United States has become more acute, more visible, and more widespread as women's economic responsibility for themselves and their children has increased. This impoverishment is associated with the dramatic rise of single-parent, female-headed households with children. But it is not confined to single mothers with young children. All female-headed households are more likely to be poor. While the rate of poverty among families headed by white males decreased by 51 percent between 1960 and 1981, the number of persons in poor female-headed families increased by 54 percent. Among female-headed families with children under eighteen, 68 percent of the black family members were poor, 67 percent of Hispanics, and 43 percent of whites.[1]

Increased economic responsibility does not inevitably mean the pauperization of women. The question is, Why are added economic obligations pushing women, and their families, into poverty? Answering that question forces us to look at two closely related social practices: the

Thanks to Carol Brown, Mary Fillmore, Nona Glazer, Heidi Hartmann, Nancy Hartsock, Marian Lowe, Julie Matthaei, Susan Ostrander, Frances Fox Piven, Mary Stevenson, Judy Wittner, Robert Wood, and two anonymous reviewers for comments on earlier drafts. This article was originally prepared for a conference of the International Working Group on Women and the Transformation of the Welfare State, Bellagio, Italy, August 1983. The conference was supported in part by the Center for European Studies, Columbia University. Revision of the article was supported in part by a Radcliffe Research Fellowship and the Murray Research Center, Radcliffe College.

1. Commission on Civil Rights, *A Growing Crisis: Disadvantaged Women and Their Children*, Clearinghouse Publication 78 (Washington, D.C.: Government Printing Office, 1973), p. 2.

sexual division of labor and the low value placed on both paid and unpaid "women's work." Expansion of economic responsibility among women occurs in a context in which the unpaid work of maintaining a household and taking care of children remains women's work and is assumed to be done "naturally" by women, regardless of their resources, time, or energy. Those who adhere to the earlier model of two-parent households expect "men's work" to bring in sufficient money for the entire family; women's work, supported by men's wages, is to care for and maintain family members and the household. Without access to men's wages, single mothers rely primarily on the state or their own earnings. The state apparently places a low value on domestic women's work; stipends are paid at a level that keeps women and their children in poverty. Single mothers who enter the labor market—or, as is increasingly the case, remain in their jobs—find that the wages paid in the female-intensive occupations do not provide an adequate living.[2] Women's work is paid on a lower wage scale, as if all women have access to men's wages. Indeed, a 1977 government study "found that if working women were paid what similarly qualified men earn, the number of poor families would decrease by half."[3] The low wages paid for women's work set one of the basic parameters of women's poverty.

Comparable worth is a concept that rejects the premise of a separate and lower wage hierarchy for women. It disagrees with both the notion that women's work is inherently worth less than men's work and the related assumption that workers are paid according to their needs and that women need less money than men. It argues that people should be paid according to the worth of the work they perform—its value to the employer—regardless of sex, race, or other characteristics.[4]

At first glance, comparable worth appears to be a very limited reform, one that could be used to legitimate further the existing hierarchy of wages and could easily degenerate into sterile debates about methods for determining what a job is worth. Yet despite its liberal origins and its potential simply to make capital more rational, comparable worth has the capacity to initiate far-reaching changes. These changes will be important for women of color as well as for white women, for manufacturing and

2. Of the ten jobs held most commonly by women, only one was less than 70 percent female in 1980 (Nancy F. Rytina and Suzanne M. Bianchi, "Occupational Reclassification and Changes in Distribution by Gender," *Monthly Labor Review* 107, no. 3 [March 1984]: 11–17, 15).

3. Patricia Sexton, *Women and Work*, Research and Development Monograph no. 46 (Washington, D.C.: Department of Labor, Employment and Training Administration, 1977), cited in Karin Stallard, Barbara Ehrenreich, and Holly Sklar, *Poverty in the American Dream: Women and Children First* (Boston: South End Press, 1983), p. 9.

4. Donald J. Treiman and Heidi I. Hartmann, eds., *Women, Work and Wages: Equal Pay for Jobs of Equal Value* (Washington, D.C.: National Academy Press, 1981), p. 70.

service workers as well as for professionals. Comparable worth has radical implications because it initiates an end to women's economic dependency and questions the market basis of wages. In doing so, it exposes the way gender hierarchy is incorporated into the organization of the economy, the traditional strategies of the labor movement, and the ideologies of gender in the United States; it provides the basis for an attack on the sexual division of labor and gender hierarchy; and it lays the foundation for a reordering of gender relations throughout social life.

I recognize that this is a sweeping claim. I do not, of course, mean that comparable worth is a complete solution to women's poverty or that alone it will transform the gender system. But I do believe that the liberation of women from poverty as well as from social, economic, and political subordination depends on the revaluation of women's work and that comparable worth provides one way in which we can struggle to accomplish that revaluation. In this article I will make a case for that claim in order to encourage debate about it. I will review the history of low wages for women in the United States, discuss the anomalies that comparable worth reveals, and conclude by addressing the social and political implications of comparable worth.

The History of Low Wages for U.S. Women

Low wages for women are closely linked to the sexual division of labor, which predates capitalism and is found in all known historic and contemporary nonindustrial cultures. In most societies only males do men's work, only females do women's work. The assignment of work on the basis of sex creates an equation between biological sex and gender and helps to determine the social patterns of appropriate behavior for men and women in a particular culture. Doing men's work or women's work becomes part of the definition of manliness or womanliness; thus the expression of one's gender identity reinforces and helps to maintain the sex-based division of labor. An occasional male or female doing the work of the opposite sex does not challenge this division of labor; instead it raises questions about the gender identity of that individual.[5]

Men's work and women's work are not only differentiated in content but also ranked in value. Whatever the particular content of the work, notwithstanding even its economic importance for group survival, men's work is valued above women's work.[6] It is the combination of the sexual

5. This discussion draws heavily on Julie Matthaei, *An Economic History of Women in America: Women's Work, the Sexual Division of Labor and the Development of Capitalism* (New York: Schocken Books, 1982).

6. See Norma Diamond, "Collectivization, Kinship and the Status of Women in Rural China," in *Toward an Anthropology of Women*, ed. Rayna Rapp Reiter (New York: Monthly

division of labor and the associated gender hierarchy of value that under-
lies women's low wages.

Alice Clark found that in sixteenth-century England, female agricultural workers were paid at most three-quarters of the wages paid to
males and often considerably less.[7] Even in colonial America, where the
harsh conditions of life and the sexual division of labor made women's
work essential for men's survival, settlers were allotted less land for a
womanservant than for a manservant.[8]

The early development of manufacturing in the United States, beginning with the spinning and textile mills of New England in the 1820s,
was promoted by mill owners and statesmen on the grounds that it would
keep women and children from idleness and permit them to earn wages
to contribute to their own support.[9] By the 1820s the prevailing wages in
the mill towns covered what women needed to live respectably (a major
concern, which led to the establishment of boarding houses) and to send
money home to the farm. This encouraged farm families to send their
unmarried daughters to the mills. Although conditions in the early mills
were superior to those in industrial England, the philosophy involved was
not so different from that of English coal mine owners, who preferred to
hire women rather than horses for pulling coal cars because women cost
less to maintain.[10]

With the wider development of industrial capitalism in the United
States, men became the predominant labor force.[11] Theoretically, the law
of capitalist development is to lower the cost of labor as far as possible by
treating all workers the same. Initially, it seemed as if capitalism might
indeed reduce all workers to the same level. Marx predicted that the lower

Review Press, 1975), pp. 372–95, esp. pp. 388–89; Michelle Zimbalist Rosaldo, "Woman,
Culture, and Society: A Theoretical Overview," and Peggy R. Sanday, "Female Status in the
Public Domain," in *Woman, Culture, and Society,* ed. Michelle Zimbalist Rosaldo and Louise
Lamphere (Stanford, Calif.: Stanford University Press, 1974), pp. 17–42 (esp. pp. 18–19),
189–206.

7. Alice Clark, *Working Life of Women in the Seventeenth Century* (New York: Arno Press,
1968), pp. 60–64.

8. Mary P. Ryan, *Womanhood in America: From Colonial Times to the Present,* 3d ed. (New
York: Franklin Watts, Inc., 1983), p. 23.

9. Edith Abbott, *Women in Industry: A Study in American Economic History* (New York:
Arno Press, 1969), pp. 35–53.

10. Note, however, that by the 1840s New England mill girls were organizing them-
selves in opposition to oppressive conditions in the mill towns (see Lise Vogel, "Their Own
Work: Two Documents from the Nineteenth-Century Labor Movement," *Signs: Journal of
Women in Culture and Society* 1, no. 3 [Spring 1976]: 787–802).

11. The attempts of male trade unionists to exclude women from industry during this
period in England are analyzed in Harold Benenson, "Victorian Sexual Ideology and Marx'
Theory of the Working Class," *International Labor and Working Class History* 25 (Spring 1984):
1–23.

wages of women and children would make them more attractive to employers and force down the traditionally higher price of men's labor.[12] Such changes threatened the family patterns of the working class, which rested on the value of men's labor, and that value was, in turn, the basis of the man's preeminent position in the family.

The capitalists, however, lacked complete control of the supply of labor. Resistance came from many quarters. Married women avoided industrial employment whenever possible. As early as 1835, skilled men led the fight to exclude or restrict the labor of women and of children.[13] By the 1870s they did so through their unions, using such tactics as barring women outright, requiring long apprenticeships, organizing women into separate subordinate unions, or leaving them unorganized. Even as union members, women were treated differently. Although women were being organized into the United Garment Workers in the 1880s and 90s, union leaders "often demanded higher pay and shorter hours for the cutters and operators, skilled jobs held by men, and ignored the women buttonhole makers and finishers."[14] Through their unions, the men fought for wages that recognized their traditional claims as skilled craftsmen and for conditions of work that accommodated their manliness.[15] What they did not do was to aid women in organizing themselves to fight for comparable pay and conditions.

The political strength of the craft unions and the value of their members' industrial skills forced the capitalists to respond. When they did respond, they consolidated the gender and generation hierarchies of the family, long traditional in the workplace, as features of the labor market. The results were male job monopolies that excluded women and children (and later all members of particular ethnic and racial groups) and an institutionalized gender hierarchy of wages, which left men the main breadwinners and women the economic dependents.

These struggles ensured that sex segregation, male domination, and lower wages for women would become an integral part of industrial capitalism in the United States. If men's work was to be both part of the definition of manliness and something that only men could do (at higher

12. Karl Marx, *Capital* (New York: International Publishers, 1967), 1:386–402.

13. Heidi I. Hartmann, "Capitalism, Patriarchy and Job Segregation by Sex," in *Capitalist Patriarchy and the Case for Socialist Feminism,* ed. Zillah Eisenstein (New York: Monthly Review Press, 1979), pp. 206–47; Ruth Milkman, "Organizing the Sexual Division of Labor: Historical Perspectives on 'Women's Work' and the American Labor Movement," *Socialist Review* 10, no. 1 (January-February 1980): 95–150, esp. 108–23; and Philip Foner, *Women and the American Labor Movement* (New York: Free Press, 1979–80), esp. pp. 213–69.

14. Foner, p. 226. For other examples of skilled male workers' hostility to women, see Abbott, esp. pp. 250–61.

15. David Montgomery identifies "manliness" as one of three central aspects of the craftsmen's ethical code (see *Worker's Control in America: Studies in the History of Work, Technology and Labor Struggles* [Cambridge: Cambridge University Press, 1979], p. 13).

wages), sex segregation was crucial. Working-class men had to maintain the exclusivity of men's work in order to press special claims on their own behalf. Their activities were aimed not at lowering women's wages but at maintaining higher wages for men.[16] If men's work was to be better paid, it also had to be of inherently higher value, requiring skills and strengths that women could not acquire. The ideology of men's work as skilled meant by definition that women's work was not skilled and therefore was worth less.

While skilled craftsmen used their industrial skills and political strength to fight the capitalists, the pressure to limit employment of women and children was increased by humanitarian protest against harsh conditions in the factories. The unions added their voices to these calls for protective legislation, in a convenient coupling of self-interest and reform. Such resistance was strengthened by appeals to the now-dominant ideology that understood woman's place to be in the home.[17]

One problem remained. How were families to survive in urban environments, where women could no longer contribute by raising food and carrying out other traditional forms of economically important women's work? The solution that the labor unions urged was the family wage.[18] The family wage was a man's wage. It provided the necessary income to support both the wife, who would provide household services and raise children, and the children, who would no longer need to begin wage labor at age eight or ten. The family wage made possible a standard of living that was impossible for women living on their own wages or for men who lacked the unpaid labor of wives and daughters. But this solution institutionalized men's domination in the labor market and the family, treated as unfortunate aberrations those households that lacked access to men's wages, and set the stage for the impoverishment of women, and especially women with children, who were without the wages of a man.

The family wage also confirmed that the ideal sexual division of labor in marriage included a man as full-time breadwinner and a woman as full-time homemaker. This arrangement became the standard of success

16. For examples, see Mary H. Blewett, "Work, Gender and the Artisan Tradition in New England Shoemaking, 1780–1860," *Journal of Social History* 17, no. 2 (December 1983): 221–48, esp. 223, 237; and Foner, pp. 215, 226.

17. See Blewett; and Foner, p. 234.

18. On the family wage, see Michelle Barrett and Mary McIntosh, "The Family Wage: Some Problems for Socialists and Feminists," *Capital and Class* 11 (Summer 1980): 51–72; and Heidi I. Hartmann, "The Unhappy Marriage of Marxism and Feminism: Towards a More Progressive Union," in *Women and Revolution*, ed. Lydia Sargent (Boston: South End Press, 1981), pp. 1–40, esp. pp. 19–29. See also Jane Humphries, "The Working Class Family, Women's Liberation and Class Struggle: The Case of Nineteenth Century British History," *Review of Radical Political Economics* 9, no. 3 (Fall 1977): 25–41; and Milkman.

in urban family life early in the twentieth century, although many, especially immigrants and people of color, could not achieve it. Ironically, during this same period, the numbers of women in paid work began to increase rapidly as the unmarried daughters of white, native-born families responded to new opportunities in the expanding urban economy. Clerical and sales jobs for women increased, attracting many recent high school graduates, while the new professions of social work and librarianship attracted the "new women" graduating from colleges. More and more women were doing paid work at least until marriage and, as time went on, until their children were born. The two world wars accelerated women's movement into industrial work. Although women were accepted into men's jobs as temporary substitutes and were expected to leave in peacetime, the experience of doing this work and earning real wages changed women's understanding of their own potential.[19] In addition, even in peacetime a wedge of women remained in jobs that were not women's work.

Following World War II, inflation, supplemented by changes in consumer patterns and other social forces, dictated that families needed a larger income than even most men's work provided. More and more women entered the labor market. Most were working to earn money for their families, though a privileged minority were seeking satisfactions not available in homemaking. Whatever their motivation, the vast majority entered women's jobs: clerical, sales, and service work and the women's professions. Their experience brought new awareness of their ability to earn income and new awareness of the limits on the income they earned.

Scholars have debated whether women's increasing presence in the labor force undermined the sexual division of labor at home, but all agree that the sexual division in the work force remained strong, as did the gender hierarchy of wages. Indeed there is evidence of continuing occupational segregation by sex and of a stagnation in women's earnings relative to men's—especially men involved in men's work.[20] All studies show a strong association between low wages and women's work.

19. See Alice Kessler-Harris, *Out to Work: A History of Wage-earning Women in the United States* (New York: Oxford University Press, 1982). On World War I, see Maurine Greenwald, *Women, War, and Work: The Impact of World War I on Women Workers in the United States* (Westport, Conn.: Greenwood Press, 1980); on World War II, see William H. Chafe, *The American Woman: Her Changed Social, Economic and Political Roles, 1920–1970* (New York: Oxford University Press, 1972), pp. 135–95.

20. For a review of the literature on occupational segregation by sex, see Treiman and Hartmann, eds. (n. 4 above), pp. 24–43, 52–62. See also Francine D. Blau and Wallace E. Hendricks, "Occupational Segregation by Sex: Trends and Prospects," *Journal of Human Resources* 14 (Spring 1979): 197–210; and Heidi I. Hartmann and Barbara F. Reskin, "Job Segregation: Trends and Prospects" (paper presented at the Conference on Occupational Segregation, Ford Foundation, New York, June 1982).

Although the low wages paid to women have always been a disadvantage, in an earlier period many women gained access to a family wage through marriage. Now, through divorce, nonmarriage, and widowhood, as well as the insufficient number of men's jobs that pay a family wage, many women have lost that access. A growing proportion of women are taking on major breadwinning responsibilities. As they do, because they are paid women's wages, they and their families become poor.[21]

Why is women's work still being paid such low wages? What can be done about it? The comparable-worth or pay-equity approach offers a specific answer to the first question and implies an agenda for action. Its foundation is an analysis of social institutions. Women still earn low wages because they labor within a tradition that has treated women as temporary and supplementary workers, devalued women's work, and rationalized low wages as all that women qua women need. This approach sees women as confined largely to low-wage sectors, as does labor market segmentation analysis. But it goes further to argue that, even when women are in high-wage sectors, they are confined to low-wage women's work within those sectors and within specific firms. Thus the problem is not simply that women are in the wrong sectors of the economy. Nor is it that women bring inadequate "human capital" to their work. I argue that low wages for women result directly from the sex/gender system—that is, the exclusion of women from "manly labor," which keeps women a separate and cheaper labor force. This system results in sex segregation within firms at a level even greater than that within certain occupations or industries.[22]

The sex/gender system maintains a sexual division of labor and a gender hierarchy that systematically undervalue the work and skills of women. Shifting women into other areas of employment will not necessarily mean higher wages in the long run. Within the sex/gender system, whatever work is done predominantly by women is or becomes sex typed in content, prestige, and wages; it comes to be seen as women's work. The question is not whether to eliminate occupational segregation or to implement comparable worth. Both are necessary. What comparable worth offers is a new concept of the worth of women and of women's work.

21. The large proportion of women and children among the poor is not a new phenomenon. A 1904 study found that two-thirds of the individuals in a sample of poor households in New York were women and children (cited in James T. Patterson, *America's Struggle against Poverty, 1900–1980* [Cambridge, Mass.: Harvard University Press, 1981], p. 8). What is new is the growing number of single-parent female-headed families.

22. On wage differentials, see Treiman and Hartmann, eds., pp. 13–43. On wage differentials and sex segregation by occupation and industry, see Mary Stevenson, "Women's Wages and Job Segregation," in *Labor Market Segmentation*, ed. Richard C. Edwards, Michael Reich, and David M. Gordon (Lexington, Mass.: D. C. Heath & Co., 1975), pp. 243–55; by firm, see Francine Blau, "Sex Segregation of Workers by Enterprise in Clerical Occupations," in Edwards et al., eds., pp. 257–78.

Comparable Worth: Theory and Practice

The theory underlying comparable worth begins with the observation that the sex/gender system as it is incorporated into the economy has created a context in which women's work, whatever its content, is systematically devalued. This position implies that there is a value of labor that derives from the content of the work itself, that this value can be determined, and that it ought to be the basis on which labor is compensated. Stated formally: "The relative worth of jobs reflects value judgments as to what features of jobs ought to be compensated, and such judgments typically vary from industry to industry, even from firm to firm. Paying jobs according to their worth requires only that whatever characteristics of jobs are regarded as worthy of compensation by an employer should be equally so regarded irrespective of sex, race or ethnicity of job incumbents."[23] The theory rests on the argument that compensation should be independent of the social characteristics of the workers.

In exposing the consequences of the ideology of gender, comparable worth exposes the limitations of neoclassical economics.[24] It reveals that women's low-wage position in the economy results neither from technical forces inherent in the organization of work nor from inexorable workings of economic laws analogous to those of the physical world. If economic forces were the sole regulator of the labor market, we would expect the capitalist drive for cheaper labor to create an almost uniform wage structure, not one characterized by continuing sex and race differentials. In particular, one would not expect wage differentials by social factors such as sex and race where workers' levels of education or skill are equal or where they run counter to the wage structure.[25] Comparable worth argues that, since the unexpected is precisely what we find, we are operating not in the context of economic laws but within a system of segmented labor markets. The structure of the market incorporates historic customs, prejudices, and ideologies that connect the worth of different kinds of work with ideas about the inherent worth of workers who vary by sex, race, age, ethnicity, and other social characteristics. It is these customs, prejudices, and ideologies, modified by the effects of struggles between

23. Treiman and Hartmann, eds.

24. For neoclassical economists' explanations of women's earnings, see Jacob Mincer and Solomon Polachek, "Family Investments in Human Capital: Earnings of Women," in *The Economics of Women and Work*, ed. Alice H. Amsden (New York: St. Martin's Press, 1980), pp. 169–205; and Solomon W. Polachek, "Discontinuous Labor Force Participation and Its Effect on Women's Market Earnings," in *Sex, Discrimination, and the Division of Labor*, ed. Cynthia B. Lloyd (New York: Columbia University Press, 1975), pp. 90–122.

25. According to Treiman and Hartmann, the "human capital" factors used by neoclassical economists account for usually one-quarter and never more than one-half of wage differentials (Treiman and Hartmann, eds., p. 42).

workers and employers, rather than the nature of work or any natural economic laws, that have shaped the basic framework of wage determination. This process has systematically disadvantaged women, who have been seen as people whose primary attachments are or ought to be to home and family.

Both the theory and methods of comparable worth reveal anomalies in the relationship among wages, women, and paid work. The first is that there is no relationship between the skills involved in women's work and the wages paid. A well-documented case involves the entirely sex-segregated Westinghouse plants of the late 1930s. In establishing company-wide labor grades and wage scales at this time, Westinghouse management specified procedures for their plants. Each job was to be first evaluated on a point system and then assigned to a labor grade, without regard to sex of the worker, on the basis of its point rating. This created labor grades of jobs with similar ratings. Then wages were to be assigned to each grade.[26] However, in assigning wages, men's jobs were to be separated from women's jobs; women's jobs were to be paid on a lower scale. The separate scales ensured that all women's jobs, whatever their labor grade, were paid less than the lowest paid men's jobs were. After Title VII passed, prohibiting separate classifications by sex, the wage scales were combined. As of 1975, all women's jobs were assigned to the five lowest steps, while men's jobs began at step five.[27] The firm claimed it paid women less than men for jobs with equal ratings "because of the more transient character of the service of the [women], the relative shortness of their activity in industry, the differences in the environment required, the extra services that must be provided, overtime limitations and the general sociological factors not requiring discussion herein."[28] These women were being paid less than the men on the basis of stereotypes, beliefs, and statistics about female labor force participation, without regard to the actual work they were performing. Such practices imply an argument that women qua women should not be paid as much as men regardless of the worth of their jobs to the employer; that is, the ratings of women's jobs had bearing only on their location within the hierarchy of women's work but had no relationship to men's jobs of equal or even lower ratings.[29]

26. The description of the Westinghouse case is found in Winn Newman and Jeanne M. Vonhof, " 'Separate but Equal'—Job Segregation and Pay Equity in the Wake of Gunther," *University of Illinois Law Review* 2 (1981): 269–331, esp. 292–96. This method is typical of job evaluation systems. For a discussion of how these techniques are related to wages, see Treiman and Hartmann, eds., pp. 69–90.

27. Newman and Vonhof.

28. *The Westinghouse Industrial Relations Manual: Wage Administration*, November 1, 1938, and February 1, 1938, quoted in Newman and Vonhof, p. 293.

29. Recent data show that traditionally female jobs, rated equal to or above traditionally male jobs, continue to receive substantially lower wages (see Commission on Civil Rights [n. 1 above], table 3.7).

The second anomaly is that the economic laws that are supposed to describe the relationship between workers, work, and wages do not operate in the same ways for women's work as they do for men's work. According to the popular view of neoclassical economics, increased demand for workers will raise wages.[30] Both historically and today we find that, where women predominate in an occupation, increased demand for them as workers rarely leads to higher wages. In the nineteenth century, women were recruited into some previously male-dominated professions (e.g., teaching and librarianship) to meet an increased demand. From the start, however, the women received lower wages than men had when the demand was lower.[31] A similar pattern occurred in the federal civil service. The first women clerical workers employed by the federal government received one-half to three-quarters of the wages paid to men.[32] This pattern was established even though the women were acknowledged to be as good or better workers. More recently, in *Lemons* v. *City and County of Denver*, it was established that nurses were paid considerably less than all other medical professionals with comparable training and experience (e.g., pharmacists), even though there was a high demand for nurses.[33] The judge ruled that the wages were not discriminatory because they were similar to the wages paid to nurses by other employers. This suggests that there is a ceiling on women's wages that operates as part of the sex/gender system and is impervious to the demand for workers.

A third anomaly is that the particular skills required in many women's occupations are not recognized as skills. Much of women's work involves recognizing and responding to subtle cues in the work process or in other people, yet women's ability to do so is devalued. For example, the work of housewives, secretaries, teachers, aides, and nurses is geared toward understanding other people's needs and assisting them in realizing their goals. But this work is judged less skilled or less important than

---

30. For neoclassical economists themselves, however, this finding is not an anomaly since the relationship between supply and demand assumes "other things being equal." For a discussion of the meaning of women's access to the professions under changing conditions, see Michael J. Carter and Susan Bostego Carter, "Women's Recent Progress in the Professions or Women Get a Ticket to Ride after the Gravy Train Has Left the Station," *Feminist Studies* 7, no. 3 (Fall 1981): 477–504.

31. On teaching, see JoAnne Preston, "Feminization of an Occupation: Teaching Becomes Women's Work in Nineteenth Century New England" (Ph.D. diss., Brandeis University, 1982). On librarianship, see Dee Garrison, "The Tender Technicians: The Feminization of Public Librarianship, 1876–1905," in *Clio's Consciousness Raised*, ed. Mary Hartman and Lois Banner (New York: Harper & Row, 1974).

32. Marjorie Davies, "Woman's Place Is at the Typewriter: The Feminization of the Clerical Labor Force," in Eisenstein, ed. (n. 13 above), pp. 248–66, esp. p. 252.

33. Joy Ann Grune with Ellen Cassedy, "Introduction: Organizing and Bargaining," in *Manual on Pay Equity, Raising Wages for Women's Work*, ed. Joy Ann Grune (Washington, D.C.: Conference on State and Local Policies, 1981), pp. 139–43, esp. pp. 142–43.

that of the persons being assisted.[34] Though transformation and reorganization of work in the twentieth century has obliterated certain skills and created a large proportion of routine jobs, the labor force is still not reduced to one level. Jobs remain differentiated as "skilled," "semi-skilled," and "unskilled." The failure of capitalism formally to subordinate labor by making all workers virtually interchangeable has been seen as evidence of workers' successful struggles to retain their prerogatives, even though these distinctions have been used by capitalists to encourage divisions among the workers. However, few analysts note, as Anne Phillips and Barbara Taylor do, the strong association between male workers and the category "skilled" and female workers and the category "unskilled." Philips and Taylor argue, "Far from being an objective economic fact, skill is often an ideological category imposed on certain types of work by virtue of the sex and power of the workers who perform it."[35]

The fourth anomaly is that women are not seen as fully entitled to fair wages.[36] It is as if the notion of how a woman is to live is totally different from the notion of how a man is to live. The difference is that a woman is supposed to be economically dependent on a man; therefore, the principle of adequate or fair wages does not apply to women. While this double standard assumes a sexual division of labor in which women ideally do not do paid work, it is applied precisely to those women who engage in paid work. It implies that women are not working for subsistence in the labor market; they are supplementing, helping out, getting new experience—anything but supporting themselves, their husbands, and their children. At the same time, women's poorly paid work is deemed necessary to the economy. This view of women and their paid work is revealed in some objections to comparable worth. In *Lemons* v. *City and County of Denver*, the judge ruled against the claim of nurses who were paid less than sign painters and related building maintenance staff. He said that the concept of comparable worth was "pregnant [*sic*] with the possibility of disrupting the entire economic system [of the United States]."[37] Although he acknowledged the history of sex discrimination, he argued that Congress did not "intend" that federal courts should

34. Dorothy Smith offers a perceptive analysis of this feature of women's work (see "A Sociology for Women," in *The Prism of Sex: Essays in the Sociology of Knowledge*, ed. Julia A. Sherman and Evelyn Torton Beck [Madison: University of Wisconsin Press, 1979], pp. 135–87, esp. pp. 151–52). See also Evelyn N. Glenn and Roslyn L. Feldberg, "Women as Mediators in the Labor Process" (paper delivered at the American Sociological Association Meetings, Boston, August 1979).

35. Anne Phillips and Barbara Taylor, "Sex and Skill: Notes Towards a Feminist Economics," *Feminist Review* 6 (1980): 79–88, 79.

36. See Barbara Wootton's classical analysis in *The Social Foundations of Wage Policy*, 2d ed. (London: Unwin University Books, 1962), esp. pp. 145–47, 162–63.

37. Quoted in Margaret Moses, "Equal Pay for Work of Comparable Value: Status of Litigation," in Grune, ed., pp. 68–70, p. 68.

"restructure the economy of the country." In effect, this ruling says that women should bear the cost of discrimination because remedying the situation would be too expensive and disruptive, presumably for employers.

Some Implications of Comparable Worth

Comparable worth provides a framework for developing and pressing alternative claims. Although it has radical underpinnings and implications, the framework is traditionally liberal because it argues for equal treatment. Demands for higher job ratings and higher wages rest on established procedures of job evaluation and seek equitable wages within the existing wage hierarchy. The attempt to use the comparable-worth approach—whether through collective bargaining, government regulation, legislation, or litigation—has been opposed by conservative groups since the comparable-worth principle was enunciated by the War Labor Board in the 1940s. Subsequent efforts to make comparable worth a feature of legislation outlawing discrimination in wages were defeated throughout the post–World War II period. The relatively weak Equal Pay Act of 1963 does not mention this principle; apparently it was sacrificed in order to attain any legislation in this area.[38] Despite conservative opposition, the meaning of comparable worth outside of the gender system is not clear. Three sets of questions about its social and political implications must be addressed. The first set concerns the relationship between comparable worth and the status quo, the second set concerns the legal basis of comparable worth, and the third set concerns the effects of comparable worth on relationships among groups of women and between women and men.

Comparable worth is related to the status quo in both the overall degree of inequality in the society and the hierarchy of wages. It can have only a modest effect on the overall degree of inequality because it does not attack all forms of inequality. It does attack gender inequality in the wage system, which is, as the earnings gap shows, a major component of gender inequality in the United States. The possibility that other forms of inequality will become more visible (e.g., similar patterns of wage differentials by race or age or inequities arising from the distribution of wealth) as a result of a lessening of gender inequality is not an argument against working for comparable worth. Indeed, struggles for comparable worth may set the stage for attacks on other forms of inequity.

How comparable worth will affect the hierarchy of wages is more difficult to foresee. On the one hand, it does not directly challenge the

---

38. Dorothy Haener, "Letter to the Women's Bureau," in Grune, ed., pp. 66–67.

concept of a hierarchy; in fact, its insistence that jobs be evaluated implies a hierarchy. On the other hand, its rejection of the market as an adequate basis for determining wages initiates a discussion of how value is assigned to jobs independent of the market and which job dimensions are worthy of compensation. Advocates of comparable worth have challenged prevailing standards of evaluation. They have pointed out that formal job evaluations were first developed in industrial settings and tend to give considerable weight to tasks such as heavy lifting and the operation of expensive equipment. As a corollary, the skills and knowledge more typical of women's work are often unacknowledged or less heavily weighted. Researchers studying the *Dictionary of Occupational Titles for 1974* found striking instances of this imbalance, such as child-care workers being rated lower than parking-lot attendants, foster mothers rated below horse pushers, nursery school teachers far below marine mammal handlers, practical nurses below the offal man, and nurse-midwives below hotel clerks.[39]

While comparable-worth advocates eschew questioning the principle of a hierarchy of wages, arguing only that they seek more objective, less sex-biased measures of job worth, the issues they raise provoke a broader debate. This debate does not, as opponents have tried to argue, concern the feasibility of setting and applying such standards.[40] Employers have been engaging in that activity for centuries. Rather the debate is about social values and priorities underlying the wage hierarchy. Is the labor-intensive work of caring for people less valuable than the work of caring for buildings or cars? How large a wage difference is reasonable between positions in the hierarchy? Or, to put it differently, what ought to be the relationship between wages and position in the job-evaluation hierarchy? What is the value of labor, and what social considerations ought to guide decisions about wages? These fundamental questions reveal how priorities are embedded in the market, where historical conventions and social and political, as opposed to purely economic, forces enter the process of setting wages.

The major legal questions concern the definition of discrimination and its relationship to established employment practices. Where these practices are long-standing, they are often seen by judges as well as by employers as arising naturally from economic laws or from differences among groups of workers. This perspective masks discrimination and

39. Mary Witt and Patricia K. Naherny, *Women's Work—Up from 878; Report on the D.O.T. Research Project* (Madison: University of Wisconsin Extension, Women's Education Resources, 1975), cited in Louise Kapp Howe, *Pink Collar Workers: Inside the World of Women's Work* (New York: G. P. Putnam's Sons, 1977), pp. 246–49.

40. E. Robert Livernash, introduction to *Comparable Worth: Issues and Alternatives* (Washington, D.C.: Equal Employment Advisory Council, 1980).

creates difficulties for women who bring charges of unfair wages. The conflict is highlighted in both *Christensen* v. *State of Iowa* and *Lemons* v. *City and County of Denver*. In the former, the University of Northern Iowa was paying its secretaries less than its physical plant employees, although the university's own internal job evaluation awarded both categories the same labor grades. The Eighth Circuit Court ruled that these differences in pay were not evidence of discrimination because they reflected prevailing wage rates in the local labor market. Such legal opinions imbue the operating principles of the economic system with the force of natural law.

Comparable-worth advocates argue that the market is a historic development rather than an expression of natural law. Conventions within the market, including wage-setting practices and labor market divisions, perpetuate a historic discrimination against women and women's work. Without contesting the principle of hierarchy in wages, they advance the notion that wage hierarchies for women can be categorically lower than those for men only because they are discriminatory.

If comparable worth does succeed in raising women's wages, how will it affect relationships among groups of women and between women and men? Will it further divide women, stringing them out along the same hierarchy that divides male workers? If so, will it reduce our common ground and create new barriers to collective action?

First, all women should not continue to suffer from certain inequities simply because the proposed solution will not eliminate all inequities. Second, having said that, I believe it is crucial that we guard against further divisions both as a matter of simple justice and to prevent the gains from being eroded. The whole strength of the comparable-worth approach rests on cooperation among women. As long as some areas of women's paid work are devalued, the potential exists for all women's work to be devalued; consider the way in which arguments about married women not needing a living wage have been used against all women.

Third, comparable worth can further divide women where they are already divided into separate occupational categories. For example, insofar as registered nurses tend to be white women and licensed practical nurses and nurses' aides tend to be women of color, comparable-worth attacks on inequities in nurses' wages could perpetuate and exacerbate divisions. There is no abstract, general solution for this potential problem. To the extent that the occupational distribution of white women and women of color has become more similar in the post–World War II period, the possibility is lessened. However, such structural shifts cannot eliminate the problem altogether. Divisions will be contained only by careful political analysis and concerted action. In the above example, the use of comparable worth to attack inequities based on gender provides the opportunity to develop conceptual and political tools that can also be used to address racial inequities among women. If gender-based inequities are eliminated between nurses and, for example, pharmacists, the same reasoning should be useful in attacking inequities between nurses and aides. That is not to say that comparable worth will create an egalitarian wage structure, but it will provide the grounds for eliminating wage inequities between groups doing comparable work.

A related concern is that comparable worth will become a class-specific strategy—advantageous to college-educated women at the expense of their high school counterparts and the latters' husbands. Again, such outcomes are possible, but there is already evidence that they are not necessary. The first comparable-worth settlements were made in manufacturing in 1969.[41] In 1979 women sewing-machine operators working in the federal bindery won their suit against the government's practice of paying higher wages to men who were journeymen bookbinders.[42] Comparable-worth suits against state and city governments have covered occupations from jail matrons in Washington state to the entire range of city workers in San Jose, California.

Women who are not members of professional associations or unions will have less access to comparable-worth strategy than will those who are. Organized workers have an advantage in using methods that require major resources. This suggests that women need to do more organizing, with the support of unions and other sympathizers, not that comparable-worth strategy should be discounted.

The last question concerns relationships between men and women. Would comparable worth be disadvantageous for men? Would attempts to implement comparable worth lead to a new form of gender politics? Comparable worth could be relatively disadvantageous to men who are paid more than the content of their jobs warrants. No one has predicted absolute reductions in wages. Instead, the wages for these men's work would rise more slowly. Any attempt to lessen inequality would involve at least this form of disadvantage for some men.

Women married to those men might feel increased pressure to enter or remain in the labor force. Yet women's economic dependence on husbands' wages has proven insufficient for a large proportion of women. Fifty-one percent of married women were in the labor force in 1982, as were almost 75 percent of divorced women.[43] In two-earner households, increases in women's wages would lessen the impact of a slower rise in men's wages, while they would improve the economic situation of the growing number of female-headed households.

41. Carole Wilson, "The IUE's Approach to Comparable Worth," in Grune, ed., pp. 89–90.

42. Beverly Jacobson, "Comparable Worth: The Working Woman's Issue for the 80s," *National Forum* 61, no. 4 (Fall 1981): 5–6.

43. Department of Labor, Bureau of Labor Statistics, *Women at Work: A Chartbook*, Bulletin 2168 (Washington, D.C.: Government Printing Office, 1983), chart 12.

The issue of gender politics is more problematic. There are already important divisions between men and women, which this article addresses. Economic self-sufficiency among women would radically alter the system of gender relations but would not necessarily exacerbate divisions. Materially, comparable worth is unlikely to work against the interests of most employed men. In fact, raising women's wages would probably raise the floor below men's wages, as the decline of a cheap labor supply in the past has bolstered wages. Furthermore, better-paid women workers would be in a stronger position to ally with men around common concerns. What comparable worth would threaten is the gender hierarchy in wages, which could be perceived as a threat to traditional notions of masculinity. Men's work and male workers would no longer automatically be seen as worth higher wages. Whether the new common standard would become a basis of solidarity or a loss of preeminence that men would fight depends in large part on the response of organized labor, especially at the local, grass-roots level.

Finally, I think that attempts to develop comparable worth claims would provide an opportunity for both organizing and consciousness raising. The history and dynamics of gender relations in the United States are such that women as well as men tend to devalue women's work. Many of us feel underpaid, yet few claim that we deserve men's wages. The few women who get such wages seem nervous, as if they occupy a position of privilege that is undeserved and might be taken away at any time. Given our experience of social subordination and low wages, it is not surprising that we are uncertain about the value of our work. The process of evaluating our own work and presenting claims on our own behalf might offer an opportunity to see our work more objectively, to appreciate its importance and its value.

Conclusions

The future of comparable worth is uncertain. Its legal foundations were strengthened by the 1981 Supreme Court ruling, in *County of Washington* [Oregon] v. *Gunther*, that claims of sex-biased wage discrimination that did not fit the narrow "equal pay for equal work" formula of the 1963 Equal Pay Act could be made under Title VII of the 1964 Civil Rights Act.[44] In 1983 comparable-worth advocates had another victory when a federal judge ruled for female state employees in the state of Washington, finding the state guilty of "overt and institutionalized dis-

44. See Newman and Vonhof (n. 26 above). A special issue of *Women's Rights Law Reporter*, vol. 8, no. 3 (1984) is devoted to comparable worth.

crimination" and ordering the state to remedy its actions.[45] However, the state of Washington is appealing that decision, and officials of the Reagan administration are preparing to support the appeal.

While conservatives have fought hard against comparable worth, radicals have been reluctant to fight for it. In part I think that reluctance stems from seeing the narrow presentations in comparable-worth litigation as the natural limits of the concept. It is true that comparable worth alone will not end women's subordination or eradicate women's poverty. There will still be unemployment, underemployment, and low-wage jobs. There will still be women outside the labor force who will need other strategies. But comparable worth is one starting point. My own initially hesitant exploration of the topic has convinced me that comparable worth has a larger, more important future. By taking seriously the value of women's work and their right to equitable wages, comparable worth not only can increase women's earnings but can also set the stage for ending their economic dependency. In the process it has the potential to redress some of the inequities among women and to initiate an open discussion of the wage system. Its theoretical and political impact will reach far beyond the liberal framework in which it was conceived and force a rethinking of assumptions underlying gender hierarchy and the dominance of the market.[46]

Murray Research Center
Radcliffe College

45. Robert D. Hershey, Jr., "Women's Pay Fight Shifts to 'Comparable Worth,' " *New York Times* (November 1, 1983); Joy Ann Grune, telephone interview, November 2, 1983.

46. Although it was brought to my attention too late to be incorporated into this article, Heidi I. Hartmann and Donald J. Treiman's "Notes on the NAS [National Academy of Sciences] Study of Equal Pay for Jobs of Equal Value" (in *Handbook of Wage and Salary Administration*, ed. Milton L. Rock, 2d ed. [New York: McGraw-Hill Book Co., 1984], chap. 63, pp. 1–16, esp. p. 16) presents a similar conclusion. For a parallel argument on the radical implications of liberal strategies regarding women's employment, see Zillah Eisenstein, *The Radical Future of Liberal Feminism* (New York: Longman Inc., 1981), esp. pp. 201–19.

The Patriarchal Relations
of the Reagan State

Zillah R. Eisenstein

This essay discusses the ways in which the Reagan administration has attempted to reconstitute patriarchal dimensions of the state that have been challenged by the increase of women in the labor force, changes in family forms, the demands of the women's movement throughout the 1970s, and the growth of the welfare state itself. Because those with power in government disagree on how best to reformulate the patriarchal aspects of the state for an advanced capitalist society, we shall see that a coherent state policy does not yet exist for the 1980s. But since New Rightists, neoconservatives, and neoliberals all identify the social welfare state as the product of excessive demands for equality and the source of crisis in patriarchal authority, the dismantling of social services remains a crucial governmental response to the "crisis of liberalism." Yet, while attacking the welfare system, the Reagan administration must try to articulate a politics that does not appear completely hostile to liberal-feminist demands.

The destruction of the social welfare state is a two-pronged effort to redefine the state's relationship to the various forms of family life. The task involves, first, a basic realignment of the connections between family

Much of the discussion in this article is more fully developed in my books, *Feminism and Sexual Equality: Crisis in Liberal America* (New York: Monthly Review Press, 1984) and *The Radical Future of Liberal Feminism* (New York: Longman, 1981). See these books for further citations on relevant and related materials dealing with this subject.

life and the state as well as a shift in the discourse about the contours of public and private life. Second, it involves a reduction of social services to the poor, which in turn affects those administering these services: middle-class white and black women and black men.

The Reagan administration has developed a covert antifeminist politics that seeks to reconstruct patriarchal privilege through the destruction of the welfare state and affirmative action law. In jeopardy are the social programs and jobs within the state itself that constituted real gains for poor and middle-class black and white women. Meanwhile, the Reagan administration argues overtly against the ERA and against abortion rights. Interestingly enough, the administration has been much more successful with its covert antifeminist politics than its open rejection of liberal-feminist demands. And this will continue to be true as long as the irresolvable tension between patriarchal male privilege and individual rights remains a part of the liberal patriarchal democratic state.[1]

The reconstitution of patriarchal relations is always a contradictory process within a society that is, by its discourse, committed to liberal individual rights. Therefore, to argue, as I do, that the state is patriarchal and is presently attempting to reconstitute itself is also to say that patriarchy is a changing system in which women always have the potential for power. Both the development and the present dismantling of the social welfare state are part of this historical flux and change. And if patriarchy is always changing through its interaction with the state, it can be changed through the actions of feminism.

Conceptualizing the Capitalist Patriarchal State

The state is both participant and mediator in the struggles within society. That is to say, the activism of the state actually stems from its attempt to mediate conflicts among the differing ideologies of capitalism, patriarchy, racism, and liberalism, and thereby to create social order and political cohesion. The liberal democratic state is currently in crisis because it has failed to create this unity.

What does it mean to say that the state is patriarchal or that patriarchy operates on the state level? Basically, it means that the distinction between public life as male and private life as female has been inherent in the formation of state societies. The state represents and defines the real separation of public and private life in terms of the differentiation of

---

1. For discussion of this point, see my essay entitled "The Sexual Politics of the New Right: Understanding the 'Crisis of Liberalism,'" *Signs: Journal of Women in Culture and Society* 7, no. 3 (Spring 1982): 567–88.

woman from man. Patriarchy thus transforms biological sex into politicized gender, giving men priority while making women "different" (i.e., unequal), or "less," or the "other." And it simultaneously establishes the sexual division of labor, the distinctness of family and market, patriarchal controls within the market, and so forth. Although the specific historical source of patriarchal control has shifted from the "father" to the "husband" to the "state" (while remaining simultaneously rooted in each), the dynamic of sexual class—the process of hierarchically differentiating woman from man—ensures the continuity of patriarchy. We cannot understand patriarchy, therefore, by simply analyzing domestic power structures (the dominance of a particular father or husband) or a static notion of biological power (strength, aggression).

The functioning of the state both reflects and constructs the relations of power in society, and yet the state does not fully reveal the entirety of such interactions. Although crucial to the reproduction of power, the state is not best understood as merely the "center" of power, because power is both concentrated and dispersed. The state, rather, condenses the relations of power in society—which function through economic, sexual, and racial hierarchies. The ruling class, therefore, is represented as a bourgeois class, although it is simultaneously white and male. The capitalist class, as the ruling class in the state, is thus actually much more than capitalist, in that it represents and protects the patriarchal and white supremacist aspects of politics.

Government, as a series of institutions, further condenses these capitalist, patriarchal, and racist relations of power by mystifying their varied loci, representing the relations of power as though they were fully encompassed in governmental institutions. Therefore, when one studies government, one has already turned to the partial and legitimized presentation of conflict within the state. In actuality, while government is an actor within state politics, it is never completely autonomous in this activity. The dynamics of the capitalist patriarchal state place constraints on government's scope. For government is not a mere reflection of a monolithic capitalist class or a set of patriarchal social relations; nor is it simply their instrument. There are different factions within the capitalist class as there are different conceptions held by this class of how best to mediate current conflicts between the capitalist marketplace, the traditional patriarchal family, racism, and the ideology of liberalism. Conflict within the state itself makes its role as a mere instrument impossible. To say that the state is only relatively autonomous from its capitalist and patriarchal class structure is to argue that the state makes choices within these class constraints. State policy reflects the conflicts that exist, given the constraints of the existing political discourse; it is not completely determined or entirely autonomous.

The relative autonomy of "the" state is actualized through a differentiation between the capitalist class and the state or governmental apparatus.[2] The same differentiation does not exist between patriarchy and the state apparatus. The governing or ruling class is made up of men representing the needs of men as a sexual class. Whereas the capitalist class functions best when it is not the governing class, there is no condensed class formation different from the capitalist class that represents patriarchal interests and distinguishes them from the state. Rather, patriarchal interests are represented by men of the capitalist class, who enforce the sexual class relations of patriarchy. These relations are represented as the natural differentiation of male and female, although we will see that integral to this presentation of patriarchal privilege—the hierarchical differentiation of woman from man—is the distinctness of state and economy, public and private, political and sexual, state and family.

The state is relatively autonomous in its relation to patriarchy[3] in that factions of the bourgeois class have different conceptions of how patriarchy is best to be protected or reconstituted—differences seen clearly in the contrasting stands of New Rightists and neoconservatives within the Reagan administration. But these differences represent not only a range of concerns within the bourgeois class but also conflicting demands within patriarchy. For instance, contrasting positions on abortion do not merely reflect different factions within the bourgeoisie; they reflect different positions among men as a sexual class, as well as among the bourgeoisie as an economic class, on the meaning of abortion.

The state as an "actor" seeks to mediate conflicts between the capitalist need for wage laborers; the patriarchal need for the "institution of motherhood," which underpins the structural, institutional, and ideological differentiation of woman from man by identifying woman within the private sphere; and the ideology of liberalism and liberal feminism, which demands equal rights among men and between men and women. It is out of these contradictory needs that the welfare state developed. That governmental form has then intensified these conflicts, as have the Reagan administration's efforts to mediate between the radical demands of the New Right and the less extreme concerns of the neoconservatives.

2. See Ralph Miliband, *Marxism and Politics* (Oxford: Oxford University Press, 1977), for a position on the relative autonomy of the state that counters the view of the state as an instrument of the capitalist class. For further clarification of the neoinstrumentalist view of the state, see Louis Althusser, *Lenin and Philosophy and Other Essays* (New York: Monthly Review Press, 1971); Sally Hibbin et al., *Politics, Ideology, and the State* (London: Lawrence & Wishart, 1978).

3. Catharine A. MacKinnon, in "Feminism, Marxism, Method, and the State: Toward Feminist Jurisprudence," *Signs* 8, no. 4 (Summer 1983): 635–59, argues that the state is not autonomous in relation to patriarchy, whereas I think it is relatively autonomous.

The Subversiveness of the Welfare State

Part of patriarchy's power has been rooted in the specific way the state mystifies its relation to patriarchy, most particularly through a discourse that distinguishes between public and private life through the differentiation between state and family. The more the social welfare state has disclosed the state's interest in family life, the more the ideological distinctions between family and state, public and private, sexual and political life are found to crisscross. As a result, the terrain of political struggle now includes areas once considered private. Ironically, the social welfare state is partially responsible for this shift and as such is subversive to its own patriarchal purposes: the separateness of public/private life, family/state, man/woman, has been challenged by the welfare state's open involvement in all of these paired realms.

What happens within capitalist patriarchal society when distinct lines between family and state are challenged? Does the transfer of male power from the father or the husband to the state mean more power for women? The state realm means the domain of men, the realm of public life, the activity of politics. And all of these are differentiated from the domain of women, the realm of private life, the activity of the family. These distinctions—which have always contained an ideological purpose and have never simply described reality—have lost much of their potency today because the social welfare state has exposed its relations to the family, to patriarchal power, to the economy.

In the same way that the welfare state eroded the distinction between the state and the economy,[4] and hence between political and economic life, so it has challenged the distinction between "the" state and "the" family, which is as necessary to patriarchal society as the distinction between politics and economics is to capitalism. The social welfare state has uncovered the state's particular interests in affirming specific family forms and functions. Although the state has always been active in defining the family realm, the social welfare state has made this involvement explicit. And this reality, the state's involvement in the family, stands counter to the liberal ideology of public/private life that presumes the separateness of state/family: if the state is viewed as actively involved in family life, the politics of family life is revealed, however vehemently the discourse of the capitalist patriarchal state proclaims the two institutions as separate.

Rather than challenging the distinctness of family from state, the

---

4. For a clear statement of this position, see Frances Fox Piven and Richard Cloward, *The New Class War: Reagan's Attack on the Welfare State and Its Consequences* (New York: Pantheon Books, 1982).

social welfare state has redefined the relationship; the terms used in doing so, particularly the terms of policies directed to single-parent families, expose state involvement more directly than earlier state family policy has done. What becomes obvious is that the existence of family forms other than the traditional nuclear family has necessitated a rearticulation of patriarchal authority on the state level. As this process occurs, the patriarchal aspects of the state become exposed and vulnerable, for the distinction between state and family, public and private, is further eroded. The social welfare state has in this way played a progressive role in exposing the state's involvement in defining the contours of (patriarchal) family life. Hence the Reagan administration's attack against it.

Reorganizing the Social Welfare State and Reconstructing Patriarchy

The dismantling of the social welfare state eliminates the supposed "new class" of welfare administrators, made up in disproportionate numbers of white and black women and black men. Expansion of the welfare state's government services increased the job opportunities for middle-class, educated black and white women. In 1976 government employed 21 percent of all women, 25 percent of all blacks, 15 percent of all Hispanics, and 16 percent of all men.[5] More particularly, government employed 49.9 percent of all female professionals and 34.5 percent of all male professionals. Therefore, government cutbacks in hiring at these levels have affected middle-class professional women at a higher rate than men. The dismantling of the welfare state and its administration is directed at reducing the gains made by these women as well as by black men.

The effects of these cutbacks are staggering: "Minority employees of the federal agencies have been laid off at a rate 50% greater than non-minority employees. Women administrators have been laid off at a rate 150% higher than male administrators. Minorities in administrative positions have been laid off at a rate about 220% higher than non-minority employees in similar positions."[6] The Reagan administration has argued that cutbacks of federal jobs will be offset by an increase in private-sector employment, particularly in the defense industry. But workers laid off in these cutbacks are not those who will be hired in private industry, which

5. Lester Thurow, *The Zero-Sum Society* (New York: Basic Books, 1980), p. 163.
6. Augustus F. Hawkins, "Minorities and Unemployment," in *What Reagan Is Doing to Us*, ed. Alan Gartner, Colin Greer, and Frank Riessman (New York: Harper & Row, 1982), p. 134. For further discussion of the Reagan administration's fiscal policies, see Frank Ackerman, *Reaganomics: Rhetoric vs. Reality* (Boston: South End Press, 1982); Robert Lekachman, *Greed Is Not Enough: Reaganomics* (New York: Pantheon Books, 1982).

has a poor record for hiring professional women and black men. The record of the public sector, on the other hand, is good. "Government employment primarily benefits professional women (both white and black) and professional minority men (about 50% of these two groups worked at all levels of government in the 1970's). Indeed, since 1950, increased public spending has been the single most important impetus behind the greater economic mobility of women and minorities."[7] In 1980, about 20 percent of black men and 28 percent of black women were classified as government wage and salary workers. The likelihood of employment in the government sector was more than 50 percent greater for blacks of both sexes than for whites.[8]

Dismantling the welfare state and attacking the "new class" constitutes a direct assault on the gains made by black men and black and white women, particularly those in the professional middle class. The gains of middle-class women are jeopardized by the state's attempts to reaffirm patriarchal white privilege through a sexual and racial hierarchy of the market. To the degree that it played an active role in providing opportunities to women, the welfare state itself, like liberal democracy, has become a subversive force challenging the patriarchal ordering of the marketplace.

In addition to the dismissal of administrators, the dismantling of the welfare state has resulted in a drastic reduction in social programs. These cutbacks particularly affect women who are underemployed, poor, and on welfare, whereas the attack on the "new class" is aimed at the middle-class white and black woman and black man. The patriarchal and racist aspects of the Reagan state are differentiated along economic class lines. A major problem for the state, however, is that a woman's economic class is partially defined by the type of family in which she lives. Black and white women are disproportionately represented among the poor, the fastest growing segment of the U.S. population. In 1979 many of these poor women were among the 5.3 million female heads of household, a group that experienced a sharp rise in unemployment from 5.6 percent to 9 percent between 1970 and 1978.[9]

The dissolution of the social welfare state, outlined in the budget cuts of 1981–84, implicitly expresses a sexual politics. That statement does more than just point out that the budget cuts have particular effects on women—although they do. It says that at the base of economic policy is a social policy on the family's function within a patriarchal society. In this

7. Martin Carnoy and Derek Shearer, "The Supply Side of the Street," *Nation* 233, no. 15 (November 7, 1981): 464.

8. James D. Williams, ed., *The State of Black America* (Washington, D.C.: National Urban League, 1983), p. 64.

9. Steven Erie and Martin Rein, "Welfare: The New Poor Laws," in Gartner, Greer, and Riessman, eds. (n. 6 above), p. 77.

sense, the Reagan budgets, while trying to deal with inflation, have sought to realign the relationship between the state and family, men and women, public and private life. These budgets attempt to limit and curtail the responsibilities of the welfare state and to increase the responsibilities (and supposed freedom) of "the" family.

The Reagan administration must attempt to redefine the relationship between family life and the state when no single policy will apply to all family forms. At present, the state seems to be articulating a differentiated series of patriarchal policies that it hopes will lead to new economic class divisions and exacerbate those already existing among women. Since a woman's marital status is increasingly the most important determinant of her economic class, the Reagan state is actively trying to redefine patriarchal controls and to devise a policy that will speak to this new social reality.

Conflict within the Patriarchal State

The conflict within the state over what to do about the changing nature of the family and the issues raised by feminism is quite real. The Carter administration demonstrated such conflict when addressing issues of the "working mother," the Equal Rights Amendment, the threat to draft women, abortion legislation, and pregnancy disability payments. These matters continue to raise significant controversy.

Whereas Carter's administration endorsed the ERA (although it did nothing to aid its ratification), the Reagan administration is balanced on a tightrope "against the amendment but for equal rights." Teetering on both neoconservative and New Right principles, Reagan supports the New Right position against the Equal Rights Amendment; yet he tries to appear supportive as well of equal rights for women, adopting the neoconservative position that endorses equality of opportunity, not equality of conditions.

Reagan's New Right stance against ERA creates as many problems as it solves, possibly more. It signals that the relations of power within the state in 1984 remain patriarchal—that those in government today think that the political system of capitalist patriarchy cannot abide women's legal equality. By protecting its interests through adherence to an outmoded form, the state draws attention to its patriarchal needs. Since a majority of Americans supports the ERA, this policy makes it apparent that factions within the state rule in their own interest. The bluntness of this contradiction—between majority opinion's approval of ERA and the amendment's legislative defeats—can only be subversive to the state in the long run. Whereas 66 percent of anti-ERA women voted for Reagan in 1980, only 32 percent of pro-ERA women did.

Because the liberal feminists demand "opportunity," which logically leads to a more progressive political stance, they cannot abide the Reagan administration's present policy of rejecting the amendment. The much-discussed "gender gap" reflects a consciousness among women that rejects present Reagan administration policies affecting them. Interestingly, the Reagan state, caught between its patriarchal constraints and liberalism's promise of equality of opportunity for women, has had an easier time rejecting welfare state liberalism than liberal-feminist endorsement of ERA and abortion rights. What becomes clear, nonetheless, is that it cannot abide equality of opportunity or conditions for women.

Sandra O'Connor's appointment to the Supreme Court shows how the Reagan administration has tried to separate the question of "women's rights"—and thus women's equality of opportunity to become even a Supreme Court Justice—from the issue of the Equal Rights Amendment itself, which supposedly will create equality in the conditions under which women and men compete. Reagan argues that the amendment would be harmful to women because it would treat men and women as though they were the same. O'Connor's appointment was intended as proof that a woman is nevertheless free to be anything she wants to be. All women supposedly need is freedom of choice—not equality. In short, O'Connor's appointment to the Supreme Court reflects the constraints in which the state operates as it attempts to restabilize the relationship between family forms, advanced capitalist market needs, and the state. Reagan's administration is not fully free to reject the ideology of women's equality within the dual wage-earning family.

Although liberalism's justification of the welfare state has been largely rejected by the Reagan government, his administration remains constrained by the demands of liberal feminism as a discourse and a public consciousness. So caught, the administration has problems in reasserting and redefining patriarchal controls, particularly when its policies mean the disproportionate firing of black and white professional women and the disproportionate suffering of poor women. To the extent that Reagan opposes the policies of liberal feminism—affirmative action, CETA programs, the right to abortion, the right to equal pay—he may find his opposition increasing among women. Although the Reagan administration considers the gender gap to be the result of a series of self-interested policy stances, I think it reflects women's developing consciousness of their identity as a sexual class with particular economic vulnerabilities. At the time of this writing, it is impossible to know whether this consciousness will be sufficiently actualized in the 1984 election to remove Reagan from office. But the possibility of doing so exists.

Department of Politics
Ithaca College

California Hearings on the
Feminization of Poverty

Elaine Zimmerman

Overview

The Women's Economic Agenda Project (WEAP), with headquarters in both northern and southern California, is a statewide mobilization effort addressing the issues of women and children in poverty.[1] The project evolved from a small group of East Bay (Oakland area) women who worked for "Women USA" in the 1982 elections by showing voters the political significance of the gender gap. Recognizing that economic concerns were at the heart of the common and critical issues among the diverse women they canvassed, its members based their strategy on linking economic issues to women's votes.

The group quickly grew into the East Bay Women's Coalition, a broad-based organization of women across lines of age, race, income, political party, and special interests. With further expansion it took on its present form as the WEAP, a project that includes AFDC mothers, health workers, union members, seniors, women of color, lawyers, community organizers, academics, public policy specialists, and homemakers. The WEAP's interest is in the deteriorating economic situation that affects all

1. For more information, call or write the WEAP offices at 477 15th Street, Oakland, California 94612 (415-451-7379), or P.O. Box 431516, Los Angeles, California 90043 (213-296-2801).

women, regardless of their present status. But it has special concern for those women at greatest economic risk: single mothers and their children; older women living on low, fixed incomes; women of color; disabled women; migrant workers; and immigrants.

The WEAP's purpose is to identify and publicize specific ways in which it is possible to reverse women's descent into poverty. The project recognizes the power that women have at the polls. Through its extensive outreach and its education program, the WEAP succeeded within a year in organizing women throughout California to develop the first women's economic agenda in the nation. This document is an enormous aid to continued voter education in the future, as well as a reflection of the present actuality of women's thinking: not only are women exercising their right to vote, but they are also voting more progressively than men on issues relating to peace, economics, and social justice. Women's voices are rising above the barriers of age, religion, income, and political party. Together women can be a single voice that legislators will have to reckon with.

Women need to come together; women literally cannot afford to be pitted against each other, and our impact is strongest when we work in numbers. We also need a broad-based educational program to alert women to present realities. Although all women are affected or are potentially affected by poverty, most are isolated from the political analysis that defines and explains our actual situation. The majority of those of us who are experiencing poverty think of ourselves as coping alone with a problem that is ours individually, rather than one we all share.

Historical Background

After the 1982 election, the East Bay Women's Coalition, made up of over fifty organizations, developed panels of women representing a range of concerns relating to class, race, and special interests. One AFDC mother, one vice-president of a union, one displaced homemaker, one housewife, and a "near-poor" working mother would go out, for example, to a women's caucus union meeting. They would all speak about the effects of the feminization of poverty on all women; however, while stressing the immediacy and general relevance of these serious economic concerns, they would also impress on the audience the political and economic significance of the gender gap. Women in attendance often became rapidly mobilized both by the panel's demands for economic equity and by a new realization of the impact women could have if organized and ready to take the opportunity right at hand.

For one year, the coalition wrote articles, presented an ever-increasing number of panels on these issues, and became quite skilled at using political and economic discussions, with their negative and positive messages, to effect public policy changes, to mobilize women, and to gather more women into the coalition. With increased experience, members of the coalition learned to present the issues so that a wide spectrum of women could find the ideas personally relevant. How, for instance, do you talk about the impoverishment of women to a professional club of "successful women"? What issues do you bring up to get them concerned and involved? What issues do you raise on a Sunday to a church congregation of senior women and men? The coalition began to face these challenges and to learn rapidly what issues, what economic concerns, brought all women together.

The Hearings of 1983: San Francisco and Los Angeles

In the spring of 1983 the East Bay Women's Coalition had an opportunity to assist in designing, organizing, and implementing the first national hearings on the feminization of poverty convened in San Francisco by Assemblyman Tom Bates, chair of the State Human Services Committee. These hearings, which are excerpted below,[2] allowed women to testify about how increasing impoverishment had affected them, their children, and their elders. The coalition got excellent press coverage for the event by reaching out extensively to the women in the newsrooms.

In the forum provided by these first hearings, women began to teach each other about the range of ways in which trends of impoverishment within the family and community have structural links to race and gender biases in our national institutions. Seniors, young mothers, working women, economists, scholars, and AFDC recipients educated the media and the public on the economic inequities hurting women. Public officials sought to speak in order to affirm both their support of this effort and their presence on the right side of the gender gap. Many legislators unable to attend the hearings had their names listed as supporters.

The East Bay Women's Coalition designed posters, fact sheets, and postcards for these hearings—materials that both legislators and the press found useful. The posters connected the problem, the feminization of poverty, with an answer, strategic use of the gender gap, in the slogan, "Two out of three adults in poverty are female. What if we were all to go to the polls?" They were used in the Martin Luther King Marches in Washington, D.C., and San Francisco and were requested by members of voter registration drives and various low-income organizing groups around the country. Recognizing that those figures, "two out of three," articulated women's concerns better than any other statement, we decided to continue to organize with this slogan in mind. Its message came through to women, particularly to women not traditionally involved in the women's movement.

2. We have made some minor changes in punctuation and spelling in these excerpts and in those from the hearings in Los Angeles. Further information on the complete testimony from the Northern California hearings is available from the office of Assemblyman Tom Bates, 1414 Walnut, Berkeley, California 94706; telephone (415) 540-3176.

Shortly after the hearings in San Francisco, California State Senator Diane Watson, chair of the Senate Health and Welfare Committee, convened in Los Angeles the second such hearings in the country, which are also excerpted below.[3] Primarily organized by women of color, these hearings included a discussion of political strategy toward the end of the day. As part of that discussion, the East Bay Women's Coalition made a presentation on the gender gap. Many women in the audience responded, and there was common agreement on the link to be made between poverty and the newfound significance of women's votes. It was recognized, however, that there would be no real use made of the gender gap unless women worked in groups and coalitions, accumulating significance through numbers.

The Women's Economic Agenda Project

Shortly after these hearings those of us in the coalition began to feel that we still lacked a program for action in our efforts to reverse the feminization of poverty by capitalizing on the existence of the gender gap. Either a candidate or an agenda was necessary for building an effective political mobilization strategy. In order to mobilize more women across age, race, and class lines while remaining nonpartisan, we began to consider developing a statewide women's economic agenda. Thus the East Bay Women's Coalition gave birth to the Women's Economic Agenda Project. The coalition decided to remain focused on local organizing, while the project's efforts expanded political activity into other regions of the state.

Sixty women cooperated in drawing up a draft agenda. Then at eight regional meetings throughout the state the draft document was critiqued and amended. On June 9 and 10, 1984, 350 self-selected delegates from the regional conferences, approximately two-thirds of whom were low-income women and one-half of whom were women of color, gathered at the state capitol for a ratification conference. Shirley Chisholm, Dolores Huerta, state Assemblyman Tom Bates, and state Senator Diane Watson acted as key speakers.

On the first day of the conference, the delegates made final changes to a document that now movingly expressed their common goals.[4] On the second day, women met in regional groups to discuss how best to implement the ratified agenda: how to educate voters about the important issues, how to increase voter registration, and how to make candidates accountable to the issues and policies recommended by the Women's Economic Agenda.

3. Further information on the complete testimony from the Southern California hearings is available from the office of Senator Diane Watson, 4401 Crenshaw, Los Angeles, California 90043; telephone (213) 295-6655.

4. Copies of the Women's Economic Agenda are available from WEAP at their Oakland and Los Angeles offices (n. 1 above).

The WEAP is the first grass-roots women's effort in California to combine an economic platform with statewide community mobilization. While still fragile because newly formed, the organization is large and rapidly growing larger and more vigorous. Churches, community organizations, poverty programs, civil rights groups, and women's groups are supporting the effort with services and, when possible, with money. Foundations are beginning to contribute. Small businesses and stores are donating food and business supplies.

The hearings in San Francisco and Los Angeles on issues relating to women's poverty created the initial momentum. And there have been more such hearings: one in Contra Costa County, near San Francisco, and one in Redding, Shasta County, situated in the rural northern sector of the state. Each hearing extends awareness of the issues to a widening circle of local communities. Meanwhile, the ratified agenda serves both to define problems in broad-based terms and to outline solutions. The political clout to implement those solutions lies in tapping the strength of the gender gap.

We hope that more hearings to raise awareness about the feminization of poverty, combined with a growth in coalitions among women, will continue throughout California and occur in other states as well. Linking the economic problem—the feminization of poverty—and the political solution—a use of the gender gap expressed through coalitions' economic platforms—can bring significant political and programmatic change in this country. Never before have women had such political leverage.

Women's Economic Agenda Project
Oakland, California

*   *   *

Excerpted Testimony from the Northern California Hearings on the Feminization of Poverty, Convened by the California State Assembly Human Services Committee, Chaired by Assemblyman Tom Bates, at the Board of Supervisors Chambers in San Francisco City Hall, April 8, 1983

Alice Denny, AFDC Recipient[5]

My name is Alice Denny, and I'm basically representing myself or Jane Doe or every woman I don't know. In 1979, I divorced my husband of four years and I applied for AFDC in order to support our two girls who were nine months old and two and a half years old; we received $400 a month from our AFDC grant and $90 in food stamps. For over a year, I paid $300 a month for rent and used the remaining $100 to pay water,

---

5. Alice Denny's testimony also appears in the newsletter of the California Commission on the Status of Women, *California Women* (June/July 1983), pp. 4–5.

garbage, gas, electricity, and phone bills. By very careful planning and time-consuming food preparation, I was able to feed my family on those $90 in food stamps. The cost-of-living increase in 1980 raised our grant to $426, but our food stamps were cut to $72 so our increase was actually $8. In late 1980, we finally got housing assistance in the form of Section 8, and I was finally able to buy shoes for my girls without worrying about which utility would have to go unpaid. In October, 1980, I was offered a job, and I enrolled my girls in the only day-care center that had an opening at that time in our town. Fortunately, it's a good one, and we've been able to stick with them. Its fees are about average for this area, and since I was allowed the full amount I paid in figuring my monthly AFDC grant, we were making it okay.

From the time I started working my oldest daughter had many bouts with illness: severe chicken pox, scarlet fever, earaches, flu, etc. Each time she was sick I had to take off time from work, but since I was allowed a supplemental grant if our income got below a survivable level we were able to weather the financial storms. My youngest also had frequent ear infections and the usual colds, but she has always been fairly sturdy even though she is usually anemic, has eczema and an innocent heart murmur. My oldest, though, continued to have more prolonged and mysterious ailments until in December, 1981, shortly before her fifth birthday she was diagnosed with a brain tumor. The first ten-day stay in the hospital she had surgery twice; once to place the shunt, and once to remove about 70 percent of the tumor. The remainder is very near her brain stem so it was decided to treat her with radiation therapy. I was unable to work during the time of her hospital stay, although I did work ten days that month after her release from the hospital; but I found I could not work and take care of her at the same time. The needs of my terrified and recuperating daughter and her daily appointments for radiation and doctor's checks made it necessary for me to quit my job.

January 1, 1982, we got tangled in the federal regulation safety net and slipped through one of the new regulations which disallowed supplementary grants when income goes down or ends for any reason. Our January grant was $40 because I'd had income in November, which, I suppose, I was to have saved for January as opposed to paying our bills and eating back in November. Our food stamps were increased to $182, but they sure didn't pay the rent or put gas in the car.

In the middle of January, I was notified by computer that our grant would be $66 in February because of my income in December. I notified welfare to end my grant, effective February 1, and planned to reapply February 2 in order to get enough to live on. . . . In the past a supplemental grant of up to 75 percent of the regular grant could be obtained by demonstrating emergency needs; that's no longer possible. January 31, my daughter Robin was back in the hospital due to a shunt infection; she ended up staying in ten weeks due to three surgeries and complications. February 2, I was in the welfare office reapplying and requesting an emergency grant of $100 to tide us over until the AFDC application was processed. I was initially denied the emergency grant as they deemed there was no emergency, but because I knew who to turn to for advice February 3, I was able to pick up a check for $100 from the welfare office.

Robin's stay in the hospital was very rocky with unexplained vomiting and diarrhea and temperatures. She was unable to eat for quite a number of days and became badly malnourished. Once she was eating she was put on a very low-salt diet because of high blood pressure caused by steroids and stress. Unfortunately, we had a difficult time getting food from the hospital kitchen that she would eat so I was making meals at home when I would go there to change clothes, and I would bring the meals back and heat them in the microwave. I spent a good portion of our food stamps on food for her, but a few months later I was informed by a new worker that we'd been overpaid in food stamps for February since Robin was not considered a part of the household as she was in the hospital that whole month. Doctors' letters stating that I had provided her food would be to no avail, I was told.

After five weeks in intensive care and another five weeks on the floor, she was sent home with a multitude of medicines and almost daily appointments with the doctors. I asked my worker about a special allowance as she was on a high-complex-carbohydrate, high-protein, low-salt, low-calorie diet. . . . But I didn't bother to apply as I was told it would only mean an additional $9 a month more for a lot more footwork required on my part. She was slowly recuperating from all the physical problems, although to this day she still is having trouble adjusting to a normal life again. She had a relapse in August when the tumor started growing again, but she is now doing well. We have avoided going back to the hospital and pray that we can continue to do so. She is now in school full-time, I am working full-time again but could not afford to except for the child care assistance I get in the form of PNSAPS (which is Private Nursery School Alternate Payments System); without it I would lose $80 a month by working.

We are unable to save for the proverbial rainy day as my income only covers the basic necessities; so if she goes back in the hospital we will be stranded. I understand now, one of the things that is being proposed is that if I apply for a grant on March 1, that I may not get the grant for thirty to forty-five days. . . . In the meantime, my ex-husband owes over $12,000 in back child support. California caught him in Nevada two years ago and, finally, December '82 he started paying child support of $100 a month. This is a third of what was originally ordered. He missed a payment in January, so his wages are now being garnisheed. His present wife is expecting a baby in October which is, of course, ironic; he pled in court that he could not afford to support his two girls. It is also ironic that he is congratulated on the impending birth of his new child, [while] I would cause outrage to taxpayers if I were to get pregnant now. Why is it that I am the only one of the two of us who must exercise responsibility? . . .

We have made it this far because I am strong enough to withstand the insinuations by society that we are freeloaders. I know first hand what life is like on welfare, and let me tell you that it is not steak and Cadillacs. Right now, I'm damned if I do and damned if I don't. In other words, if I stay home and care for my children I'm accused of freeloading, but if I work I not only face economic sanctions but a society that tells me I'm a bad mother for abandoning my children to child care and neglecting my responsibility. I am so busy trying to feed my children and do what is right for society that I don't have the time it takes to fight the system. . . .

Donna Ambrogi, Managing Attorney of the Bay Area Law Center on Long-Term Care

The problem I'm going to be addressing has been largely an invisible problem in our society: the problem of older women who are taking care of a disabled adult. It's very striking; women are the caretakers from beginning to end. It's women who are caring for their own children, women, by and large, working in the day-care centers; then when the children grow up a little bit more and the mother has to go to work, then the grandmother is very often the one who's taking care of the children. This grandmother, who may be a woman in her fifties or sixties, . . . may also be caring for a disabled parent. . . . Finally, when she is still older . . . she may be caring for a disabled spouse. . . .

We are beginning to recognize the problem of these groups like the Altzheimer's disease victims, stroke victims, people with Parkinson's disease, multiple sclerosis, etc. We have not yet sufficiently focused on the needs of the persons taking care of these people. Those of you who know anything about Altzheimer's disease know that as the disease progresses the person becomes extremely difficult, temperamental, and hard to cope with. The spouse who is caring for her husband with Altzheimer's disease has an extremely heavy burden, and the problem is that she receives virtually no help from society. . . . I would say, of course, there are some men who are caring for disabled wives, but on the whole the man, if he can work, is going to work and pay for someone to take care of his wife. The woman is expected to take care of her husband; not only is she expected to by society and her husband and her own internal pressures, but she rarely can earn enough money to pay for someone else to take care of her husband. . . .

I've been haunted since I met with a group called Women Who Care in Marin County, with the story of one woman who said for fourteen years she had been taking care of her husband who had had a stroke. He was partially paralyzed; he was incontinent; his speech was almost impossible to understand (every now and then she understood a little of it—no one else understood anything). For fourteen years she was changing his diapers, changing the sheets, getting him up with backbreaking labor, coping with his temperamental bouts and so on—never getting much sleep. Fourteen years with virtually . . . no help. In the end she finally became physically ill herself and had to put her husband in a nursing home, and is now coping with all the guilts she feels because her husband is in a nursing home. . . .

The physical burdens on these women are enormous. There's story after story about disintegrating knee joints and back disks, heart disease, increased problems with high blood pressure, even increased cancer rates, and nervous breakdowns. These women are coping with their own aging process at the very same time. . . . The result, very often, is two patients instead of one—institutionalization, at least, of the husband and much more call on the public to support the two of them.

Secondly, the emotional stresses on the care giver. Think what it would be like to be confined to your home for fourteen years taking care of someone who gave you very little emotional satisfaction, who could perhaps not communicate with you at all, who was very likely not express-ing any gratitude or concern for what you were experiencing. Your children, after a while, don't come very much. The studies show that sons, in particular, find this extremely difficult to cope with, and the children don't come often. . . .

Finally, the financial stresses. When the illness strikes the husband early, very often he gets little or no pension benefits and the woman loses all her means of support. There are very few services that are available on a sliding fee basis: either you are eligible for them because you're at SSI [Supplemental Security Income] level or you pay full fare. So people who have a little bit of nest egg that they've worked at for forty years are very quickly going to run out of their money providing any kind of help for the husband. Medicare is useless for custodial care; . . . it has very restricted home health services, particularly when there's a spouse in the home. Private health insurance does nothing for these same problems. . . .

At the moment there really are, for most women, only two options: One, put your husband in a nursing home. Or, two, care for him yourself at home twenty-four hours a day, seven days a week. It's not a very happy choice to make. What we need is a third option with real supportive services to the care giver, services which consider the needs and rights of the care giver on an equal basis with those of the patient.

*Excerpted Testimony from the Southern California Hearings
on the Feminization of Poverty, Convened by California State
Senator Diane Watson, Chair of the Senate Health and Welfare Committee,
at Los Angeles County Hearing Room 1138, June 3, 1983*

Jill Halverson, Director, Downtown Women's Center

My name is Jill Halverson and I am the founder and director of the Downtown Women's Center, . . . a center for women on skid row. That is the population of poor people that I am going to talk to you about this morning: shopping-bag ladies—aging women with swollen ankles and ulcerated feet toting bags, shuffling clothing across the street, poking into garbage cans, slumped on a park bench, dozing in doorways, sprawling across library steps, huddled among their possessions in the dreary waiting rooms of train and bus stations, poor, lonely, sick, old, afraid.

Impoverished homeless women have been with us for as long as there have been urban poor. But only recently have they appeared in large enough numbers to enter the public consciousness as a group apart. . . . Fearful or finicky people turn aside when they see one coming. The fastidious sometimes report them to the police. Youth harass them. Thieves rob them. Psychopaths burn and strangle them. . . .

Who are the women? They are women of all ages and ethnicities, religions, educational levels, family backgrounds. They are not members of some tribe peculiar to the run-down areas of large cities. They come from farms and small towns, from the East Coast to the Midwest, from Texas to California. They come from your family and mine. They are all someone's cousin and sister and daughter and mother.

How did they get that way? Most of the women suffer from some form of major mental illness and have been in and out of state mental hospitals. In the 1970s, California and other states decided to release, where housed, mental patients to community care facilities, an effort both cost effective and humane. However, only the first half of the proposal was implemented and only the first half of the result achieved. Patients were released, and it was cost effective. Community care facilities were not developed, and it has not been humane. . . .

A shared plight of all women of skid row is homelessness; most have been homeless at one time. . . . Incomes are too small and precarious to provide a cushion for a stolen or late check or a robbery. Besides homelessness, the women share an environment that is overwhelmingly male and overwhelmingly violent. In the pecking order of poverty on skid row, as elsewhere, women are on the bottom. They are the ones who are mugged leaving the check-cashing place. They are the ones who are beaten and raped. They are the ones whose rooms are broken into and possessions are stolen. They are the ones whose purses are snatched. No wonder, then, that they retreat into isolation and rags and bizarre behavior and shopping bags.

Mary Buchanan, Project New Focus Recipient

My name is Mary Buchanan, and I . . . was in Project New Focus.[6] And before New Focus came along, I've been raised in institutions from a minor to an adult. I have strikes against me. I'm a woman, and I'm a minority. For me, to be a minority and poor was just a way of life. My mother went through what the ladies have talked about . . . today, about their husbands leaving them with kids and having no way to make it. Well, I fortunately do not have kids, and thank God for that. But to watch what goes on in all cities, and I can only speak for Los Angeles, they have programs for men, and they understand men. . . . But when it comes to women, we are degenerates. We are prostitutes, and we are thieves. And that's not true.

Everytime we get our foot in the door, somebody shuts it out. . . . I've lived through it all my life. I'm twenty-five and a program was introduced, Project New Focus, that gave a lot of women a chance, and it was yanked from us, [even though] it gave us enough respect in that short time.

I did not want to go back to jail, did not want to commit crimes. I lived good committing crimes, but that's not what it's about for me today. I'm trying to make it, and it's hard with $3.35 an hour.

You know, everybody talks about welfare. I'm not eligible for welfare because I have no kids. I'm eligible to work as a waitress eight hours a day, and if I'm lucky, get a roommate to afford to rent a one-bedroom apartment. And I hear people talk about all these great fantastic things, but I don't see any action. All I hear is talk. You know, and there is not too much I can do when it comes to action. I'm not well-educated. I can talk, but to understand a lot of these things, I can't. I can only understand my feelings. . . . I just wish that women today would get it together—senators, governors, whoever, would take notice that women need help from the bottom up.

We just don't need welfare. We need to learn how to work, and we don't need doors slammed in our face when we try to take a man's job. I was trained in dry wall, and I'm good at it, damn good. But I can't get in a door. I have six hundred hours, union certified. I can't get in. I'm a woman. I'm small. I'm Hispanic. And it's just not going anywhere—you know, until we decide to stick together as a team.

6. Project New Focus is a program funded by the U.S. Department of Labor, set up to meet the needs of female offenders.

Johnnie Tillman-Blackston, President, California
Welfare Rights Organization

I'm the president and founder of the California Welfare Rights Organization and chairman of the National Welfare Rights Organization, where I still hold a volunteer position as the executive director.... Twenty years ago, it was not proper for women to identify themselves as welfare recipients, ... and I know you are not going to like this because most of the people I see in this room are women. In my day—when I became a welfare recipient, January, 1963—most social workers were women, and we caused holy hell being a welfare recipient from our so-called sisters, aunts, and brothers and cousins. That's what drove me to organize a welfare system because they were crying just like this lady is crying right here. . . .

They were crying about abuses that they got from their workers from the welfare department. And they cried about midnight raids—that you got a knock on your front door at . . . midnight, and a man flashes a badge and says, "Pardon me." In the back door, when you open up the door, here he's standing with a badge. What were they looking for? They were looking for men. Now, that is a good time to look for a man in a house. And what you had then was there were some men who tried to stay with their wives and babies. . . . It was rough on them too, especially if you were poor and black. And I don't want to get into racism. I'm going to tell it like it is. . . .

Because you know some other folks who are not black ... was catching hell too. The man had to split so you could eat. He got to come back at midnight so he could eat too. . . . You got penalized for that because they came in. They looked under the bed. They emptied the washing machine (those of us who were fortunate enough to have a wringer-type washing machine). [If] there was a dirty clothes hamper, they pulled those apart.

That's what women was crying about. Then the social worker crosses her legs whenever she got in your house and asks a lot of asinine questions. They want to know what time did you get pregnant, what position was you laying, et cetera and et cetera. And if you didn't come up with something innocent, that broad disenrolled you from the welfare role.

And when they told me all of this, I thought they was crazy. I said, "They come in?" When I had to get on welfare, everytime somebody knocked at my door, I was scared to death. There was no man there because I had left him in Arkansas. I was more fortunate than most women. Some women, the man left them. I left him. Thank God I had the sense enough to leave him. . . .

We are still at 8459 South Broadway in Los Angeles. . . . How that organization . . . has survived twenty-five years is because we never had any money. I refused to let anybody fund us publicly. Now, you can give me all you want privately but not public funds. Let me tell you why. You take that money, you have to do what they say. I don't like to do what they say. I like to be independent. . . . I plan to keep it like that. So I still sell . . . chicken dinners and chili, whatever folks want to eat. I sell it. We keep the lights on the telephone. We pay the landlord when we get it, the best we can. So far, he has been very good and not put us out.

. . . I would like to add . . . that I been fortunate. . . . I've been off the relief roles ever since 1970, I believe. I became the executive director, so I moved from $3,000 a year to $13,000 a year. I am now an aide to one of the city councils, Councilman Robert Farrow, which . . . raised my salary a little bit higher. But I still have an opportunity to do things that I now do and to be able to know people.

Celia Fire Thunder, Assembly of California Indian Women

The reason I am here is because I have been asked to talk on Indian women. Half of our Indian women are in Washington, D.C., this week because Congress has cut health care for Indians in many areas. So many women [are there] arguing right now.

My name is Celia Fire Thunder. I am a student from Pine Ridge, South Dakota. I have lived in California for twenty years, fourteen of those in the L.A. area, and the last six years I've lived in San Diego. . . . I used to be an AFDC mother back in 1967. I went to the WIN [Work Incentive Program], got my LVN [Licensed Vocational Nurse] license. At this present time, I am continuing my education, and I hope to go to law school.

I represent the Assembly of California Indian Women, which is a statewide organization of Indian women, both rural and urban. Our primary goal is to reach as many Indian women across the state as we can and teach them the legislative process. What we have found out is many times we ask our Indian women to write . . . a letter to this person and to that person, and politely they will say yes. They didn't know what we are talking about. So, we have had to go back to square one and begin to teach members of our community the whole legislative process. We have had to give names and addresses of local assemblypeople, local congressmen, and local senators. We give them out in packets. . . . I also represent the California Urban Indian Health Council, which is a statewide organization representing the Urban Indian Clinic. And I am also a chairperson of the American Indian Health Center in San Diego.

I'm going to talk about California Indian history at this time. From the years 1500 to 1820, the early Spanish explorers who went up and down the coast in their beautiful ships estimated the population of the natives to be around 400,000. From 1822 to 1848, under Mexican rule, the estimated population was 300,000. From 1849 to 1875, under Anglo rule—genocide—the untold story of California, where in twenty-six years, the population of an estimated 300,000 natives was reduced to 20,000. The 1900 census data shows 15,377 Indians in the state of California. From 1900 to 1950, there was a normal growth rate, up to 20,000. In 1950, President Eisenhower planned to . . . relocate Indians to large urban areas. His plan was for termination by assimilation, meaning he puts us in cities, and we were going to disappear. He was wrong. We always find each other.

The 1980 census . . . shows in California there are over 201,000 Indians once again here. And of those, 100,383 are women. The American Indian women in 1900 in California [totaled] 7,654. Today, we are a hundred thousand. From 1950 . . . the rate of Indian women had doubled. The Bureau of Indian Affairs at one time placed single Indian women with children in large cities. It is like placing somebody from the moon in Los Angeles or somebody from Los Angeles on the moon; it's a totally alien environment. . . .

American Indian females have been forced to assume the physical, emotional, and spiritual well-being of their families for many reasons, the most obvious being that of being deserted. The rate of Indian men deserting their families is alarmingly high, and the reasons for this are also many. And it has also been seen, even if the male or father is present, the female is still the head of the household. She is usually the one who has to interact with all the social service agencies to obtain assistance, as well as negotiate with the landlord, and tell them, "Well, I'll pay you next week. . . ."

Many of these American Indian women, especially in Los Angeles—I think the population showed L.A. City had the high somewhere around 47,000 in the '80 census—are usually from another state. . . . We are still under what we call treaty obligations. The federal government assumed a certain amount of responsibility for our health care and our education by treaties with our nation. They could be the Navajo, the Sioux, the Hopis, but they did sign a little over three hundred treaties, and they said they would provide for our health and education.

One of the other problems that Indian women have is that back on their reservation . . . they have always enjoyed the company of many relatives while at home. Well, once in a major city, they no longer have a support system. In the last fifteen, twenty years in Los Angeles and many other major cities, we have developed urban Indian clinics. Many of these Indian clinics support all the necessary support systems that one needs: advocacy, counseling, social work, health care, news/information. Sometimes [women] just go to socialize. At this time, many of these clinics, their futures are in jeopardy. . . .

We hear about AFDC. We hear about child care cuts. There is also something else called block grants that is coming down the tubes that is going to affect us. . . . If that block grant comes down . . . many, many of those things that women enjoy—our children's health care, community clinics—are going to be eliminated because the . . . government has been totally insensitive to the health needs of minorities and children. This, I suspect, is why the government has had to step in and develop the public health system. Now, under the block grant, they want to give it back to the counties, and this is another issue that we are going to have to deal with.

Reena O'Connor, California Fair Share, Men and Women against Judicial Rape

I'm forty-six years old, and I'm with California Fair Share, Men and Women against Judicial Rape. After being with my ex-husband . . . from approximately '63 to '79, he left me pregnant with our fifth son and no money. He was in show business. I'm a singer, and I was in show business also.

His income at the time of the divorce was $30,000 a year, plus he's an heir to the Montgomery Ward estate. He's an independent record producer, photographer, office manager—lots of money. He could have paid his child support. However, he stopped paying his court-ordered support money in '79. I had to go on AFDC, and, at that time, they were paying for six people $625 a month.

For the past two years for six people, I've been getting $771, $171 in food stamps. When my ex-husband was with us, the rent was $450, and, within a year and a half, I was increased to [$600]. So I pay $600 on my rent and $171 is left. . . .

With the medical cutbacks, I have an asthmatic child and a lot of his medicine he needs in order to prevent him from dying, to get to an emergency hospital, was included in the cutbacks, was no longer covered by Medi-Cal. . . . Also, my family has skin problems. You can go see a doctor for that, but there is no money to pay for the medication because Medi-Cal doesn't cover that either. What is needed is for laws to be made to prevent a lot of these problems that we are all having.

I think, with the AFDC program, the cost of living increases should be reinstated. At least these help with the inflation that has been going on. Housing is not covered by all the rent laws that they have. A landlord can raise the rent in a house whenever he wants to raise it and that's how I got caught up in that. I have no money to move.

Also, the working mother's budget should be reinstated. And I have teenage children. However, now, with Reaganomics, any money that is earned by any of us is counted toward the AFDC allowance. Therefore, there was a time that teenagers could go out and get part-time jobs to pay for some expenses, for clothing and stuff. But that's no longer possible. So that keeps the children from being encouraged to go out and work because a lot of us cannot afford to lose the AFDC, . . . having young children.

So, I don't know. Just saying that my problem was I was caught up in the situation because the system wasn't there to enforce his paying the child support, which, by the way, was reduced by the district attorney's office from $800 a month to $150 for all five children after no investigation was done on their part. . . .

And then, all the things that you hear about, being paranoid, being on AFDC from the intimidations that you get from your workers. I'm having emotional problems as well because I was afraid to go to my mailbox because every time a gray envelope was in there, you just know if it wasn't on the first or fifteenth, you just know they were going to deduct something from your allowance or cut you off. I was cut off about three times for not doing things that my worker demanded me to do, even though my child was under the age that I am supposed to be able to go out and look for work. And there is no work for anyone to support our children. You just can't go into a job instantly and get housing and medical and all of that without laws being passed by our legislators and people who I feel can help.

Kathy Dawson, Older Women's League

I am representing the Older Women's League. [I speak for] a group of women facing poverty for the first time, a new group appearing on the scene, women who are educated and middle class who never expected to be poor at any time in their lives. . . .

Older women are at a particular disadvantage in society today. They face so many disabilities. [They] lose their rights to pensions, their husbands' pensions, their support, their means of livelihood, and they face a life of discrimination in the work force not only because they have never worked before and have no recent paid work experience but because they are older.

Age discrimination in employment is a particular disability for women. When an older woman attempts to find employment, she hears so many euphemisms. I'm sure they are familiar to all of you who have recently [tried] to obtain employment . . . : "You are over-qualified." Older women know what being over-qualified means. It means you are too old. "You are under-qualified. . . ." Older women know that if they have taken time out from the work force to raise a family, of course they haven't qualifications of the woman who has never left the work force or has been able to continue working while she has been raising a family. . . .

Older women who cannot find employment are invariably not eligible for any kind of welfare. They are ineligible for social security because they haven't reached the age at which social security can be given to them. And they are left to their own resources. . . . Those women who at midlife and older need to support themselves in some fashion or another because of widowhood or divorce or some other disability find themselves without any means of support at all, without any means of obtaining an income and without, really, any means of surviving. . . .

The Older Women's League is trying, through legislation, to change the lot of the women facing midlife and older years alone and without some sort of support. It seems to me that a change in attitude, which means a tremendous social change, will have to occur before the older women will ever be given any status in a society which worships youth and particularly feminine youth. . . .

I hope that somewhere we will find the means to give some attention to these deserving members of society who have contributed a great deal and who deserve to live with a little peace of mind in their declining years.

Women's Poverty and
Women's Citizenship:
Some Political Consequences
of Economic Marginality

Barbara J. Nelson

Much of women's political activity—especially their work in community, religious, and labor organizations and their participation in social movements—remains unchronicled and undervalued because it occurs outside the realm of governmental politics. Our attention is rarely drawn even to women's involvement in the more visible political activities that might be called "statist." In the United States during the last decade, three important changes have occurred in women's political interaction with the state. First, women now have substantial clout on election day. They vote in roughly the same proportions as men and thus have, for demographic reasons, a significant advantage in the number of votes cast. Second, women now differ noticeably from men in their opinions on issues, parties, and candidates—a difference the media have labeled the "gender gap." One expression of this gap has been the consistently poorer evaluations that women have given President Ronald Reagan, largely because of his militarism and his lack of commitment to social programs.[1]

An earlier version of this paper was prepared while I was a visiting fellow at the Russell Sage Foundation. Continuing support was made available by a grant from the Hubert H. Humphrey Institute of Public Affairs. In addition, I would like to thank Nancy Johnson Häggmark for research assistance, Knut Ekker for computational assistance, and Lynne Mills and Doreen Englund Corwin for preparing the manuscript. Harry Boyte, Mary Dietz, Sara Evans, and the anonymous reviewers for *Signs* offered helpful comments.

1. William Schneider, "Despite Foreign Policy Popularity Boost, Doubts about Reagan Persist," *National Journal* (November 19, 1983), pp. 2448–49. Schneider reports on the ABC News/*Washington Post* poll results showing that in September 1983, 59 percent of men, compared with 47 percent of women, approved of the way Ronald Reagan was handling his job as president.

The third change is the increasing recognition given to the political nature of women's economic status. In the United States, as elsewhere, women are poorer than men. By itself, this fact is not new; what is new or, better said, newly recognized, is that women constitute an increasing percentage of the poor. In addition to its material consequences for women, the feminization of poverty, as it has been labeled by Diana Pearce, has important political consequences for women's connection to the state.[2] In a modern industrial nation, poverty links individuals and families to the state through a web of social and economic programs. This connection is often more durable, salient, and immediately relevant to the lives of clients than voting is to those who make the occasional pilgrimage to the polls. And it is women who constitute the substantial majority of the clients of most social insurance and welfare programs.[3] For example, in 1980, women constituted 61.6 percent of the adult beneficiaries of Social Security (OASDI) and 81.1 percent of the guardians receiving Aid to Families with Dependent Children (AFDC). While women participated equally with men in most mass electoral activities, women increasingly predominate in the less legitimate and less valued client interactions which often betoken economic marginality.

These trends—women's electoral clout, women's current electoral distinctiveness, and the feminization of poverty—are rarely discussed together. In no other Western industrial country are electoral and distributional considerations so relentlessly segregated in mainstream political rhetoric and analysis. In this essay I want to examine together the electoral and client experiences of women, that is, to analyze women's citizenship and women's poverty in ways that illuminate each other. This examination takes two directions. The first juxtaposes women's electoral and client activities, with emphasis on poor women, to show that client activities are a major component of poor women's statist political experiences. For all women, but especially for poor women, client experiences are largely determined by their positions as wives or mothers, not as independent citizens or workers, as is the case for men. The second part of the essay uses the pattern and history of women's client experiences—which are, of course, one proxy for their economic and social position—to discuss women's place in the liberal theory of the Western state. This

2. Diana Pearce and Harriet McAdoo, *Women and Children: Alone and in Poverty* (Washington, D.C.: National Advisory Council on Economic Opportunity, 1981).

3. Individuals are eligible for social insurance programs (e.g., Social Security, Medicare, and unemployment compensation) on the basis of their own or their employers' contribution to the program fund. Individuals are eligible for "means-tested" (or welfare) programs (e.g., food stamps, Aid to Families with Dependent Children [AFDC], and Medicaid) on the basis of their household's income or assets. Such programs are financed from the general revenue. Convention dictates that veterans benefits be considered insurance programs, with service in the armed forces being the payment that entitles one for benefits.

theory, so reluctant to accept women as electoral citizens, faces an even stronger challenge when confronting women in their roles as clients.

Women's Electoral and Client Activities

Resources and Participation

The great body of conventional political literature analyzing the connection between economic position and political participation focuses almost exclusively on the relationships between socioeconomic resources and voter turnout.[4] The principal finding of this research is that as a person's income and education increase, so does the probability that he or she will vote. The two factors interact in the following manner: turnout increases with income, but at each income level, turnout rates further increase as the level of schooling rises. These associations are not explanations, of course. The reasons for lower turnout among the poor and poorly educated are complex. The nature of the political system offers one: the absence of a working-class party directly tied to the mobilizing arm of unions reduces the turnout of average- and low-income people. Awareness of individual experiences gives another: electoral participation is more difficult (and perhaps less clearly worthwhile) for poor people.

Studies of voter turnout rarely if ever examine the differences between the electoral participation of poor women and poor men. Similarly they do not consider a wide range of political activities, including client experiences, within the definition of political participation.[5] This section begins to rectify these omissions by comparing women's electoral and client activities.

A word is in order on the sources of data and principal definitions supporting this discussion. Data on the use of social programs come from many different sources and are, occasionally, contradictory or incomplete. Indeed, one of the striking findings of this study is that official publications of social programs often do not report the gender composi-

4. See, e.g., Sidney Verba, Norman H. Nie, and Jae-On Kim, *Participation and Political Equality* (Cambridge: Cambridge University Press, 1978); Sidney Verba and Norman H. Nie, *Participation in America* (New York: Harper & Row, 1972); Raymond E. Wolfinger and Steven J. Rosenstone, *Who Votes?* (New Haven, Conn.: Yale University Press, 1980).

5. For material challenging the narrow definition of participation, see Barbara J. Nelson, "Client Evaluations of Social Programs," in *The Public Encounter: Where State and Citizen Meet*, ed. Charles T. Goodsell (Bloomington: Indiana University Press, 1981), and "Help-Seeking from Public Authorities: Who Arrives at the Agency Door?" *Policy Sciences* 12 (August 1980): 175–92; Samuel H. Barnes, Max Kaase, et al., *Political Action: Mass Participation in Five Western Democracies* (Beverly Hills, Calif.: Sage Publications, 1979); John D. McCarthy and Mayer N. Zald, "Resource Mobilization and Social Movements: A Partial Theory," *American Journal of Sociology* 82 (May 1977): 1212–41.

tion of beneficiaries. Information by gender on electoral activities is more readily available. The two sources of election data used here are the biennial National Election Studies conducted by the Survey Research Center (SRC) and the Center for Political Studies at the University of Michigan, and, since 1964, the Current Population Survey conducted by the Census Bureau after each national election. Results from the Current Population voter surveys are published routinely. Interestingly, the tables showing turnout by income level are published only intermittently, and tables showing the gender and income differences in voting are never published.

It is always difficult to decide which definition of poverty to employ in a study like this. Although women and children constitute a growing percentage of the poor, those experiencing poverty still remain quite heterogeneous in age, household composition, and region, and that heterogeneity is difficult to capture in any single measure. For the analysis of the 1980 election study, I classified as poor all individuals living in households with less than $7,000 total income. My use of this figure represents an attempt to balance a variety of concerns in a way that would make the results of the election study analysis roughly comparable with the information available from program reports. Contrary to popular stereotypes, poor households are not, on average, larger than more well-to-do households. Nationwide, the modal composition of a poor household is one adult and two children. In 1980 the official (and quite conservative) poverty line for a household of this type was $6,635—hence the decision to use $7,000 as the cutoff point.[6] Under this definition, some larger households with low per capita incomes were inappropriately excluded from the analysis and some smaller households with "high" per capita incomes were inappropriately classified as poor. It is clear, however, that in 1980, $7,000 did not make any household rich.

Other figures about the 1980 poverty population are useful as points of comparison. The 1980 census found that 13.3 percent of all households and 13.0 percent of all individuals fell below the poverty line. In the 1980 National Election Study, 17.4 percent of respondents to the post-election questionnaire lived in households with family income under $7,000. In the same year, the Social Security Administration reported that the average yearly AFDC payment totaled $3,453 and the average yearly Social Security payment totaled $3,602. These figures suggest that the definition of poverty used in this analysis includes most if not all the individuals whose total household income derived from public social programs.

---

6. Mollie Orshansky, "Counting the Poor: Another Look at the Poverty Profile," in *Poverty in America: A Book of Readings*, ed. Louis A. Ferman, Joyce L. Kornbluh, and Alan Haber (Ann Arbor: University of Michigan Press, 1968).

Gender Differences in Electoral Activities

When women won national suffrage in 1920, male politicians expressed two somewhat contradictory fears. On the one hand, they feared the effects of a wave of inexperienced, undisciplined citizens washing into the electorate. On the other hand, they feared that women would vote in militant unison, disrupting the existing partisan balance. Time showed that neither fear was justified.

Instead, in the period between 1920 and the mid-1970s, women held much the same political preferences as the men of their class, race, educational level, and family. As a group they voiced those preferences less frequently than men, voting somewhat less often and engaging in the campaign process significantly less often. During the post–World War II period, the National Election Surveys showed a pronounced gender difference in voting rates. In the presidential election years between 1948 and 1960, these surveys of approximately 1,500 people indicated that women voted at a rate averaging 10.5 percent less than men. In presidential election years between 1964 and 1980 this source indicated that women voted at a rate averaging 6.8 percent less than men.[7] In contrast, the Current Population Surveys of voter behavior, which interviewed approximately 70,000 people and became available in 1964, showed much smaller gender differences in turnout. This source reported that the turnout rates for men were, on average, only 2.3 percent greater than those for women in the years between 1964 and 1980. In fact, in 1980, the turnout rate for women was just slightly higher than that for men—59.4 percent and 59.1 percent, respectively.[8]

The source of the current parity in women's and men's turnout is an odd one: women's turnout declined less during the Vietnam-Watergate period than did men's.[9] In 1964, 67 percent of women and 72 percent of

7. Figures for the years between 1948 and 1976 are taken from table 2:2, "Percentages of Men and Women Voting in National Elections, 1948–76," in Virginia Sapiro, *The Political Integration of Women* (Urbana: University of Illinois Press, 1983), p. 23. The voting rates for 1980 came from my analysis of that year's National Election Survey. These figures have not been corrected for the overreporting of voting common in election surveys. In an investigation of the overreporting problem using the 1978 National Election Study, Lee Sigelman concludes, however, that "our understanding of the factors that influence voting appears to be largely unaffected by the misreporting phenomenon" ("The Nonvoting Voter in Voter Research," *American Journal of Political Science* 26 [February 1982]: 47–56, esp. 55).

8. If the 1980 data are excluded, an average of 2.9 percent more men voted than women. See table C, "Percent Reported Voted in Presidential Elections by Age and Sex: November 1964 to 1980," in U.S. Bureau of the Census, *Voting and Registration in the Election of November 1980*, in *Current Population Report*, series P-20, no. 370 (Washington, D.C.: Government Printing Office, 1982), p. 5.

9. Voting rates declined for demographic, political, and social-psychological reasons. Between 1964 and 1980, 34 million young voters were added to the electorate, 12 million of whom were made eligible by the Twenty-Sixth Amendment, which lowered the voting age to

men voted (table 1). By 1980 the overall turnout for each group equalized at 59 percent. The parity in voting is important for two reasons. First, equal voting rates give feminist activists and Democratic politicians a device for publicizing women's commitment to the electoral process, a commitment that popular culture and conventional social science have denied. Second, equal voting rates give women a large advantage in the number of votes cast because women constitute a larger percentage of the electorate. In 1980, women constituted 53 percent of all voters and cast 5.53 million more votes than men. These numbers are used to make a case that women as a group presently have an opportunity to influence elections.[10]

The case is strengthened by the fact that the policy and party preferences expressed by women are currently somewhat different from those of men. From a policy perspective, women are more interested in the cause of peace than men are, and they are more likely than men to support social programs. For example, in March 1982, only 36 percent of women, compared with 57 percent of men, were willing to support the idea of sending U.S. military advisers to El Salvador. In the same survey, 47 percent of women and 36 percent of men felt that too much money was spent on space exploration.[11]

In terms of party affiliation, the 1980 election showed that women were 3 percent more likely than men to identify with the Democratic party, but by early 1982 the difference had increased to 8 percent. What this meant is that before the congressional elections of 1982, fully 60 percent of Democratic partisans were women.[12] Women's differences in

---

eighteen. Young voters have low turnout rates, thus reducing overall turnout rates for the electorate. Alienation and dissatisfaction with government also reduced turnout, although the extent of this impact is still being debated. See U.S. Bureau of the Census, *Voting and Registration Highlights from the Current Population Survey: 1964 to 1980*, in *Current Population Report*, series P-23, no. 131 (Washington, D.C.: Government Printing Office, 1984), p. 1; and William H. Flanigan and Nancy H. Zingale, *Political Behavior of the American Electorate*, 5th ed. (Boston: Allyn & Bacon, 1983).

10. Bella Abzug, with Mim Kelber, *Gender Gap* (Boston: Houghton Mifflin, 1984); Eleanor Smeal, *Why and How Women Will Elect the Next President* (New York: Harper & Row, 1984).

11. The figures come from unpublished CBS/*New York Times* poll results from the survey of March 10, 1982. One of the first observations of women's preference for a peaceful foreign policy is found in Gerald Pomper, *Voter's Choice: Varieties of Electoral Behavior* (New York: Dodd Mead & Co., 1975). Earlier studies found no gender differences in partisanship or policy preferences. See Angus Campbell et al., *The American Voter* (New York: John Wiley & Sons, 1964); Bernard R. Berelson, Paul F. Lazarsfeld, and William H. McPhee, *Voting: A Study of Opinion Formation in a Presidential Campaign* (Chicago: University of Chicago Press, 1954).

12. Kathleen A. Frankovic, "Sex and Politics—New Alignments, Old Issues," *PS* 15 (Summer 1982): 439–48.

Table 1

Differences in Selected Electoral Activities by Gender, Election Years 1952–80 (%)

	1952			1964			1976			1980		
	Men	Women	Men Minus Women	Men	Women	Men Minus Women	Men	Women	Men Minus Women	Men	Women	Men Minus Women
Voted in election* (Current Population Survey)	N.A.	N.A.	N.A.	72	67	5	60	59	1	59	59	0
Voted in election† (National Election Survey)	80	69	11	80	76	4	77	68	9	73‡	70‡	3
Tried to influence the vote of others†	33	22	11	30	26	4	44	32	12	40	33	7
Attended political meetings or rallies†	7	6	1	10	8	2	6	7	−1	8	7	1
Worked for a party or candidate†	4	2	2	5	5	0	4	4	0	3	4	−1
Gave money to a party or candidate† ...	6	3	3	12	8	4	11	7	4	9	7	2

*From *Voting and Registration in the Election of 1982*, in *Current Population Reports*, Ser. P-20, no. 383 (Washington, D.C.: Government Printing Office, 1983), p. vi.
†Information for 1952, 1964, and 1976 is from table 22. "Political Activities of Men and Women, by Election," in Sandra Baxter and Marjorie Lansing, *Women and Politics: The Invisible Majority* (Ann Arbor: University of Michigan Press, 1981), p. 114. The 1980 figures are from my analysis of the SRC National Election Study, which is also the source of Baxter and Lansing's data. Voting figures are not corrected for overreporting except where noted.
‡Corrected for overreporting; the percentage for men would be 58 percent, for women, 54 percent, a difference of 4 percentage points.

attitude toward policy and in party affiliation seem likely to endure, confronting mainstream politicians with the old fear associated with women's suffrage: that women might vote distinctively. The relative importance of a "women's vote" depends, however, on the extent to which other groups also mobilize and vote distinctively.

In a modern state voting is as much a symbolic act as it is a method of informing the government of preferences. In contrast, campaigning for a candidate or party requires a deeper commitment to the electoral process, the availability of discretionary resources, and stronger feelings of political efficacy. (It also requires that political candidates or parties welcome and encourage participants.) Not surprisingly, gender differences in these types of activities have remained somewhat less changeable, although the gap has been narrowing. The most persistent difference in electoral activities is found in attempts to influence the votes of others (table 1).[13] In 1980, women remained 7 percent less likely than men to try to influence the choices of others.

Electoral Activities of Poor Women

Any general pattern of electoral participation glosses over important differences in the level and kinds of electoral activities undertaken by specific groups. Historically, electoral participation has been directly tied to economic and social resources. The poor and the poorly educated, along with racial and ethnic minorities and (until very recently) women, have always participated less than have privileged groups. It is not surprising, then, that people living in poor households (for simplicity called "the poor") participated less in a whole range of activities connected with the 1980 elections (table 2). Three particularly interesting gender differences in electoral participation occurred among the poor. First, poor women voted slightly more frequently than poor men. The figures are within the margin of error for analyses on populations of this size, but it seems reasonable to assume that poor women actually did vote more frequently than poor men. Poor women are somewhat better educated than poor men, and educational differences are a major influence on turnout within income levels. Moreover, since women face more downward mobility than men through aging and divorce, it is likely that many poor women have had life experiences that encourage voting.

Second, poor women participated in almost every type of electoral activity except voting less frequently than did poor men. Although the

13. Only respondents whose voting records were validated by National Election Survey staff were considered validated voters. All others, including those whose votes could not be validated for administrative reasons, were considered nonvoters. This is the most conservative procedure for defining the voting population in the 1980 National Election Survey.

number of people participating in these activities was quite small overall, poor women as a group were less likely than poor men to try to influence the votes of others, to have others try to influence them, or to attend political meetings or rallies. Interestingly, though, political parties contact poor women more often than they contact poor men, perhaps because women are more accessible through social benefit offices.

Third, poor single heads of households (all of whom were women) participated in active politics—voting, attending political meetings, working for candidates, or giving money—less frequently than all women and, of course, less than men. At the same time however, they reported engaging in political conversations (trying to influence others and being influenced by them) more frequently than all women, and often more frequently than men. From these findings it appears that poor women who head households have a strong interest in politics but may be constrained by resources and responsibilities from participating actively—a view supported by the fact that in this survey only 2 of the 68 women heading households alone attended a political meeting, worked for a candidate, or belonged to a political organization. Both of these women had incomes over $25,000.

In sum, this analysis suggests that, while poor women vote slightly more often than do poor men, they are even more detached from other forms of electoral participation than the men of their "class." This detachment is particularly evident among poor women who are single heads of households; they apparently discuss elections regularly but rarely have time to participate actively in them.

The Limited (Re)distributive Purposes of Social Programs

Claiming benefits from public social programs is a political as well as an administrative act. Applying for client status involves threading one's way through a large, obviously public bureaucracy, in search of publicly financed benefits. In addition, it usually takes some effort to retain one's client status, although the effort required varies from program to program. For instance, Social Security checks are routinely mailed to beneficiaries, but recipients of unemployment checks must pick them up in person and give assurances, however pro forma, of their attempts to find work. If maintained regularly, client status is a rather durable political role. For some programs (like unemployment compensation) it is self-limiting, but for others (like the retirement part of Social Security) it lasts for the rest of a person's life.

A surprisingly high percentage of American households receive public social benefits. In 1982, 38 percent received benefits from one or more of six programs: Social Security, Supplemental Security Income, veterans benefits, AFDC, unemployment compensation, and food

Table 2

Electoral Activities of Individuals Living in Poor Households, 1980 (%)

	Total Population (N = 1,407)	Individuals Living in Poor Households						
		All (N = 220)	Men (N = 69)	Women (N = 150)	Whites (N = 168)	Blacks (N = 50)	Living in Households with Single Head (N = 31)	Living in Other Households (N = 188)
Voted in elections (not controlled for overreporting)	71.4	56.2	56.5	56.0	54.2	64.0	35.5	59.6
Voted in elections (controlled for overreporting)	55.3	40.6	36.2	42.7	41.0	40.0	22.6	43.6
Was registered but did not vote (controlled for overreporting)	6.1	11.5	16.0	9.3	11.4	8.0	3.2	12.8

Influenced others to vote	36.1	29.7	39.1	25.3	29.9	29.4	35.5	28.7
Was influenced by others to vote	44.0	34.5	40.6	31.8	52.6	29.4	48.4	32.3
Attended political meetings or rallies	7.5	6.4	11.9	4.6	6.5	5.8	3.2	6.9
Worked for party or candidate	3.6	2.7	4.3	2.0	3.6	0.0	0.0	3.2
Had campaign button or sticker	6.7	5.9	5.8	6.0	6.5	3.9	3.2	6.3
Was member of political organization	3.3	1.4	2.9	0.7	1.2	2.0	0.0	1.6
Was contacted by political party	24.4	15.5	10.1	18.0	15.7	16.0	12.9	16.0
Gave money to a candidate or party	8.0	2.7	1.4	3.3	3.6	0.0	0.0	3.2

Source.—1980 SRC National Election Study.

stamps. The actual figures covering the entire range of social programs (which would be easy to derive through a national survey) may be as high as 45–50 percent.[14]

The cost of social benefits is not small. In 1979, the share of the federal budget devoted to social welfare (using the Social Security Administration's definition, which includes educational expenses) was 55 percent. In that year, the federal government together with states and localities spent $428 billion on social welfare, a sum equivalent to 18.5 percent of the GNP.[15]

Public benefits never make anyone rich; often they do not even provide minimal living requirements. Neither have they increased overall income equality during the last twenty years.[16] Public benefits have, however, had a pronounced effect on the number of people living below the magical "poverty line." Congressional Budget Office figures for 1976 show that income transfers from benefit programs reduced the households in poverty from 27.0 percent to 11.5 percent.[17] The patchwork of programs cushions primary-sector workers (mostly men) from the worst impacts of the business cycle, provides a minimum income for the elderly and for mothers with young children, and provides some protection for low-skilled laborers against further exploitation of their wage rates.[18]

In 1982, almost half the income available to the bottom fifth of the population came from public social benefits. As Frances Fox Piven and Richard Cloward have recently written, "The poorest people in the country are now as much dependent on the government for their subsistence as they are on the labor market."[19] Some programs (those described as

14. In a national survey undertaken in 1973, 38 percent of the adult population (not households) received benefits from the sixteen major nonmedical social programs. With the growth in coverage seen during the last decade, it would not be surprising if 45–50 percent of all households now received part of their income in benefits. See Barbara J. Nelson, "Help-Seeking from Public Authorities" (n. 5 above), "Clients and Bureaucracies: Applicant Evaluations of Public Human Service and Benefit Programs" (paper delivered at the American Political Science Association meeting, Washington, D.C., September 1, 1979); Saad Z. Nagi, "An Epidemiology of Disability in Adults in the United States," *Milbank Memorial Fund Quarterly: Health and Society* 54 (Fall 1976): 441–43.

15. Ann Kallman Bixby, "Social Welfare Expenditures, Fiscal Year 1979," *Social Security Bulletin* 44 (November 1981): 3–12, esp. 9, 10.

16. Together public benefits and women's employment have kept the income distribution in the United States stable in the postwar period. See Lester Thurow, *The Zero-Sum Society* (New York: Basic Books, 1980), pp. 155–57.

17. U.S. Congress, Congressional Budget Office, *Poverty Status of Families under Alternative Definitions of Income* (Washington, D.C.: Government Printing Office, 1976), p. xv.

18. See Pearce and McAdoo (n. 2 above), pp. 1–5; Benjamin I. Page, *Who Gets What from Government* (Berkeley and Los Angeles: University of California Press, 1983), pp. 61–91; Frances Fox Piven and Richard A. Cloward, *The New Class War: Reagan's Attack on the Welfare State and Its Consequences* (New York: Pantheon Books, 1982), pp. 1–39.

19. Piven and Cloward, p. 15.

means-tested) are targeted to the poor; others (the social insurance pro-grams) are ostensibly blind to the economic need of beneficiaries, who are eligible to payments by "right," that is, by virtue of their own or their employer's prior contribution to the program fund. In recent studies, Sheldon Danzinger, Robert Haveman, and Robert Plotnick have calcu-lated the proportion of 1974 expenditures in social programs spent on the "pre-transfer" poor—those who were below the poverty line before they received benefits. Not surprisingly, means-tested programs went primarily to the needy: the poor received 91.8 percent of AFDC benefits, 83.0 percent of food stamps, 65.0 percent of housing assistance, and 77.8 percent of old age assistance, aid to the blind, and aid to the permanently and totally disabled (programs now superseded by Supplemental Security Income). Insurance programs, which make up two-thirds of all transfer payments, direct a much lower proportion of their benefits to the pre-transfer poor: the poor received 58.8 percent of Social Security, 45.2 percent of workers compensation, 43.0 percent of veterans income sup-port, and 20.8 percent of unemployment insurance.[20]

Gender Differences in the Use of Social Programs

By maintaining a two-tier benefit system, the United States has per-petuated the idea of legitimate insurance beneficiaries and illegitimate means-tested recipients. The dual benefit system reflects the dual labor market. Workers in the primary economy have access to insurance ben-efits on the basis of their *individual* work records, regardless of the re-sources available from other members of their households. Insurance beneficiaries do not face the social stigma of being dependent on public resources, although they often suffer bitterly from the loss of self esteem that accompanies the loss of employment. In contrast, welfare bene-ficiaries are granted benefits on the basis of inadequate *household* income, and they face enormous scorn for their public dependency.

Women predominate as beneficiaries of most social programs, a finding which by itself is politically important (table 3).[21] Women consti-tute well over half the users of most major social programs. For example, 64.8 percent of the recipients of Medicare are women, and 70.0 percent of housing subsidies go to female-headed households or women living alone. The last figure underestimates the number of women benefiting from programs like housing subsidies. Most means-tested benefits are distributed on the basis of household income, and figures describing the benefits are reported by major household "types"—women living alone,

20. See Page, table 10, "Major Income Transfer Programs and Benefits to the Pre-Transfer Poor, 1965 and 1974," pp. 65–66.
21. Figures on women's use of social programs in 1982 are available from the author.

female-headed households with children, male-headed households with children, and men living alone. Women live in most of the households labeled male-headed (indeed, they are frequently the ones who apply for benefits), and they may directly or indirectly receive some of the benefits going to male-headed households even though they are invisible in the reporting system.

A closer examination of the specific distribution of women across the benefit system reveals other politically relevant findings. First, women constitute a larger proportion of the beneficiaries of means-tested programs than they do of insurance programs. For example, 81.1 percent of AFDC guardians are women, while women make up only 41.4 percent of unemployment compensation beneficiaries. Access to unemployment

Table 3

Use of Selected Social Programs, 1980

	Yearly Beneficiaries— Individuals (N in Thousands)	Female Users— Individuals (%)
Insurance programs:[a]		
Medicare	28,100	64.8
Social Security (OASDI)	30,500[b]	61.6
Unemployment compensation[c]	2,844/week	41.4
Veterans benefits	3,196[d]	N.A.[e]

	Yearly Beneficiaries (N in Thousands)		Female Users— Households (%)[f]	
	Individuals	Households	Definition 1	Definition 2
Means-tested programs:[g]				
AFDC[h]	N.A.	3,428	81.1	N.A.
CETA[i]	2,871	N.A.	50.0	N.A.
Food Stamps	19,625	6,769	56.7	73.3
Housing	6,842	2,777	70.0	80.0
Medicaid	18,966	8,287	56.0	71.9
Supplemental Security Income[j]	4,142	N.A.	65.5	N.A.

SOURCES.—Based on latest census data or annual program reports. For details, contact the author.

[a] Insurance program statistics are generally reported on individuals, not households.

[b] 1981 figures.

[c] Includes all types of compensated employment.

[d] Includes compensation and pension benefits.

[e] Veterans Administration staff indicate juust over 1.0 percent unofficially.

[f] When the percentage of female users is based on households rather than on individuals, two definitions are used. Definition 1: Female-headed households or female-only households. Definition 2: Female-headed households or female-only households, plus one-half of married couple households with one or more beneficiaries.

[g] Means-tested program statistics are generally reported on households, not individuals.

[h] 1979 figures.

[i] Excludes Job Corps. 1981 figures.

[j] Includes federally administered payments. Generally reported on individuals, most of whom live in households described by definition 1.

compensation or other social insurance benefits is limited for many women because they are not employed in jobs that are covered by social insurance.

Second, and even more important, many women make their claims for social benefits on the basis of their functions as mothers or wives (implicit mothers). In AFDC, this connection is explicit and direct, but the link to motherhood is also made indirectly in other programs. Any program whose benefits are applicable to those on or below the poverty line encourages AFDC recipients to apply. Sometimes AFDC mothers or families are specifically targeted for certain kinds of aid. For example, in 1981, 25 percent of the people in CETA (Comprehensive Employment and Training Act) job training came from households receiving AFDC.[22] The link to motherhood is evident in social insurance programs as well. The Social Security Administration reports that only 54 percent of female beneficiaries make claims on the basis of their own as opposed to their husbands' work records. In other words, 46 percent of the women receiving Social Security benefits make their claims as wives.[23]

The poorer a woman, the greater the likelihood that she makes a claim for benefits on the basis of her position as a wife or mother. The dual benefit system and the dual labor market dictate this situation. Men, even poor men, rarely make claims for benefits solely as husbands or fathers. My point here is not that all claims for social benefits should be "individualized," much less that the state should fail to recognize the needs attending child care and homemaking but, rather, that social programs reproduce and reinforce existing economic and social inequities.

Connection between Electoral and Client Activities

When we consider together the 1980 patterns of electoral and client activities, we discern poor women's limited attachment to the state through voting, their marked detachment from the active campaign process, and their pronounced dependency on public economic resources. For many poor women, client activities are surely their regular connection to statist political activities. It would be very instructive to know the extent to which poor women engage in both electoral and client activities and how the two together inform their understanding of and judgments about government and politics. Unfortunately, to my knowl-

22. See table 2, "Selected Characteristics of CETA Participants, Fiscal 1981," in *Employment and Training Report of the President* (Washington, D.C.: Government Printing Office, 1981), p. 30.

23. Table 60, "Women Beneficiaries: Number and Average Monthly Benefit Amount, by Type of Benefit and Race, at the End of 1980," *Social Security Bulletin: Annual Statistical Supplement*, 1982, p. 131.

edge, no existing data set asks the same individuals questions about both electoral and client activities.

Household rather than individual data gathered in a recent survey provide a brief but important glimpse of the connection between these two spheres of activity. In March 1982, the CBS/*New York Times* poll asked a national sample of adults if anyone in their household was currently receiving Social Security, Supplemental Security Income, veterans benefits, AFDC, unemployment compensation, or food stamps. The results, previously noted, may be startling to many people: 38 percent of American adults live in households where these benefits are received. These benefits, which include both means-tested and insurance programs, reach households across the economic spectrum: 29.6 percent goes to households with less than $10,000 family income; 37.9 percent goes to households with incomes between $10,000 and $19,999; 20.0 percent goes to households with incomes between $20,000 and $29,999; and 12.5 percent goes to households with incomes of $30,000 or more.[24]

Despite their economic diversity, respondents in households receiving benefits were considerably more likely to evaluate Reagan's performance in office negatively. In March 1982, 42 percent of the general population disapproved of Reagan's performance, but 53 percent of respondents from beneficiary households gave him a negative evaluation. During this period, the media focused a great deal of attention on proposed and actual budget cuts in social programs. Placed in such a context, this group's more negative judgment of Reagan demonstrates that client concerns can and do bear on the evaluation of elected officials.

In many ways, this survey is a turning point in the study of mass interactions with government. By including questions about client experiences as well as about electoral preferences, the survey acknowledges that modern political life includes distributive as well as classically democratic components. But the findings raise more questions than they answer. As worded, the survey results give a good and previously unavailable measure of the impact of six major social programs on American households. But because the questions ask about use of these programs by anyone in the household, it is not possible to learn anything further about the actual beneficiaries. Hence we cannot comment on gender differences in program use, or on gender differences in clients' evaluations of Reagan. I expect, however, that future research on individuals rather than households will show that women clients, particularly poorer women or female users of welfare programs, evaluate unsympathetic politicians more negatively than men do. In the meantime, current data do provide a benchmark measure of the correspondence between a household's use of

24. In the March 10, 1982, CBS/*New York Times* poll, 554 respondents answered both the program utilization and household income questions. The distribution is calculated on the basis of these data.

social programs and the evaluation of an elected official. Wise politicians will keep this correspondence in mind.[25]

Women and Citizenship

The juxtaposition of poor women's electoral and client activities has theoretical as well as practical importance. Women's electoral participation constitutes a "permanent embarrassment" for liberal political theory, which consistently defines free and equal "people" as free and equal men.[26] So too, liberalism is uneasy when confronted by claims for collective rather than individual economic responsibility and is particularly confused by those claims when they are made in the name of motherhood. Beginning in the Progressive Era, claims based on the special needs and character of motherhood began to be recognized as valid. These claims placed women in a special relationship with the state—a relationship different from that available to men and much less independently powerful.

Women are not natural citizens of the Western liberal democracies. The ideology of liberal theorists, and others, largely excluded women from the public sphere, and nowhere was that exclusion more complete than in political life. In fact, many political philosophers felt women were by nature incapable of joining public life. They believed that if by chance or design women were permitted to do so, government and even society would be in grave danger.

These views were widely held by the social critics who most shaped Anglo-American political discourse. Locke acquiesced to patriarchalism, believing that husbands (more specifically, husbands who were also fathers) were the only legitimate political beings.[27] Even John Stuart Mill, the early and passionate promoter of women's rights, believed that most women would continue to choose marriage and motherhood as a career, a choice that Mill felt was inconsistent with informed political participation.[28] Similarly, Hegel asserted that when "women hold the helm of

25. Current efforts to register poor voters may greatly change American partisan politics. See Frances Fox Piven and Richard Cloward, "Toward a Class-based Realignment of American Politics: A Movement Strategy," *Social Policy* 13 (Winter 1983): 2–14; Theresa Funiciello and Tom Sanzilli, "The Voter Registration Strategy: A Critique," *Social Policy* 14 (Summer 1983): 54–58.

26. Teresa Brennan and Carole Pateman, " 'Mere Auxiliaries to the Commonwealth': Women and the Origins of Liberalism," *Political Studies* 28, no. 2 (June 1979): 183–200, esp. 183.

27. Ibid., pp. 195 and passim.

28. John Stuart Mill, "The Subjugation of Women," in *Essays on Sex Equality*, ed. Alice S. Rossi (Chicago: University of Chicago Press, 1970), p. 146, cited in Carole Pateman, "Feminism and Democracy," in *Democratic Theory and Practice*, ed. Graeme Duncan (Cambridge: Cambridge University Press, 1983), p. 209.

government, the state is at once in jeopardy." Kant believed that women are "mere auxiliaries to the commonwealth," and, more recently, Freud wrote that women are "hostile to" civilization.[29] In all, there were very few champions for the idea of extending individual freedom and equality—citizenship, as it is known in the political arena—to women.

For men, the emblem and measure of citizenship has always been the vote, but for women no such universal standard existed. Women's "political" status implied a contradiction with their "private" status. If women were sufficiently free and equal to be able to vote, were they not also free and equal in the family? Framed this way, voting rights for women implied that power relations within the family needed to be reconsidered and realigned. The earliest demands for woman suffrage were thus profoundly radical acts—so radical, in fact, that property qualifications and racial barriers to male suffrage were eliminated scores of years before women won the vote.[30]

With the passage of the Nineteenth Amendment, American women formally achieved the much-coveted emblem of political citizenship. (Other aspects of citizenship were still denied to many women, however. The amendment did not grant women the right to sit on juries, nor did it allow them an independent claim on national citizenship, transferable to their children and separate from their foreign-born husbands.)[31] But then, as now, women's citizenship remained tenuous in practice. The exercise of citizenship by women was and is constrained by their precarious economic position and by a particularly American philosophy of the state that is, de facto, hostile to women's claims and experiences. The economic and philosophical explanations of the fragility of women's citizenship are deeply intertwined, and both deserve more attention.

The first section of this essay shows that economic limitations reduce women's participation in many electoral activities. These findings, and the larger pattern they represent, do not greatly trouble many adherents of liberal theory. Indeed, there is a strong elitist strain in liberal theory

29. The quotes are from: Sigmund Freud, G. W. F. Hegel, and Immanuel Kant. Freud, "Civilization and Its Discontents," in *Standard Edition of the Complete Psychological Works*, trans. J. Strachey (London: Hogarth Press, 1961), 21: 103–4, and Hegel, *Philosophy of Right*, trans. T. M. Knox (Oxford: Oxford University Press, 1952), addition to par. 166, cited in Carole Pateman, "'The Disorder of Women': Women, Love, and the Sense of Justice," *Ethics* 91 (October 1980): 20–34, esp. 20, n. 2, and p. 26, n. 14. Kant, *Kant's Political Writings*, ed. H. Reiss (Cambridge: Cambridge University Press, 1971), p. 139, cited in Brennan and Pateman (n. 26 above), p. 196, n. 53.

30. Literacy tests and poll taxes limited the franchise of black men (and later black women) in such a way as to negate partially de jure access to the franchise.

31. See Virginia Sapiro, "Women, Citizenship, and Nationality: Immigration and Naturalization Policies in the United States" (paper delivered at the Midwest Political Science Association meeting, Milwaukee, April 29–May 1, 1982); J. Stanley Lemons, *The Woman Citizen: Social Feminism in the 1920s* (Urbana: University of Illinois Press, 1973), pp. 63–84.

that reflects a history of fear and dismay at the prospect of increased political participation by the masses. All the general arguments against any increase in participation have been used at various times to explain and justify women's exclusion. Nonparticipation, it is argued, is a measure of popular satisfaction with government. When that argument fails, elitist liberals suggest that increased participation would mobilize the politically incompetent, subject the polity to the instability caused by the expression of a greater number of transitory or basely egotistical interests, or distort the representative nature of politics through coerced participation.[32]

In the liberal tradition, it has been appropriate to limit women's political participation for one additional, and very crucial, reason: women lack a sense of public justice. In a very persuasive article, Carole Pateman has distilled and interpreted this attack against women's political participation. "Liberal theory," writes Pateman, "presupposes the opposition between nature and convention (i.e., contractual relations) but the opposition can neither be admitted nor its implications pursued." This opposition is based on the idea that when women participate, they subvert the state through their commitment to families. In other words, women, according to liberal tradition, do not have a universalistic standard of justice and are not capable of developing one.[33]

The inherent tension in liberalism between women's commitment to (and responsibility for) families and their full exercise of citizenship has become more severe as the mature capitalist state has increasingly undertaken distributive responsibilities. Industrial capitalism worsened the economic status or material reality of many American women. The economic relationship of marriage was something of a partnership in the family farm society. As the economy changed, the interests of wage-earning women and men often clashed, even though the members of working-class households were mutually dependent on each other's earnings. In the nineteenth century, wage-earning women made less than wage-earning men and were largely restricted from unions. Professional women faced enormous legal and social barriers to receiving training and earning their livings and were shut out of the newly formed professional

32. For a summary and critique of elitist liberal views on increased participation, see Dennis Thompson, *The Democratic Citizen* (Cambridge: Cambridge University Press, 1970), pp. 67–72. See also Pateman, "Feminism and Democracy" (n. 28 above); Charles E. Lindblom, *Politics and Markets* (New York: Basic Books, 1977), pp. 162–66. For a review of how these arguments have been applied to women's electoral participation in the two decades after World War II, see Susan C. Bourque and Jean Grossholtz, "Politics as Unnatural Practice: Political Science Looks at Female Participation," *Politics and Society* 4 (Winter 1974): 225–66.

33. Pateman, "'The Disorder of Women'" (n. 29 above), and p. 32 passim. For a current, more psychological version of this discussion, see Carol Gilligan, *In a Different Voice: Psychological Theory and Women's Development* (Cambridge, Mass.: Harvard University Press, 1982).

societies. Bourgeois wives and daughters who did not work for wages had little independent access to economic resources. This picture makes it easy to understand why the first wave of feminists fought for a constellation of civil and legal rights for women.[34]

Early in the Progressive period, mainstream arguments for women's rights took a conservative turn and began, in the suffrage movement, to emphasize the advantages of adding the maternal sensibilities of white women to political life. At the same time, government initiated judicial and legislative policies that gave mothers a special, separate status in relation to government. These policies, most notably the *Muller* v. *Oregon* Supreme Court decision and the rapid adoption of mothers' aid pensions, acknowledged women's marginal economic status in the form of their maternal responsibilities.[35] Such policies, adopted at a time when women had very few civil rights, created a quasi-coverture for women within the redistributive functions of government.

Consider for a moment the *Muller* v. *Oregon* decision. The case, argued before the Supreme Court in 1908, challenged an Oregon statute limiting the workday to ten hours for women employed in factories and laundries. Louis D. Brandeis wrote his famous sociological as well as legal brief outlining why women's working hours should be limited. When the court held the Oregon law to be constitutional, Progressive reformers rejoiced.

Muller belongs to a period of judicial history called "the *Lochner* era" after a decision that struck down a maximum work week statute in New York state.[36] The *Lochner* decision underlined the courts' stand against any limitations to workers' freedom of contract—that is, workers could sell their labor under any conditions they "chose." *Muller* constitutes one of only two exceptions to this policy.[37] Even though the *Muller* opinion states that "it is the law of Oregon that women . . . have equal contractual and personal rights with men," the reasoning of the arguments suggests that it is proper to limit women's freedom to contract in the name of the social value of motherhood.[38] Note that the argument does not consider decent working conditions, nor does it address the relative power differences between employers and workers:

> [A woman's] physical structure and a proper discharge of her maternal functions—having in view not merely her own health, but

34. See Brennan and Pateman (n. 26 above), p. 198; see also Heidi Hartmann, "Capitalism, Patriarchy, and Job Segregation," *Signs* 1, no. 3, pt. 2 (1976): 137–70.
35. Muller v. Oregon, 208 U.S. 412 (1908).
36. Lochner v. New York, 198 U.S. 45 (1905).
37. See Holden v. Hardy, 169 U.S. 366 (1898), which allowed maximum hour legislation for miners because mining was considered an extremely hazardous occupation.
38. Muller v. Oregon, at 418.

the well-being of the race—justify legislation to protect her from the greed as well as the passion of men. The limitations which this statute places upon her contractual powers, upon her right to agree with her employer as to the time she shall labor, are not imposed solely for her benefit, but also for the benefit of all.[39]

At best, *Muller* suggests that women's interests as individuals are subordinate to those of their actual or future children. Such a view is very much at odds with the ideal liberal notion of independent and equal civic standing as the basis of citizenship. Feminism supports the belief that society has important responsibilities for ensuring the well-being of families, even while providing critiques of family definitions, structures, and processes. Hence, it is not the outcome of *Muller*—the legality, in 1908, of the ten-hour day for women only—that is important for this discussion, but the recognition that the decision was based on the belief that women's rights should be abridged because of their maternal functions.

The mothers' aid pension movement did not involve a question of fundamental rights as did *Muller* v. *Oregon*. Nonetheless, this movement constitutes the second important source of women's special separate, maternal relationship with the state. First established by legislation in Illinois in 1911, the idea of a mothers' aid pension spread rapidly to other states. Its funds were designed to provide financial support to mothers of unblemished character who had lost the income provided by their husbands. The pensions (actually grants-in-aid financed through the general revenue) acknowledged the reality of turn-of-the-century living conditions. Women, who were often widowed (or deserted) while their children were young, faced a terrible dilemma: whether to (continue to) work for wages, leaving their children unsupervised, or to give up custody of their offspring. The 1909 White House Conference on Dependent Children articulated the principle guiding these pensions: "Children of parents of worthy character, suffering from temporary misfortune and children of reasonably efficient and deserving mothers who are without the support of the normal breadwinner, should, as a rule, be kept with their parents, such aid being given as may be necessary to maintain suitable homes for the rearing of the children."[40]

The Great Depression nationalized mothers' pension efforts through the joint federal-state Aid to Dependent Children (ADC) title of the Social Security Act. Like the mothers' aid pensions, ADC was designed to give mothers a special, though limited, claim on public resources. Originally, the purpose of ADC (now AFDC) was to keep mothers out of

---

39. Muller v. Oregon, at 422.

40. *Proceedings of the Conference on the Care of Dependent Children Held at Washington, D.C., January 25, 1909*, 70th Congress, 2d sess., 1909, S. Doc. 721, p. 9.

the paid labor force, allowing them to devote all their energies to child rearing. (The social purposes of AFDC are more complex today. In the mid-1960s legislative changes that reduced the tax rate on recipients' earned income encouraged AFDC mothers to work. While maintaining the ideology of work, budget cuts and program changes initiated by the Reagan administration have eliminated the financial incentives for AFDC recipients to enter the paid labor force.)[41]

In contrast, the Social Security retirement program was consciously structured to respond to the needs of white male workers. The original law merely provided rather modest benefits for retired workers. It was not designed to provide a minimum income for all elderly people, nor did it provide additional benefits for dependents or survivors until 1939. The 1939 amendments made the benefits more adequate but introduced a long-standing bias in favor of homemaking wives (implicitly mothers) and against working women, married or single.[42]

In the United States, cash benefits, whether made on the basis of motherhood or of work history, suffer from a lack of legitimacy more pronounced than in other industrial nations. Without either a successful socialist tradition or a conception of the good collective, the American political system falls back on the Anglo-American concept of the state for justification of governmental redistribution. This philosophical and judicial tradition does not distinguish clearly the state from the rest of civil society. The state is conceptualized as analogous to the market, the almost accidental or epiphenomenal consequence of the citizenry's choices at any given time. The state, like the market, deals with individuals as though they have neither memories nor histories. In such a state, it is hard to find support for the idea of governmental redistribution with its implications of long-range consequences.[43] It is not surprising that the American concept of the state is hostile to women's redistributive claims: women embody the future in a state with a limited vision of tomorrow.

Thus an individual's productive capacity in the market becomes the only legitimate method by which a citizenship-based claim for social benefits can be made. Put succinctly, the ideal of the (male) citizen-worker

41. Gilbert Y. Steiner, "Reform Follows Reality: The Growth of Welfare," *Public Interest* 34 (Winter 1974): 47–65; Tom Joe, *Profiles of Families in Poverty: Effects of the FY 1983 Budget Proposals on the Poor* (Washington, D.C.: Center for the Study of Social Policy, 1982).

42. Martha Derthick, *Policymaking for Social Security* (Washington, D.C.: Brookings Institution, 1979), pp. 260–63.

43. Kenneth H. F. Dyson, *The State Tradition in Western Europe: A Study of an Idea and an Institution* (Oxford: Martin Robinson, 1981), pp. 25–47; Jennifer Nedelsky, "Individual Autonomy in the Bureaucratic State: Toward a Reconception" (paper delivered at the American Political Science Association meeting, September 1–4, 1983), and "Confining Democratic Politics: Anti-Federalists, Federalists, and the Constitution," *Harvard Law Review* 96 (November 1982): 340–60; Albert O. Hirschman, *Shifting Involvements: Private Interest and Public Action* (Princeton, N.J.: Princeton University Press, 1982), p. 77.

has replaced the ideal of the (male) citizen-soldier in the realm of redistribution through benefits. The reality of women's poverty and the limits to women's citizenship in a liberal democracy coalesce to disempower poor women. Their electoral participation, particularly their campaign participation, has been constrained through lack of resources. Their claims for public aid are made primarily on the basis of their maternal responsibilities and the assumption (if not the requirement) of limited labor-force participation. Poor women, indeed most women, are doubly disadvantaged in the political world.

Hubert H. Humphrey Institute of Public Affairs
University of Minnesota

About the Contributors

Mari H. Clark, doctoral candidate in the Department of Anthropology, University of North Carolina, Chapel Hill, recently coedited a special issue of *Women Studies* on "Gender Bias in Feminist Fieldwork." She prepared a literature review for the Urban Development Department of the World Bank on household economic strategies of the poor, with an emphasis on the needs of woman-headed households, and is planning research in Kenya on this topic. For the past four years, she has been involved in the training of those who train nurses in Africa and the Middle East, developing manuals with CHP International for the Peace Corps.

Mary Corcoran is an associate professor of political science at the University of Michigan. Her research interests include sex-based wage differences, intergenerational mobility, and poverty. She is coauthor with Christopher Jencks and others of *Who Gets Ahead* (New York: Basic Books, 1979).

Greg J. Duncan, associate research scientist at the University of Michigan, is primarily interested in the dynamic aspects of poverty, welfare, and labor markets. He is the principal author of *Years of Poverty, Years of Plenty* (Ann Arbor, Mich.: Institute for Social Research, 1984), which summarizes findings from the Panel Study of Income Dynamics project. He is also codirector of that project.

Zillah R. Eisenstein teaches feminist theory and political thought as a professor of politics at Ithaca College. She is the author of *Feminism and Sexual Equality: Crisis in Liberal America* (New York: Monthly Review Press, 1984), *The Radical Future of Liberal Feminism* (New York: Longman, 1981), and editor of and contributor to *Capitalist Patriarchy and the Case for Socialist Feminism* (New York: Monthly Review Press, 1978).

Jana Everett, associate professor of political science at the University of Colorado at Denver, is author of *Women and Social Change in India* (New York: St. Martin's, 1979) and has published articles on women's movements, women's leaders, and feminism in India. Her research interests include women and development, social movements, and children and public policy. Currently, she and Mira Savara are writing a book on women and credit programs in India.

Roslyn L. Feldberg, a Radcliffe Research Scholar, is interested in the institutions that shape women's employment. Her studies on clerical work have approached the subject from many angles: the implications of technological change, the experiences and consciousness of women clerical workers, and historical shifts in the nature of work. She is currently coauthoring a book on clerical work in large enterprises and doing research on the changing lives and attitudes of women clerical workers from 1955 to 1980.

Martha S. Hill is an assistant research scientist at the Institute for Social Research at the University of Michigan. Her research includes longitudinal analyses of poverty, unemployment, and divorce, as well as intergenerational analysis of

NOTE: This biographical information is not current, but was extracted from the SIGNS issues in which the articles first appeared.

economic attainment and welfare dependency. She examined the economic well-being of children in "Trends in the Economic Situation of U.S. Families and Children: 1970–1980," an article prepared for the National Research Council.

SHEILA B. KAMERMAN is professor of social policy and planning at the Columbia University School of Social Work. In addition to teaching courses in social policy and planning, family policy, and social services, she codirects the Cross-national Studies Research Program; serves as a consultant to various governmental agencies, foundations, and international organizations; and lectures extensively. Her current research includes work on comparative social policies, on child care services, on "occupational" or "corporate" welfare, and on single-mother families. Her most recent books, coauthored by Alfred J. Kahn, include *Income Transfers for Families with Children* (Philadelphia: Temple University Press, 1983), and *Maternity Policies and Working Women* (New York: Columbia University Press, 1983).

MURIEL NAZZARI, a Ph.D. candidate in Latin American history at Yale University, is the author of "The Significance of Present-Day Changes in the Institution of Marriage" (*Review of Radical Political Economics*, vol. 12 [Summer 1980]). She is presently writing her dissertation, "Women and Property in the Transition of Capitalism: The Disappearance of the Dowry in São Paulo, Brazil."

BARBARA J. NELSON, associate professor at the Hubert H. Humphrey Institute of Public Affairs, University of Minnesota, is a political scientist with interests in social policy and social movements. She is the author of *Making an Issue of Child Abuse: Political Agenda Setting for Social Problems* (Chicago: University of Chicago Press, 1984) and *American Women and Politics: A Selected Bibliography and Resource Guide* (New York: Garland Publishing, 1984). Her current projects include "Women and Citizenship: Dilemmas of Participation in the Modern State" and "Comparable Worth and the Political Process: The Consequences of Implementation." Her essay in this issue won the 1984 Western Political Science Women and Politics Award.

DIANA M. PEARCE, director of research at the Center for National Policy Review, Catholic University Law School, coined the phrase "the feminization of poverty," which is the title of her first article on women in poverty (*Urban and Social Change Review*, 1978). Since then she has written or spoken on women in poverty and related topics, including women and welfare policy, and has researched the relationship between school desegregation and housing discrimination.

ROSEMARY C. SARRI, professor of social work at the University of Michigan, has focused her research on the feminization of poverty as well as on juvenile justice and the management of human service organizations. Her final report of a major study funded by the Ford Foundation on the impact of AFDC reductions on working welfare women was made available in the fall of 1984. An interim report entitled "Working Female-headed Families in Poverty," written jointly with the Center for the Study of Social Policy and published in the spring of 1984, covers the experiences of women in Michigan, Georgia, and New York City.

MIRA SAVARA, a free-lance researcher, journalist, and activist, received her Ph.D. in sociology from Bombay University in 1982. She is primarily concerned with the topics of health and population policy, prostitution and sexuality, and the effects of development on various groups of women. Her study of NET-EN, an injectable contraceptive being tested in India, is forthcoming.

JOAN SMITH is an associate professor of sociology and a research associate at the Fernand Braudel Center, State University of New York at Binghamton. She and Immanuel Wallerstein are currently acting as principal investigators in a project on household structures and labor force formation, funded by the National Endowment for the Humanities. Smith, Wallerstein, and Hans Dieter Evers have also coedited a book on this topic, recently published by Sage Publications.

ELAINE ZIMMERMAN, codirector of the California Women's Economic Agenda Project, has focused her organizing efforts on linking the accelerating impoverishment of women and children to women's newfound voting power in order to gain political leverage. This interest is graphically demonstrated in her voter registration drive poster, designed by Sandy Chelnov, which uses the slogan, "Two out of three adults in poverty are women. What if we were all to go to the polls?" Her articles include "The Odd Couple: Feminization of Poverty and the Gender Gap," *California Women* (June/July 1983), and "The Good News: Women's Votes Make a Difference," *Matrix* (Santa Cruz) (September 1983).

DEBORAH K. ZINN, a doctoral candidate in sociology and social work at the University of Michigan, is concerned with economic stratification in the United States and has focused her policy and research interests on public welfare programs. Part of her work in progress, a study of the political language of public policies, particularly the concept of "welfare dependency," will appear as an article in an upcoming issue of the *Journal of Social Issues*.

Index